JUST

LET ME

LOOK

AT YOU

*also by Bill Gaston*

NOVELS
*Bella Combe Journal*
*Tall Lives*
*The Cameraman*
*The Good Body*
*Sointula*
*The Order of Good Cheer*
*The World*

SHORT STORIES
*Deep Cove Stories*
*North of Jesus' Beans*
*Sex Is Red*
*Mount Appetite*
*Gargoyles*
*Juliet Was a Surprise*
*A Mariner's Guide to Self Sabotage*

POETRY
*Inviting Blindness*

DRAMA
*Yardsale*

NON-FICTION
*Midnight Hockey*

# JUST

# LET ME

# LOOK

# AT YOU

## ON FATHERHOOD

BILL GASTON

HAMISH HAMILTON

an imprint of Penguin Canada, a division of Penguin Random House Canada Limited

Canada • USA • UK • Ireland • Australia • New Zealand • India • South Africa • China

First published 2018

www.penguinrandomhouse.ca

LIBRARY AND ARCHIVES CANADA CATALOGUING IN PUBLICATION

Gaston, Bill, author
Just let me look at you : on fatherhood / Bill Gaston.

Issued in print and electronic formats.
ISBN 978-0-7352-3406-2 (softcover).—ISBN 978-0-7352-3407-9
(HTML)

1. Gaston, Bill.  2. Gaston, Bill--Family.
3. Authors, Canadian (English)--20th century--Biography.
4. Fathers and sons--Canada--Biography.  5. Fatherhood.
I. Title.

PS8563.A76Z84 2018      C813'.54      C2017-904426-5
                                        C2017-904427-3

Cover and interior design by Lisa Jager

Printed and bound in the United States of America

10  9  8  7  6  5  4  3  2  1

Penguin
Random House
HAMISH HAMILTON CANADA

TO CONNOR BOB

*If I chance to talk a little wild, forgive me;*
*I had it from my father.*

—WILLIAM SHAKESPEARE

# SOME FIRST WORDS

THIS YEAR FOR CHRISTMAS my two boys gave their mother Dede a beautiful gift, a double frame holding two photos. In one, three-year-old Connor sits in a yellow plastic laundry hamper, holding up baby Vaughn by the armpits. Connor smiles proudly and Vaughn isn't sure what's going on. In the second photo, the present-day boys, in their early twenties, sit in and crush the yellow plastic hamper, legs splayed. They're dressed as before, Connor in black T-shirt and shorts, Vaughn a red onesie. The background scatter of chair and table legs is painstakingly recreated. Connor has Vaughn by the armpits, and they copy their expressions of proud and clueless. The gift moved Dede to laughter and tears. It's likely the closest to gushy we'll ever see from these two young men, who took her hugs in stride.

The thing is, they didn't also give it to me. I know why, but can't explain it, except that it feels like a son's gift to a mother just like it doesn't feel like a son's gift to a father. If I were to ask either of them why they didn't also give it to me, at most I'd get some grunted irony. And that would feel natural too. My gift from them was a selection of odd craft beers, one with kelp. They know me.

Maybe this book is about how fathers and their children do, and don't, communicate. That is, maybe this book is about yearning.

———

If I'm going to write something from memory, best start now. I've turned sixty, and this truth shocks me from my hair to my feet. Age doesn't have much going for it as far as I can tell. Maybe I've calmed down in a way that lets me admit how little I know, which I suspect is wisdom's first door. My father knew this kind of humility sooner in life—but I don't think he valued it or saw it as a door. Maybe he did, in ten-second blooms of clarity. Alcoholism does have its moments, though they're so well erased they don't count. I recently heard a good one: alcohol gives you wings and takes away the sky. In any case, my father wasn't *allowed* to not know something. His was an era when a man's only pose was to know everything. A father's pose? Even more so.

I'm hoping he'd forgive my scrutiny. The lens I'll have him under. But I had him in sharp focus the whole time. Parents watch their growing kids for strengths and flaws, but kids also eye their parents, and of course in adolescence the scrutiny kicks into high gear. It's part of love, isn't it? A parent's fault-finding is seen as a facet of love, so why not a child's? His hot disgust over a father's stumble wouldn't happen if he didn't feel so deeply. His turning from a father in fury, hyperventilating as he drives away—isn't it a manifestation of love?

Despite all these years I doubt that I've learned how to live my life, let alone anyone else's. And yet when I lay out my father's life the air will be thick with judgment. I don't know how to avoid this. It's what I felt. I don't claim that I could have lived his life better than he did, and I'm aware that I'm seeing someone's agonies from the safety of distance and the clarity of time.

# ONE

*Directly after God in heaven comes a Papa.*
—MOZART

I begin my voyage to Egmont today and, ten minutes in, something in the sky makes me stop.

This trip has been thirty years in the making. Egmont—a marina, a store, a few houses—is eighty miles across the Salish Sea and up a remote inlet. It's where my father and I learned to mooch for salmon together. It's where I came of age, and he slid downhill, and it's where we grew apart. It's not a dangerous journey, unless I get caught in a storm, or misjudge a rock. *Sylvan*, my boat, is a piece of junk.

Dead slow through the channel out of the bay, the engine's contained growl feels like my own excitement. Forget the thirty years—I've waited two weeks for this break in the weather. I emerge into the Salish Sea and a blue, windless morning, the kind of soothing spirit that gave the Pacific its name, the kind of day that suggests a benevolence bigger than us. I breathe deep and eye things. A creamy haze obscures all distant landforms, including the B.C. mainland to the east and Vancouver Island to the west, and also Texada Island, thirty miles north, its lone mountaintop poking up through mist, black. I point *Sylvan's* bow at it.

There's something strange there in the sky, up ahead.

I grab the binoculars and get it in focus. A tumult of great wings, almost overhead now. I don't need the binoculars anymore. I put the boat into neutral. It's a bald eagle and two great blue herons. At first I think cranes, because herons fly with necks and legs tucked and these herons are in, well, spread-eagle mode. They flap and hover as if standing up, necks outstretched and wingspan on full heraldic display, as in a coat of arms. The eagle flaps five or six times to gain a bit of height then goes into a quick dive, unfurling its talons.

I didn't think I believed in omens, but maybe I do.

My father had an affinity with herons. He was six-five and skinny, and this might be a reason he admired them. Where he grew up, in Mukilteo, Washington, a heron was a "shittaquart," a graphic description of what might happen if you got close and it took flight. I remember his fond chuckle and *"Shittaquart"* when we motored near one and it launched, shot its alarming stream of white, and squawked at my dad laughing.

Driving home the day after his cremation, when a heron flew out of a ditch and veered not away from my car but toward it, looming into the windshield, I instantly thought of him. I knew that in the mystical East the cremations of significant people often attracted unlikely visitations of both rainbows and birds. No rainbow for my dad, but a giant bird he identified with.

I probably do believe in signs. A year ago, we bought land on Gabriola, an island lying off the east coast of Vancouver Island. As we walked the property, unable to decide, toeing the weeds, I watched a heron land on the deck overhanging the pond. Ted, the owner, a bird photographer and man of few words, remarked that he'd never seen this in his two decades here. The heron was so close, and why land on the deck? As for me—buying this place was possible only because of my late father's lifetime of work and frugality—I took the heron as meaningful. Ted might have too. When the sale was complete, after packing up his two decades and moving away, Ted left behind one thing only: a framed print of a great blue heron. This picture now hangs over the mantel, and in my head I refer to it as "Dad."

The gangly herons dodge the eagle's next small dive and, when the eagle is below them, try to fly a bit. They head out to sea. I wonder at this strategy because I doubt they can swim—they're waders with three-foot legs, and their feet aren't webbed. But eagles can't swim either. Is this an avian game of chicken? The herons hover as the eagle climbs again, dives, misses. The herons stay together. During the next diving attack a sabre-like bill jabs at the eagle in defence, but otherwise the herons look helpless. They are just birds but my heart is in my throat. Another climb. A dive. Finally, unbelievably—*whack*—this time the eagle makes contact. The stricken heron goes into a long, almost horizontal glide, down, down, gradually down, not once flapping a wing. The other heron knows, tucks its neck and legs, and starts flying landward. Finding it in the binoculars, I watch the wounded heron splash down maybe two hundred metres away. Now the eagle goes into a longer dive too, and with steady wingbeats picks up velocity along the water's surface. It hits the heron with talons out, trying to lift the larger bird as it would a two-pound fish—but the eagle topples into the water, stuck fast.

I put the boat in gear and approach slowly. I wonder if I should disturb nature—nature at both its best and its worst. Putting closer, I can see the eagle perched on the downed bird as on a wobbly raft. Its white head plunges a couple of times, stabbing or taking bites.

I can't see the heron at all. I draw closer. But what am I really seeing? Is it possible that this all *means* something? If this is an omen, is it good? Is it bad? Is it saying there will be trouble if I make this journey in a wounded boat? Does it mean I've killed my fear of water and it is waving me on my way? What really gives me pause is the notion that, in making this voyage back in time and writing about it, I am attacking my father all over again.

I'm closer. It's just a meaningless eagle standing wobbly on its prey, on water a kilometre deep. When I'm thirty metres away the eagle takes off. Because of me or because the heron sank out of reach, I don't know, because I circle around and find no heron. The exhausted eagle flies landward, and soon out of sight. I feel stupid for making a natural drama a little bit about me. A belief that the world is communicating with you is seductive, but it's also a mark of schizophrenia.

My dad's favourite colour was grey-blue, but that has to be coincidence.

I hit the throttle and point out into the Salish Sea again. I aim the bow at the black mountain peak of Texada Island, some hours away. It's a beautiful day. It'll be my first time sleeping on *Sylvan*. I'm going boat-camping. I'm having an adventure.

The boat reaches cruising speed. I hear, and feel in my feet, a cylinder misfire. Now, almost as if I was too dense to understand a message and need a more obvious sign, an engine belt begins to squeal. I check the temperature gauge—thar she blows, the engine overheating, the needle rising fast.

I'm only twenty minutes into this trip.

———

After decades without, I finally bought myself a boat. My dad would approve.

Because of him I grew up on boats. When I was young I fished from them with passion. In my late teens and early twenties I lived most summers on a boat, in small marinas up the coast, starting with Egmont. On *Cormorant* I fished and guided. I also played lots of solitaire, partied, and wrote my first two books on board, clunking away on the typewriter as a fluid world moved underneath.

I loved sleeping aboard, likely for what are narcotic or even return-to-the-womb reasons: a dark enclosure and softly rhythmic motion. After we met, my wife Dede, who knew none of my past, saw me fall into a trance if we happened near a marina. I'd have to study the boats, eyeing their features for those I'd like, wondering if they had a writing table or much of a galley. Lately I check to see if they have downriggers, winch-powered cables that send your cannon ball-weighted lure down to the deeps to troll for salmon.

Boats are magic. That metal or fibreglass can float is a marvel, one your life depends on. It's not a romantic thought, I feel it in my body. It's easy to find bygone power in the word *vessel*.

*Sylvan* is an old fibreglass tub with a big back open cockpit for fishing. Its twenty-six feet include a miniature bowsprit, a railed platform shooting off the bow where, if someone else steered, I could teeter onto and declare myself king of the world. It has a small cabin with V-berth, tiny sink and enclosed bathroom, or "head."

I'll avoid nautical terms. At marinas you run into people with boats smaller than mine who say "helm" and "starboard" and, of course, "she." My boat's an it. *Sylvan* is its brand name, painted on the stern, like a big *Ford*. Its navy canvas top highlights the seagull shit. It's powered by a big, gas-gulping inboard, plus a small outboard, or "kicker," for trolling. Both motors are old and the big one has begun burning oil. Many of the switches—for instance the horn, running lights, inside heater, windshield wipers—don't work. I've duct-taped rips in the canvas.

I bought the boat on a whim, but one that felt fated. Out of the blue, after forty years, I was contacted by an old high school teacher. I'd had a crush on her, a Texan who'd moved north for political reasons. She had prematurely greying hair, wore serapes and went barefoot. It was she who'd implanted the idea of writing. In any case, she apparently liked my books, and after I blamed her for inspiring them, her next envelope contained a cheque for ten thousand dollars. I tried to decline it but she insisted, explaining that it was something she did every year, sending this amount to whomever she felt like, from Patch Adams to Obama to unknown poets. She told me to use it on "something missing in your life." After I had two downriggers installed, *Sylvan* cost exactly ten thousand dollars.

The boat is decent in moderate waves, and once the motor gets going it tends not to quit. I keep *Sylvan* in Silva Bay (how fitting is that?) at the cheapest marina and the only one without a waiting list. Reportedly my berth bottoms out in extreme tides, but I'm assured it's soft mud down there.

The transaction that brought us our place on Gabriola felt fated too. When our father and then mother died, my brother and I sold their condo and, not seeing a wiser investment, bought a place here for the exact amount, to the dollar, we got for the condo. Our two families share it. Somehow it felt right, and also practical, both of those. When I sit on the cabin's sundeck and view the small orchard and pond, or when I walk the hushed trails through the woods, there's a palpable sense that this is the fruit of my father's hard work. His imagined link to this land keeps him alive in ways I can feel. Less poetically, I know I bought this place with his money, feel like a spoiled brat, and imaging him liking it here eases the guilt a bit.

———

I have an image that catches him perfectly. Not an image really, but a mid-eighties Japanese comic book. I came upon it again a week ago, digging through his stuff. Not knowing how to read Japanese, I think of it as The Big Bob of Mystery Beer Fishing Art Book.

I'm about thirty, still living in Vancouver and over for a morning visit. My dad is late-fifties, newly retired. Morning is the best time. I find him at the dining-room table flipping through what appears to be a comic book he's just got in the mail. Unlike our comic books, this one is thin, fragile paper, including the cover. And it's in Japanese. My dad looks befuddled.

The captions are all Japanese characters. Every page or two has a sidebar or sometimes a full-page drawing, rough but artful, of various fish. The cartoon boxes depict a young man, an artist, on a fishing trip, sketching everything he sees.

"Hey," I say. "This is that trip you took last year. That charter out of Egmont."

"Right. Right."

"I remember you telling me about some Japanese artist guy? Drawing everything? He got stung by a rock cod?"

"Right, right. Drawing everything. I remember that guy now."

I recall it was a business perk, my dad and some other executives wooed with a freebie aboard a forty-foot aluminum houseboat. He'd come back from the weekend with stories about "this funny little Jap" who didn't fish at all but got all excited when a fish was caught. He'd lay tracing paper on the fish and run charcoal over it.

"It was really something," he'd said. "It showed all the scales."

Always instructive, I said, "A 'rubbing.'"

"He sure was a funny little guy." My dad had sounded almost affectionate.

It's too perfect that the comic is Japanese. He still hated them. They were sneaky, they weren't to be trusted. I didn't blame him for these feelings. He'd been in a war, he'd had friends die. If I occasionally wondered aloud that they couldn't be all bad, that some were forced to fight, he'd turn away. Fine. I'd never been in a war. An American, my father joined up right after hearing the radio broadcast about Pearl Harbor. He tried the air force, was too tall to be a pilot, so he joined the navy.

But he hated whoever he *thought* was Japanese. Koreans and Chinese and Inuit were "Japs." It was sadly funny that for decades he lived beside Layton Wing, a shy family man who was unfailingly friendly to my father, who was only reservedly friendly back. After a few beers, in private, my dad would rail against "that Jap" next door. He'd settle down when I explained again that not only was Mr. Wing Chinese, but that the Chinese hated the Japanese probably more than he did. But he'd forget, and he'd grumble about "that Jap" whenever Layton appeared to be trying to keep up with the Joneses, like when he installed a pool. I actually thought it a good thing that Layton's pool was a bit smaller than ours. Again, I found it more funny than sad. It was the big, American stupidity, that of not learning who your enemies really are.

I can't say I believe in the more colourful kind of karma, the one that says if you're a pickpocket you're bound eventually to get your pocket picked, if not in this life then the next. But I have to wonder about my dad and his hatred of Japs and those he mistook for them. Near the end, when he broke a hip and suffered a stroke in surgery, he could no longer walk or talk and ended up in a facility where he was tended almost exclusively by Asians. Most were Filipina, some Vietnamese. I never saw a Japanese caregiver, but I did see a certain look in my father's eye as they spooned him his food, plumped his pillow, and all the rest, bantering in halting English. He wasn't all there but I know his pride remained, and I can't imagine how he felt when, chirping, "How you today *Bob*, you look *good*," they washed him and changed his diaper. It would have been an odd hell.

And now we're looking at the oddest comic book. It's part graphic novel (though I don't think they existed yet in the West), part natural science guide to Pacific Northwest fish, with those cool charcoal rubbings. The story boxes show the artist landing at the Vancouver airport, lugging his art supplies, tongue sticking out with effort, cartoon sweat shooting off his brow. It shows a bus ride, a first meal with clumsy knife and fork, mishaps with mysterious money. Egmont scenery in the background, it shows the houseboat, and him stowing his gear. A seagull wanders close, begging. Overleaf the gull is rendered, full-page and fine art. It really is bizarre. It gets more bizarre when, early the next morning, he wakes up as the houseboat lurches, nearly tipping. He rushes out to encounter a giant climbing aboard. In one hand the giant clutches a beer and the other he holds out to be shaken, "I'M BOB!" emblazoned in caps on his T-shirt in such bold lettering I can hear my dad's basso profundo voice in the letters. In the next box the artist suffers a crushing handshake and falls to his knees under the giant's shadow.

The only English in the entire comic book is the "I'M BOB!" on his shirt. The artist has nailed my father's likeness, though exaggerated: twice the height of everyone else, he wears a skewed cap, and loudly gets in everyone's face. He appears to lurch like John Wayne. His nose is red. It's hilarious.

Turning pages, my dad chuckles nervously.

The story shows the men fishing, eating, drinking. My dad is never without a beer. Now he wears the captain's hat, a ball cap with gold braid, and the captain wears my dad's hat and doesn't look happy about it. One box is just my dad's face, his eyes closed and stars and birds circling his head, passed out. But he is also helpful, showing people how to fish. Near the end he's battling what appears to be a whopper, and then, chagrined, holds up a minnow.

My dad closes the book, snickers insincerely and flicks it so it spins and slides three feet across the dining-room table. Partly he doesn't recognize this version of himself, this BOB the rest of us have known for years. And partly he just doesn't remember that weekend, not a thing.

———

My problem is, he never told me any of it. Not what mattered. Not what made him who he was. All I had were a few generic facts, delivered cheerfully by my mother: he grew up in the Pacific Northwest, mostly in a tiny place called Mukilteo, without a father. He was poor, even by Depression standards—which made his present situation so remarkable. By this she meant *my* present situation, her curtly lifted eyebrows indicating my nice clothes and the swimming pool out back, all due to my father's hard-won success. Then she continued with his story, about his basketball scholarship, where he finally got enough to eat and went on to be a star centre. In those days, six-five was tremendously tall.

I did ask him things. When I was a boy I asked him about his father, what he was like and what he did. Without looking at me, my dad said his father died when he was ten. How did he die, I persisted, hungry for this rare stuff. My dad's voice had an odd tone as he told me how his father was on a lunch break and sitting on a curb, in Everett, and suddenly a fire truck came flying around the corner and the ladder came loose and swung off and hit him on the head and killed him. His father's name was Ozro, and I didn't know until later what a strange name that was.

I savoured this colourful tale and didn't learn it was fabrication until after my dad himself had died, when I heard the truth from my mother. The only true part about my dad's story was his being ten, which isn't when his father died, but when my father, his sister and his mother fled him in fear. Ozro was a drinker. He sold Burroughs business machines (working for writer William Burroughs's father) and I've heard rumours that he'd been a professor. In any case, all my dad ever told me about his dad, my grandfather Ozro, was untrue.

But from my dad I did hear some highlights: how he fished for salmon off Mukilteo, rowing with the line wrapped around his foot; about how while playing centre for Gonzaga in a Final Four game during March Madness he had his front tooth knocked out in Madison Square Garden, and he'd always punctuate the story by flashing the false front tooth, discoloured and framed in gold; about how in WWII in the South Pacific he watched a kamikaze-flown "Jap Zero" plunge into the sea just short of his ship. Even as highlights, these were pretty good. Other details I got from my mother, when in her last years certain never-before-mentioned family secrets came tumbling out.

One true thing my dad did tell me about his childhood was that he grew up beside the pristine waters of Puget Sound north of Seattle and that, as soon as he could hold a rod, he loved to fish. He had a favourite story about the time he hooked a huge ling cod while jigging a handline off the village wharf. I can picture my dad, alone, lying on his belly, staring down into the water, wholly eager and entertained, his fist jigging up and down. Then the strike, and him screaming at the unbelievable weight. It was thirty, maybe forty pounds, and ling cod fight hard. They are also ugly, with massive heads and bucket mouths full of teeth. But they are firm white meat, and taste great. It took a half-hour to land after walking it back, climbing down onto the shore, and dragging it up onto the gravel. Then he ran home for his wagon, he said, adding that he hated his wagon, he was humiliated when he used it to trade food stamps at the grocery store and haul the food home along the length of Mukilteo's main street. I could easily picture him in this task. He's taller than his years and painfully skinny and weak, so skinny, according to my mother, that he was a target for bullies. But he pulled the giant fish home, a neighbour helped him nail it by the tail to the backyard laundry post and, proud as could be, he proceeded to skin it. It felt great because his family was poor and needed this food, he added, meeting my eye, making sure I understood that, strange as it might sound to a slightly tubby kid who could make himself a sandwich and grab some cookies whenever he felt like it, hunger had been a real part of his life. But, halfway into the skinning, he could see the ling was lousy with worms. Inedible and useless. He was devastated, and he cried. When he told me this, about the crying, he boozily shook his head and mock-whimpered. Ten-year-olds don't cry, but that was how upset he was over that useless giant fish.

Only recently did I learn that, while most of this ling cod story was true, that wasn't the way it ended, not at all.

I wonder why he didn't tell me what really happened. The bad stuff. God, why didn't he? He could have told me, and he could have cried for real. I would have cried too. It would have changed everything.

———

Just like him, fishing was my favourite thing. I was four when we first vacationed at Three Mile Lake, just north of Toronto, a modest resort with a safe little beach, and rowboats. It had outhouses, I remember. I suspect we were there only because of the rowboats. My mom read mysteries in a lawn chair while my dad rowed us out not far from shore. The quarry was perch and sunfish.

Even when I was an adult my parents loved regaling company with how little Billy took to fishing.

"His eyes were big as saucers, looking at those damn things."

"He'd sit out there all day happy as could be. I'd worry about you two guys."

"He'd *study* them. He'd hold open its yap, stare right down its throat."

"He'd sit on your chest in the morning and bounce to get you up."

"He'd smell them and poke them. He'd stick his finger in it! He *licked* one!"

None of this was exaggerated. I remember those first fishing expeditions clearly and they were serious business. As clearly as I can conjure up the smell of apple pie, I can smell the smell of a sunfish. To this day the odour of a freshwater fish remains one of the most distinct smells I can think of. It's funny that saltwater fish, which can be much bigger and look more bizarre, have hardly any smell at all. Why is that? I heard the reason but I've forgotten. It might have to do with salt.

I was enamoured of these hidden creatures pulled from the depths. Sunfish are stunningly pretty—stained glass in a church comes to mind but falls short. Perch have a pretty green-and-yellow pattern, and the smaller fins are brilliant orange. All fish are pretty. Even a brown fish is in some way radiant. It's also their shape, their symmetry. Bullets of balanced muscle, darting through water.

One reason a fish is more beautiful than stained glass is that it's alive. Stained glass isn't *vital*. Though I was caught by this beautiful hidden mystery life, I didn't yet respect it *as* life. At four, I was unconcerned as a fish flapped feebly on the boat's wooden floor, slowly dying. I ripped a few apart, alive, to check out their inner workings. A few years later, in Winnipeg, I would catch big minnows in nearby ditches, lifting them from the bucket one by one to drop into a jar of hot tap water to see how fast they jerked and died. Fish death didn't bother me a bit.

———

But, *fishing*. I'll try to explain. I inherited my love of it from my dad and I'd bet we inherited it from Cro-Magnon forebears. It feels more like *need* than love, and I'll bet the deep tug in the gut has to do with finding food, and survival itself. That explains why we fisherfolk want to catch bigger fish and more fish. At the cleaning table you can tell the successful angler from his legs-apart stance, bloody knife flashing. Most fish mean best caves, most desirable mates, more and bigger offspring. . . . But, no, if fishing were this fundamental, we'd all love it, and we all don't.

I do. I enjoy the technical side too. The underwater world is a vast question mark but there are things we can know. I like learning bottom terrain. I like guessing what lure most resembles what they're eating today. The challenge is to think like a fish in order to first find them and then fool them. Basically it comes down to this question: Where and when and what are they eating? You try to find them and, if you do, you hover over their restaurant with a menu.

Picture a fish. It looks built to be both predator and prey. It's born elusive. Its underside is bright white, so from below it looks like the sky. Its back is dark, so from above it looks like water. And its eyes: lidless, always wide open. A fish is built to hunt, and be hunted. It looks exactly like a lure, and I am wholly taken in.

But I'm just as excited pulling up a stupid crab trap as I am fighting a salmon. I'm excited pulling up the trap simply because I don't know what's in it. Therein lies the secret to my joy. It's about anticipation, that most patient hunger. It's about being surprised, by something from that invisible, unbreathable world. In traps I've pulled up rock crabs, Dungeness crabs, thirteen-armed sea stars weighing ten pounds or more, and mudsharks all twisted inside the cage, which I then might kill and remove the ureic skin and grill with lemon and garlic. Once I hauled up a huge Irish Lord, the most pompous and frilly of the sculpins. More often I pull up nothing. Which is what whets the appetite, and deepens the surprise, and makes pulling a crab trap a never-ending joy.

Fishing grabs into the unknown. I don't think I'm any happier than when a line gets baited and goes in. Ready, set . . . *ready*. That's enough. I'm dumbly content. I want for nothing more than to sit in this state of want. Back east a friend bought a house on the Nashwaak River solely because it held a few salmon and he could fly-fish every morning from his yard. There weren't many salmon, and he was never much good at it, but he had a favourite saying: Fishing is prayer.

The best time is the strike. I'm content waiting for a strike, but when the rod tip goes crazy—a strike—I go a little crazy myself. It's beyond fun, it's primal. My meat, my game, for which I am seriously hunting, has come. In that moment of the strike, I am a Cro-Magnon having his peak experience. Reeling it in is a lesser thing.

But it feels odd to be getting back into fishing at this time in our history. Venturing onto our fragile sea in this old gas guzzler. Fishing, I contradict my self-image almost violently. I drive a car so tiny it might as well be electric. Our household recycles everything. I love my four children to death but cringe at our family footprint. I not only live in North America's first Green federal riding, but my vote helped make it so. The world really doesn't need an extra guy out there burning gas and killing wild salmon. I know it looks bad. It looks so bad that Dede, the more religious of us two when it comes to environmental concern, has said nothing negative. That's how bad it looks. I know it gave her pause, me and my big boat. It made her wonder who she married and what he's reverted to. I recall an identical silence issuing from my mother when my dad bought *Cormorant*.

*Cormorant* was the closest my dad ever came to spending money on something luxurious. Or as my mother would see it, *unnecessary*. They saved their money and never did unnecessary things. I can't help remembering this when I'm up here at our Gabriola place which is so beautiful, so unnecessary and, again, bought with the money they didn't spend.

And now I have *Sylvan,* not so beautiful but just as unnecessary. And *Sylvan* is what triggered this trip to the past, to Egmont. If it stops overheating. If I make it.

———

I went down to the pond to do most of my Egmont daydreaming and planning. I'd heard some time ago that Vera died. Of course any surviving Egmonsters will be old men now. I wonder if the Suzukis still have their place. The area is fished out, but is it still full of eagles? I flash on the time my dad and I tied up to a kelp bed, to keep from being sucked into the Skookumchuck Rapids, and as the current grew, rippling off *Cormorant's* stern with the sound of a creek, so did the fear on his face.

The pond is my favourite place to sit and stare. I grab a handful of fish food from the pail, stomp my foot on the creaky deck five times, toss the food grandly in, and watch it float. Eventually something small grabs a piece, *plip,* and then there's nothing but the ring, widening out.

Here at the pond I spend a lot of time engaged in fishing of another sort. It's a beautiful pond, and it used to be full of fish.

Ted, the previous owner, put his heart into how he designed these ten acres, over twenty years ago. *Designed* maybe isn't the word, because I use it to include his choosing to leave things alone—eight acres is untouched forest, with a few trails through the fir, cedar, salal, and fern groves. Some of the fir and cedar are upward of three and four feet in diameter, so it's real raincoast forest.

It's designed as, literally, *paradise,* which originally meant "walled garden." In this case, two cleared acres are surrounded by a circular wall of forest. It's a delight to see no neighbours, no roads. The cleared land has an idiosyncratic orchard—plum, pear, cherry, Persian mulberry, hazelnut, six kinds of apple—that slopes down to the pond. The size of a city lot, the pond has a small island on it, reached by two bridges. The bridges and deck and gazebo are badly faded and rickety so they look natural, foresty. Around the pond Ted planted other interesting trees, some for their fall colours, others for their fruits that attract birds. I don't know the names of many of them. When Ted toured me through I remember him saying "swamp cypress" and "corkscrew willow." But I would rather not know the names of all these wonderful, unnecessary trees.

The pond is the focal point, and the focal point of the pond is its fish. The kind of fishing I do at the pond is simply the waiting part. I throw food, then sit and wait to see something rise. Ghost usually shows first, and she's almost always followed by Stalker, who's also cream-coloured but with a black saddle. Both koi are about six inches long. I bought them as babies and they have grown a bit.

Last fall a tragedy befell the place. When we bought it we also inherited the pond's fish, most of them koi carp, as Ted called them. There were eighteen big ones, five or six pounds apiece, and many middle-sized and small ones, because they'd been breeding. Lilli, thirteen at the time, named the big ones: Tiger, Gopher, Boogerhead, Monroe, who was white with blue eyeshadow.

Friends or visitors were forced to come down and watch me feed the fish. I'd stomp my foot and they'd rise and swirl and I'd toss the pellets. Tiger started gobbling first. Monroe was often next, and then there'd be five, then a dozen. Sometimes one of the three big turtles would magically surface and join in, studiously taking a pellet at a time.

All of this would have delighted my father, lying there belly-down on his Mukilteo wharf, watching the perch and shiners circle the pilings, darting from their seaweed shadows for the bits of mussel he's tossed in. When he was on in years he discovered bird feeders and hung a few in front of the window where he spent most of his sober time, eating breakfast, doing the daily crossword, and playing penny-a-point rummy with my mother. He loved watching the birds, the loud jays especially. They'd yell and he'd yell back. He even liked the starlings, though he pretended not to. But my mother hated the mess the birds made underneath the feeders, and one day she took them down.

In any case, last fall an otter came to our pond.

We'd seen otters. Sometimes two, one big and one small. They began to shit in the same spot on a nearby trail. Ted had mentioned that otters came and went, so I wasn't worried. Then I found some fish scales in the grass. Scales the size of a quarter, translucent orange. Koi scales. One day I heard noisy chewing on the other side of the island, and I snuck up to surprise the otter eating the stomach out of a big orange koi. Seeing me, it dove under. The koi swam slowly away, stomachless, its back an inch above water, until it nosed into the opposite bank, tail waving weakly.

I hid behind trees, chunk of wood ready to throw. Twice I was close enough to do damage, but I think I threw to miss. A mammal is of a different order than fish, and an otter is a different order of mammal. Big-eyed, playful, able to feel pain just like us. And I wasn't going to eat it, I was merely mad at it. For eating my fish. Luxury fish, unnecessary fish. But everyone loved these fish. Lilli had named them. Ted had raised them. They were worth lots of money.

On the phone from Victoria, Lilli told me I wasn't allowed to kill the otter.

"I think it just ate Tiger," I said, sinking this low.

When she repeated, "You can't kill it," I could hear tears in her eyes.

I bought the biggest live trap I could find, asking the salesman if it could catch otters. He informed me that it was illegal to trap an otter, but he met my eye significantly and said otters had accidentally been caught in these, yes.

I baited it with store-bought trout, rubbing trout skin all over the trap to hide my scent. That night I caught a cat, and the following night a raccoon which, I learned, can cry like a baby. Both animals were released unharmed and newly wary.

And the otter cleaned the pond of its fish.

Over the past year I've been stocking it. Young koi are expensive, thirty bucks for a three-incher, and it doesn't help my spending mood when I suspect I'm only buying otter food. And, when they're this small, heron food and kingfisher food. I also bought various crazy-patterned goldfish—they aren't koi but they grow to a foot or more. And when they surface to the food I toss they'll surprise me.

Some days nothing comes up, but it seems I can wait endlessly. That's maybe the main thing I shared with my father.

Our solid little house has a fine sundeck. A favourite viewpoint is to lean back in a recliner and look straight up: I'm at the bottom of a bowl that's ringed by lordly trees and, above me, a perfect circle of sky. I feel like I own this land no more than I own that sky.

I wish my father could have seen what he bought for us. He would have loved it. I do have a sense that when I enjoy this place, this paradise, I enjoy it with him. We nod and agree that buying this place, like *Cormorant*, like *Sylvan*, was necessary. Sometimes, as darkness falls, he guzzles beer here with me on the deck, just the two of us. I match him beer for beer, and then some.

# TWO

*Sons have always a rebellious wish to be disillusioned
by that which charmed their fathers.*

—ALDOUS HUXLEY

I'm barely a mile from Gabriola, Egmont still a distant fantasy. An eagle
has killed a heron, the engine is squealing as well as overheating—I
want to end this farce right now. I picture my sundeck, a beer, and my
bed. But I throttle back to trolling speed, slide the stick into neutral. The
squealing lessens not a bit. The word *banshee* comes to mind. The noise
sounds like crisis, like emergency, and it's hard to believe in the bigger
picture all around me—the perfectly calm water, the blue sky.

I go below, hunting a bar of soap. The banshee out back makes me
stumble and hurry and toss charts, cups, blankets aside as I root through.

All spring the overheating was intermittent, and the belt squealed
briefly but then mysteriously stopped, and I went online to see how
you might fix one. First, you could buy a proper torque wrench, and a

new belt, and install it. Second, with that same wrench you could loosen the alternator and adjust the belt tension. Third, from the band-aid school of temporary mechanics, you can spray it with WD-40. This sounds like it would make the belt even more slippery, but apparently it eats into the belt and makes it grabby—before fatally weakening it. I have no WD-40. The last way, today's way, is to rub the belt with soap. This sounds slippery too and makes no sense either, but soap I do have—I find a bar in the frying pan under the sink.

Lifting the engine cowling I stoop before the big black howling beast, and press the soap against the zipping belt. It instantly cuts a groove into the soap bar, and seconds later the howling stops. I love the internet. I keep the bar hard to the belt, letting it apply more soap to itself, enjoying the engine's ordinary rumble. I look around to take in the immense and lovely day again.

Returning to the controls I see that after all this time at idle the engine temperature has fallen to normal. My breathing falls back to normal too. I throttle forward gently and point the bow at the black peak of Texada Island. I'm off again.

But something's ruined. I feel that hot tight knot in my gut, from the engine trouble. Despite the perfect day, my *gut* understands I'm plowing an iffy old boat across a span of water where there's no shelter if the wind comes up. No harbour, not a single island to tuck behind. Because of one rough solo voyage long ago, I'm still very afraid of wind and waves. That is to say, I'm afraid of drowning. Which is reasonable, you say. But my fear borders on silly. It would take something truly freakish out here, in late summer, to capsize a twenty-six-foot boat. I'm also afraid of my fear. By this I mean I'm afraid of a storm but just as afraid of how it will make me feel. I'm afraid of the painful panic.

It's one reason I want to do this trip—to confront my fear. I want to go back to Egmont, and revisit my younger self, and my father's story, but I also want to get back on the horse I fell off about forty years ago.

The spring my father bought *Cormorant* we decided that when my semester ended I would drive it from Vancouver up the Strait of Georgia then north to Egmont, which is where we fished, and where we'd moor it. He'd meet me up there in a week. Piece of cake—two years before, when I was eighteen, in a fit of fishing-addict lunacy I'd made the same trip in a twelve-foot aluminum car-topper. This new boat, twenty-six feet, *could go anywhere*. It was almost a yacht. It had a bathroom. It even had a name.

On a beautiful morning in late May I cast off. Steering up on the flying bridge under a beaming sun I cruised with pride and swelling adventure through Vancouver Harbour. I dodged freighters and sailboats, with no idea what all the colourful buoys meant, following the law of "get out of the way of anything bigger." From my cleaving vessel I knew what Cook and Vancouver had also felt—an intoxicating freedom from land—as I gazed upon stately Stanley Park to my left, ritzy West Van to my right, and my bright future dead ahead. I motored under the majestic Lions Gate Bridge into open water. And, I noticed, a stiff headwind.

Maybe it's called a headwind also because of the way it blows your hair back and empties your head of everything but fear. Of course it means a wind you are heading into, impeding your progress. But both happened when I passed under the bridge into English Bay. Stiff wind became strong wind and two-foot waves became six. Waves I'd been plowing through now had the attitude of plowing through me. They got bigger still, and the wind stronger.

I had no clue what this boat could handle. Mostly, I didn't know if it could safely turn around, to go back. Turning around would mean briefly going broadside to the waves, and that is when a boat can capsize. Plowing straight-ahead cut through the wave somewhat, though it was a rodeo ride. I planted my feet wider apart so I wouldn't fall. The bow plunged into wave after wave and the spray drenched me, ten feet above. Salt water stung my eyes. Ahead lay endless giant, growing waves. Wind blasted my face. I couldn't turn around! This death-trap tub inched forward at maybe two miles an hour. I whimpered like a small child.

A roar above my head—a coast guard helicopter. It had slowed to watch me. Its hover had an attitude of, "Do you have any idea what you're doing out in this?" Barely able to tear my eyes from the next oncoming wave, I did glance up, no doubt wearing an expression that made them wonder aloud why that boat down there was being piloted by a terrified child.

White-fisting the wheel, soaked, lurching up and down, I aimed for a distant island, hoping I could angle into the waves without further endangering things. I didn't know at the time that, steering from up top, things felt way worse than if I'd steered from below, where the pitch and roll was less. But even had I known, it would have been impossible to get down the ladder. So I quartered into the waves, the little brown island my beacon. Hellish though they were, the waves weren't getting bigger. The wind wasn't noticeably stronger. Heading into it, *Cormorant* could apparently survive this much.

It took an hour to make the island, which I cut in behind, into the lee, or what sailors call the side of a landform that's blessedly out of the wind. Exhausted, breathing hard, I praised the beauty of the rocks, the trees. I adored the calm water. I could still hear the wind out there, and this glassy surface miraculously contradicted it. Mostly, the awful, awful wind wasn't blowing into my ears and eyes. It was the wind that was the worst. It was the wind that made you crazy. I nudged up tight to the shore and dropped the anchor. I wasn't going to die today.

The story wasn't over. I waited hours for the wind to die before continuing undramatically on to Egmont. But even after my cramped muscles let go later that night, and stopped being sore a few days after that, the storm continued. If I was on land, any hint of wind grabbed me in the stomach. Even if I was standing in a Saskatchewan field and a breeze came up, I would feel a clench in my very middle. On the water, little waves troubled me. *Ripples* made me hesitate about going fishing in my twenty-six-foot boat that could go anywhere. When I did go out in them, they wouldn't let me relax, let alone enjoy myself.

That storm turned me into a weather baby, a wind chicken. Here I am, forty years later, still reluctant to go out in any kind of blow. Most friends are fine with this. Even though I find myself with *Sylvan*, another twenty-six-footer, I listen to the marine weather forecast every hour before venturing out, and any rumours of a breeze over ten knots will convince me that actually it's time to get some mulch into those tomatoes.

So that storm still wedges in my gut, a wary, vigilant clam that squirts adrenalin at any hint of wind. At sixty, I'm too old to get caught out there helpless, whimpering like a child. In Silva Bay I've noticed that other boaters my age have boats that look clean and cared for. I own the roughest-looking scow at the dock and, like a teenager skiing in old jeans, I'm proud of it—the stains, the duct-taped canvas, the wires connected to nothing. But the radio is often only static. The horn is dead. And the ignition is wonky—I often have to turn the key ten, twenty times before it sparks. I do have to finally just admit that the other skippers are simply smarter, and better prepared not to drown out here on the Salish Sea.

You'd think that after so many years of partial employment I'd be a better mechanic. I lived with barely running cars well into my forties. I could jump-start a standard vehicle and replace spark plugs, but that was about it. Once I changed out a starter motor on *Cormorant*—it involved taking off, and then putting back, two bolts—and my dad bragged to friends about it.

On *Sylvan* this spring, fishing with a friend—Terence—a downrigger seized and he visibly brightened. He liked fishing as a kind of sleepy activity, but probing an unknown machine was worth waking up for. Terence enjoys taking apart his WWII–era British motorcycle whether it needs fixing or not. Needless to say, he had the pesky downrigger running in a jiffy, and I suspect he prodded and tightened extra things just to make the experience last longer. (I've learned that *jiffy* is an actual unit of time, and used by physicists. It lasts approximately a half-second.)

Weeks later I was once again shamed, by a different friend—Steve—but the same downrigger. This time it just quit. I opened the housing, exposing the motor (I'd watched Terence and knew how). Steve prodded and jiggled. I tapped with a wrench, then considered the duct tape.

"Why don't we just call them?" said Steve.

"Call who?"

Steve leaned and read the downrigger's logo. *"Scotty."*

Steve is two decades younger than me so he not only knows how to turn on a smart phone but knows what they're for. We were trolling way out on the Salish Sea and here he was talking to a receptionist and then a techie, discussing the diagram that magically appeared on Steve's screen. I was amazed, and imagined how amazed my dad would have been, a man for whom a screwdriver was technology and expertise was having one on board.

Determining there was no short, and no wires loose, the techie posed a question that, if our problem were a computer, would have been, "Is your computer plugged in?" The question he asked was, "Is your transom button on?"

On *Sylvan*'s back wall, or transom, are two silver buttons, one for each downrigger. You pull them out to turn the power on. Someone's knee, mine, had pushed one in. I bent over and pulled it out. The downrigger started humming.

"There," I said to Steve. "I fixed it."

Steve eyed me over his glasses, trading whispers with the techie.

———

If I'm a lousy mechanic my father was worse. My bar of soap would have impressed the hell out of him.

It shouldn't have been this way, because it brought him endless grief. He was ex-navy, an athlete and all-American male. After getting married, he went to work at Sears, in Seattle, and before I turned one he was transferred north, to Canada, and made manager of the hardware department in Burnaby, a Vancouver suburb. Sears sold Craftsman tools, a respected brand with a famous lifetime guarantee, and it's hard to imagine him talking tools with expert, monosyllabic contractors. He no doubt read all the manuals, but he really didn't know how tools worked. As we moved from city to city and he climbed the corporate ladder, every house had a "Dad's workroom" full of Craftsman tools hanging from hooks over a spotless workbench. These tools stayed clean. But he was from an era when a man who wasn't handy was less than a man, and it must have grated on him. It occurs to me that his main motivation for advancing so quickly from managing a hardware department to managing an entire store was that he got tired of faking competence with tools.

He lacked a certain visual logic to be handy. When I was sixteen he bought a fancy new and powerful car, a Buick Riviera—"the Riv," as my friends came to call it. It could lay a long strip of rubber from a standing start—not that my father ever knew this about his car. But once when I was in the passenger seat while he drove, he angrily shook a finger past my chest at a discovery he'd made, the words printed on the passenger-side mirror: OBJECTS MAY BE CLOSER THAN THEY APPEAR.

"Why would they *do* that," he said.

"What?" I said.

"Instead of fixing the damn thing, they write some crap on it." He shook his head. "This is an expensive car."

It took me a moment to see that he didn't understand a fish-eye mirror, which makes things smaller in order to give you a wider field of vision. My dad thought it was some sort of flawed mirror they for some reason hadn't bothered to rectify.

I didn't say anything. Just like I didn't on *Cormorant* after it broke down, an awful knock starting as we motored in after a day of fishing. The reason marine engines don't last, a mechanic once explained to me, is because, while a car has wheels and can roll along with little resistance, the water on a boat's hull is constant drag, which is why, to get the boat moving at all fast, you have to "keep it floored," as if it were a car forever labouring up a steep hill. I relayed this to my dad as we crippled in to the dock, a rhythmic banging coming from the injured eight-cylinder monster we had captive under the deck. I ventured also that maybe we'd "thrown a rod," because I'd once seen a movie where a hot rod's engine banged like that, and the anguished greaseball kept moaning that he'd "thrown a rod."

We banged to the dock, me steering, my dad going through the beer as if to make up for our lack of pace. Normally he would have kept this stuff to himself, embarrassed to own a faulty engine, but the knocking made it public. Almost at the dock slip, he shouted at a guy his age who was spraying down his boat.

"We threw a rod!"

The guy turned and looked at my dad, then at *Cormorant*, blankly.

As I tied up, and another fellow strode past with two salmon en route to the cleaning table, my dad explained to him that these damn marine engines don't last long because of the way they're always going uphill. With a hand he illustrated the shape of a hillside, and earned a quizzical nod. I saw that he thought my mechanic's "uphill" referred to how a boat sat in the water pointing slightly up, which wasn't the logic at all, and made no sense.

He was drunk by now, and didn't give a shit about the engine or anything else, and wanted only to amble down to the cleaning table to "give 'em the gears," as he put it. Me, I was still cringing and hissing to myself, angry at the knots I couldn't get quite right. It was awful how he needed to cover things up, to lie, to fake it—because he wasn't any good at the mechanics of that either.

———

My dad was freed from the Sears hardware department when he was transferred to Winnipeg, bumped up the ladder to middle management. On the entire continent of North America, Winnipeg is about as far as you can get from salt water, and it was hard to be a fishing addict there.

To this day, whenever I come upon hidden creeks or ponds I realize how fishing is in my blood. I'm instantly drawn to what might be *in* them. It's not a curiosity roused otherwise—I don't see a cave and wonder about bats, I don't see a huge old tree and wonder what's living in its branches. I might remark on a grand old house but I don't wonder at the people inside. It's water that draws me, and all my life I've needed to know what's living in it. The creature doesn't need to be brightly coloured, and it doesn't need to have eyes—though eyes make a smarter, more worthy prey. I don't necessarily need to catch or kill it, it's enough just to see it. What's living there, under water?

Springtime in Winnipeg, walking home from school I'd be excited, in fact fevered to the blood, if the ice was melting in the ditches. I could see through the ice to the water beneath and I could smash through it with a boot. Under there, I knew, were beetles, water bugs, maybe minnows. Hunting, I needed to see these jewel-like prizes. My hands grew dead numb in the search. I'd get distracted and float some sticks—my future boats—in the streams I'd uncovered. My boots would be full and I wouldn't care. It was the best of times.

Summer I'd walk to the muddy trickle of the Seine River with a length of string, tied with a nail for weight, and piece of raw bacon for bait, to catch crayfish. (My dad called them crawdads, which was American.) At age seven and eight I caught them all summer. Sometimes I'd build a Roman Coliseum of rocks and drop several in together to see if they'd battle, but only rarely did they please the Emperor.

I don't know if my father was stricken with the same malady but I think he was. The thing my father disliked most about Winnipeg, besides winter, was the distance you had to travel to fish. The rivers intersecting the city—the Red, the Assiniboine, the tiny Seine—were so muddy and polluted that, so we believed, if you fell in you had to instantly go to the hospital. Fishing was never an option. If we wanted to fish we had to drive a fair distance.

A few times we drove east to the Brokenhead River. The Trans-Canada was just a two-lane road in those days and we fished right off the highway bridge. It was on this bridge that my dad had me perform surgery on him. I was nine.

There were bass and pike in the Brokenhead, and we were casting red devil spoons. We weren't getting anything and I was bored. I jigged and fooled around, and my lure got snagged on the bottom right below our feet. Usually I was good at getting unsnagged, but eventually Dad had to grab my rod and do it himself. He pulled and pulled, impatient with me for getting snagged in the first place. He gave it a mighty, rod-breaking pull, the lure tore free at speed, shot up, and one of the big treble hooks sank deep into the back of his hand.

He yelled, he swore, he stomped his feet, but hunched over, protective of his hand, which he cradled with the other, at the same time holding tight to the lure so it didn't wobble and hurt him more.

*"Jesus."*

"Is it okay?"

*"Goddammit."*

I asked if I could help and he turned his back on me in case I came close. The barbs on hooks work. It's amazing anyone ever loses a hooked fish.

He told me to get the fishing knife out of the tackle box. It was actually more hunting knife than fishing knife. I'd cleaned a perch or two with it last time and it wasn't sharp and I could smell it. Dad tried gingerly nicking enough skin to free the hook. He couldn't bring himself to make the slice that would do the job.

"Here," he said, thrusting the knife my way. "You do it." He didn't look at me.

He pulled steadily on the lure to keep the hook from jiggling.

"Fast."

I knew the knife was sharpest closest to the handle, as dull knives often are, and when I positioned that part over the target area he asked me what I was doing and I had to explain. He said nothing. He closed his eyes. A semi whooshed by and honked long but neither of us moved. If there was ever a perfect time for a slug of bad whisky and a bullet to bite, this was it, and I've never seen a Hollywood bullet extraction without thinking of the Brokenhead River bridge, which itself sounds like a corny western.

It's hard cutting into a father's flesh with a big, dirty knife. Freud could've come up with a pithy paragraph about it. My half-hearted sawing made Dad wince and grit his teeth and finally hiss, *"Do it"*. So I gritted my own teeth and put some muscle into it, gouging. Out it popped, and blood flowed.

He didn't congratulate or thank me. He found a bandage in the tackle box and we kept fishing. I believe he picked up pace on the beer.

That same day I caught a memorable fish. I'd gone down the bank and around a bend in the river, out of sight of the bridge and my dad, which made it a bit scary, but also a small joy—there was a well-trod, shaded clearing where, I could tell from a few old lure packages, people fished. I dug up a worm and fished it with a bobber, and I don't think the line was in the water two minutes before the bobber shot down and a giant golden fish leapt up thrashing. It was a great big carp.

It was one of the best fish-fights of my life. It was five or six pounds, and carp do put up a tussle. I held my breath the whole time, especially when it jumped, and I somehow yelled for my dad. He arrived just as I got it up on the bank, and I knelt admiring it until it was time to pack up and go home. A beautiful burnished gold. Dad said carp were too bony to eat, but I insisted on taking it with us. The ride home was quiet and it was the last time we fished the Brokenhead River.

For some reason I was forbidden to cook the carp at home so I took it across the street to Mark's. Mark was two or three years older than me, so we weren't exactly friends, but he fired up his family barbecue. I don't know where his parents were. I proudly gutted the fish in his sink, and we made a tray out of tinfoil. I insisted we put slabs of butter on it, which gradually melted as the fish sizzled over the coals. When it was done, the knob of the severed backbone lifted free of the tender flesh, taking a perfect, delicate skeleton with it. It tasted better even than pickerel, or mahi mahi, and no one will ever convince me otherwise.

———

One fall my dad took me on a strange trip maybe an hour's drive out of Winnipeg, to a small, dark village on a dammed river. Why we spent the night in a hotel I have no idea. Maybe in those days an hour's drive home was something you didn't try at night. Maybe my dad knew he'd be having a few. I sensed my mother made him take me along. The whole trip felt pinched and tawdry. It was raining and cold when we left home. But I was excited to be going fishing.

The top of the dam was the town's main street and you fished from the sidewalk, leaning on a rail, hanging a line in. The prey was pickerel and its smaller relative, sauger. It rained the whole time, strange for the prairies, and it was miserable. We caught nothing, and weather drove us back to the hotel. The tiny room was wooden, and musty. No TV or radio, and the one small window was too high for me to see out.

We ate a bad hamburger downstairs. I had extra fries, even though they were dry, because there was nothing else to do. Back in the room, my father stood not looking at me, jingling the change in his pocket, something he did when nervous.

"What's there to do?" I whined. I had no book to read, no comics, nothing. I could sense my dad's helplessness and I milked it, because it was all his fault.

"What's there to *do?*" I flopped on the one big bed, whining, almost crying, acting younger than my age. It was all his fault, because I knew he didn't want me here in the first place. Kids know things like that, they can feel them. My dad stood at the foot of the bed, edgy, trying to think of something to say and failing.

He could hardly wait to get to the bar, I know that now. Most likely the whole trip had been a getaway. Fish a bit, drink his fill, no one's the worse for wear. But he was stuck with me—probably my mother's last-minute demand, a gambit to staunch his solitary fun.

He left and came back bearing a pencil and two paper placemats.

"You like drawing," he said hopefully. This was true, but I didn't want to hear it from him.

"It's not *an HB.*"

I said this to his back as he left, closing the door quietly. He didn't come back, not till sometime in the deep of the night, when I woke to hear him stumbling around, clumsier than usual. Soon he was snoring beside me.

———

I really liked Winnipeg and my dad really didn't. I lived there from age six to twelve, and it was a time I remember well—pack of friends, hockey, reading, innocent of the hormones just around the corner. For my dad, Winnipeg was as far from his west coast as he could find himself.

I have a photo of him near the end of when we lived there. He's standing before our house, a basketball trapped with his wrist against his hip so casually it's like he doesn't know it's there. His checked shirt doesn't go with the basketball. He's scowling, his face sallow. He looks angry, sad, and depressed. He's skinnier than in any other picture I've seen, including those from his college beanpole days. His crew-cut hair is mostly grey, and in another year or two it would be all grey and heading for white. He's thirty-nine. He looks mid-fifties.

Even while in Winnipeg, my mother told me that my dad missed the ocean. She added that at work he was surrounded by "some real go-getters" who would stab you in the back to make themselves look good.

One year my dad's mother visited us, all the way from Washington State. It was the only time I saw my grandmother. She "wasn't herself" during the visit. A bit senile, was the word. I learned later that she'd brought hidden packs of salt, despite a heart condition. I was ten, and she could never remember my name, and talked to herself in quiet half-sentences. She was thin, and pale, and too small to be the mother of someone so big. She smelled like powder. I never knew what to say to her.

I don't recall my dad talking to her at all. I didn't see how he greeted her. It was all fascinating to me because I'd never known or even seen a relative before, let alone a grandparent. Most interesting of all, only two days into her visit my dad and some Sears friends flew on a seaplane to a remote lake in northern Manitoba to go pickerel fishing. His mother was gone by the time he returned. He brought back with him a dozen quart milk cartons filled with pickerel fillets frozen in water.

Years later, when I talked to my mother about that time I met my dad's mother, she brought up his sudden fishing trip but only because it had put her out, having to entertain her mother-in-law and keep her away from that hidden salt. I asked her why she thought my dad went fishing: Was he refusing to cancel a long-planned trip, or was he fleeing his mother?

My mother looked away and chirped, "Well I don't know!" in the voice that said she wasn't going to tell me.

Recalling my grandmother's state—stick-thin, sneaking salt, not making sense—I wondered if he couldn't handle what she'd become. Or he couldn't take the memories she kindled, because he hated his past that much. It was confusing. By this time I knew more about his mother, how she slaved to raise my dad and his sister Margaret, cleaning houses, and working in the cafeteria lunch line at Everett High School, where she got fired for repeatedly serving her too-skinny adolescent boy extra food despite warnings, simply unable to control herself. It was hard to reconcile that story in particular with my dad's reaction to her visit in Winnipeg. I remember his silent brooding after she left. I have no proof but, from what I know now, I can imagine that this is when the drinking took off. Or took hold.

Not long after his mother's visit, late one night when I was in bed reading, I answered the phone and it was him.

"Billy? Is that Billy?" His voice sounded robotic, and echoing, like he was in a gym. It sounded like he was talking carefully to a phone, and not to me.

"Dad?"

"Go get your mom." He sounded serious, even afraid.

"What's wrong?" I asked, afraid myself.

He was at the hospital—a car accident, he said. I'll never forget the sound of his voice. A zombie finding it difficult to talk.

He spent the night at the hospital. Driving home from a poker game he'd hit a patch of ice and totalled the car (our sky-blue 1960 Chev), knocking over a wooden power pole, or what we called a telephone pole. He'd hit his head on the windshield and broken his nose and got knocked out. The doctors told him how lucky he was to get away with just the broken nose, which, he joked, had been broken on the basketball court more than a few times before, anyway. The city made him pay for a new pole. For years, I'd laugh pointing to "Dad's pole" when we passed it on Archibald Street. Its wood was newer, blonder than the other poles. My dad would chuckle half-heartedly. My mother not at all.

When I found out the real cause of the accident—he'd blacked out at the wheel, drunk—of course it only made sense. I'd always wondered how a patch of ice could cause a car to veer sideways in a new direction. "Dad's pole" was planted along a stretch of road as straight as a ruler.

——

A car is one place a father can hold an old-fashioned power. When my son Connor was little, he loved the first time he saw me turn on the high beams, instantly illuminating a forest, ice-white. His astonished *"woah!"* included the notion, *Dad knows how to do that.* Just like you knew the multiplication tables, and you could skate backwards, and you somehow seemed even to know things about his future. But best yet, you can light up that forest. What *couldn't* you do? You trip the high beams a few more times, until the *woah* loses some of its joy. You eventually show him the lever, but you aren't quick to reveal that you don't really understand the mechanics of it. It feels too good, this pure admiration from your little boy. You already sense that these moments are gold coins, and the supply might not be endless.

The first time my dad stuck me between his legs and let me steer, I was nine. We were en route to fish at Lac du Bonnet, the place we vacationed every summer. Pickerel and pike. Sometimes I used live frogs for bass, which would shoot up from the depths and attack my bait as it frog-kicked along the surface, trying to escape the hook in the skin of its back. It is not a lucky thing to be live bait.

My mother wasn't with us, and that's likely why I got to drive. We were on the main highway north out of Winnipeg, not a lot of traffic but certainly not empty. It was the sky-blue 1960 Chev.

We idled on the gravel shoulder. I clambered into position. I wasn't going to push the gas because I couldn't reach. But I was going to steer. I took some breaths. I didn't like that we were on the highway.

"Just go straight," my dad said.

When he saw no cars in either direction he floored it. I turned too sharply left to get us off the shoulder and onto pavement, and there was some swerving before I got it straight. He didn't let up on the gas. I was yelling, "*Ahhhhhhhhh!*"

"Thirty!" he yelled.

The car went faster, and faster. Every new level of fast needed a new kind of steering. You had to be *instant*. You had to steer *small*, or flip. You don't breathe.

"Okay?" he yelled. He was laughing and his body against mine felt reckless. He could have grabbed the wheel at any time but still nothing felt safe. The engine noise grew higher, harsher.

"Faster!" I yelled.

His "okay-ay" was the wary singsong but he kept his foot down. Faster.

"Fifty!" he yelled.

"Faster!"

The car was shaking.

"Sixty!" he yelled. And took his foot off the gas.

We decelerated, and I managed to get the car back onto the shoulder. Now I could breathe. I marvelled and laughed there between his legs.

It had been his idea. He'd simply kept it floored the whole time, till we hit sixty, and then just as simply taken his foot off the gas. Looking back, I find this a bizarre way to teach your kid how to drive. Stranger still, he was a conservative, even poky driver. I'm not sure, but I don't believe there was beer involved.

It was really fun.

The following year, on that same strip of highway—which, by the way, still passes both a never-ending underground fire and the world's largest garter-snake colony—another odd car incident took place. I own a perversion that's truly a mystery to me, and I thank God it visits only rarely.

I was in our car with my dad and two of his business friends, one of whom was his boss at Sears, Mr. H. We were going fishing. The thing is, I liked Mr. H. He was friendly, pudgy, and liked to joke, plus he asked me about hockey and let me talk about myself, there in the back seat. He was up front with my dad, who was driving. He sat there not saying much and chuckling a lot.

I knew Mr. H was Catholic. I don't know how I knew, maybe from a conversation. The point is, for some reason, apropos of nothing, I suddenly leaned forward, planted my face between my dad and his boss Mr. H, and announced,

"I *hate* Catholics."

I didn't hate Catholics. In Winnipeg, most of my friends were Catholics. I eventually married one and live with her still.

There followed a confused silence. I was made to apologize, and later when my father asked me what in the world had come over me, I didn't know what to say. "Mysterious perversion" wasn't in my vocabulary yet. Nor did I know how to say that, as a child in the back seat, I saw a strange fear and submissiveness come over my dad in the face of authority, for instance a boss. Even a nice boss. I saw my dad go weak. I didn't understand it, and I wanted to explode it.

———

He got two weeks' vacation and we spent it at Lac du Bonnet, where we did little but fish. Pickerel for Mom to fry up for dinner, or we'd drift the weedbeds hunting big northern pike, casting spoons. My dad pronounced the place "Lack Da-*bon*-ny." The fridge opened and closed a lot once we were off the water, and my dad went to bed earlier than usual. Other than fish, my brother and I swam, and hacked around in the woods catching frogs or plinking a BB gun. If the goldeye were running we'd spend hours chasing grasshoppers and fill a jar. My mother joined us for the goldeye hunt, sitting in the bow with a mystery novel in one hand and a rod in the other.

Goldeye are strange fish. They school in great numbers and don't seem to occur anywhere but the Winnipeg River, which is actually a slow-flowing chain of prairie lakes. Winnipeg's pro baseball team was The Goldeyes. A panfish, like sunfish or black bass, they're silver like salmon, their irises bright gold. They're oily, bony and best eaten smoked. When the goldeye were running, the resort owner fired up his smoking shed and strung hundreds of the fish on stinky old poles through the mouth and one gill, so they all came out with heads on an identical tilt. Rumour had it they were a delicacy in New York and Paris.

We'd anchor in the ripples of a visible current and bobber-fish them with our grasshoppers. When a school came through we'd have goldeye on all four rods at once, running and jumping, frisky as hell, my mother lost in her book, oblivious to her rod whipping and yanking, barely noticing the rest of us at our peak fun.

One day my dad was under the weather and didn't want to go out so my brother and I went on our own and found some. I fought something a little bigger, stronger, and when I saw it I yelled:

"Master Angler Award!"

To win a Master Angler Award you had to catch a near-record fish, a freak. Eight pounds was the mark for pickerel, and most pickerel we caught were one or two pounds. Eighteen was the weight for northern pike. I had all the weights memorized. Once when my dad hooked a huge pike, and I saw it and shouted, "Master Angler Award!" I must have convinced him because we zoomed right back to weigh it—the pike was only thirteen, so five pounds shy.

The weight for a goldeye was two pounds, two ounces. This looked close. But I wasn't that excited—a two-pound fish simply isn't a big fish. We didn't zoom in to weigh it, but when we did, it was two pounds, one ounce. I went behind the dock shack for some pebbles to force-feed my fish. Weighed it again. It needed more pebbles. Eventually it weighed two pounds, two ounces. My dad was strangely still in bed so Mom was my adult witness. I sent in the forms and a month later received a certificate and bronze medal declaring me a Master Angler. I wasn't that excited getting it in the mail—not because I was a liar but because it was, again, a smallish fish. Even at that age I had a sense that lying was an honourable part of angling tradition. My twenty-pound salmon still become twenty-five-pounders, often by the very next day.

———

The first time I took any of my own kids fishing, they were as small as I was when my dad first took me on Three Mile Lake. Aware that

I was sparking a torch and passing it, he was very much on my mind. We were living in New Brunswick. A friend had a place up the Nashwaak River, and a rowboat. There were rumours of bass and trout. I borrowed two tiny rods, some small hooks and bobbers. I dug a jar of worms.

We took the boat out mid-river and anchored. I discovered that I didn't have life jackets for the kids. But I told myself that the river wasn't fast, and it was barely knee-deep—plus, I'd bet any amount that I didn't have a life jacket on when my dad took me. Truth be told, I just wanted to fish. It had been years and years.

One thing you quickly forget is how much hassle fishing can be. Especially in unknown water, with unfamiliar gear. There on the Nashwaak with my two companions, one a toddler, I encountered hurdles. The boat proved hard to anchor in the current because the rocks were round and slick. My eldest, Lise was patient and dutiful, but little Connor wanted to do everything himself and wasn't capable, so when he insisted he let out not twenty feet of line but two feet, there his line stayed, inches from the boat, useless. Lines got tangled. Tantrums bloomed. Forbidden to stand on the seat, Connor eyed me while he placed one, and then a minute later, two feet onto the seat, and then he would slowly hoist himself to standing, until I yelled. We replayed this glacier-paced game as Lise gripped her rod, irritated by any bites she got because they didn't feel right compared to the smoothness of *not* having them. Over on the friend's lawn, Dede, cradling Vaughn in her arms, waved and shouted suggestions, but I couldn't hear her over the river's wash.

We caught a few tiny trout, three and four inches long. Some had swallowed the small hook and would slowly die after I tore it from deep in their throats. I didn't like this part at all and I hoped the kids weren't noticing. I made a big show of getting the trout back into the water quickly, singing cheerily, *"There* it goes," as it drifted out of sight. I was glad that Connor wanted to hold one and that he showed brow-knit interest in the mystery, shape and beauty—the life—in his hands.

But I really wanted them to hook into a sizable trout or bass and feel the thrill of the fight, where a thrashing fish had just as good a chance of getting loose as getting caught. That didn't happen, but it looked like the kids had some fun.

Though not enough, apparently. A year later, a nice sunny day, I asked if they wanted to go fishing, hinting that this time we'd catch something big. They both declined. What I got from them was my first taste of kids turning me down and looking apologetic, aware that I was excited and not wanting to hurt my feelings.

How easy it gets, though, this turning down your father and his idea of fun, with apologies.

# THREE

*Fathers should be neither seen nor heard.*

—OSCAR WILDE

About three miles into the Salish Sea, I can't believe I'm doing this this. I'm actually doing it. I'm sixty, and voyaging solo, in my junker, to Egmont. Where my dad and I learned to fish. Where we spent the most time together. That place of swirling rapids and dark weather.

I feel—I feel great. The weather is holding. It's like being on a vast liquid mirror, surrounded on all sides by distant cotton wool. Blue mirror, white wool, blue sky above. I can see no sign of other humans. To the west and east, above the cotton, are hazy mountains. I keep *Sylvan* pointed north, at a black peak called Texada.

Completely alone. I haven't done something like this in years. Decades. I feel . . . *young*. I want to shout, or take off my clothes. But that's unnecessary. This is enough. I want to say I could die happily now, but that would be untrue. The truth is, because of times like this I never want to die.

On this calm water I can see forever and the coast is clear of logs, so I bungee-cord the steering wheel pointed dead ahead. I'm hungry, go below. And I'm excited just to look around. I love the compact life of a cabin cruiser. I nudge with a toe my cooler of food that doesn't need cooking and can be eaten while motoring: bag of mini-carrots, plums and apples from my own trees, a gypsy sausage I can eat one-handed as I steer. In a garbage bag on the V-berth, a change of clothes. A fluffy pillow rides atop a mound of blankets. A Lorrie Moore novel beside a history of the Captain Beefheart band, which apparently had over thirty members at various times, so crazy was the Captain. My laptop, and an adapter to plug into the boat's dash.

A case of bottled water. The boat has a freshwater tank and small sink, but last winter when I drained it I put in line cleaner and then couldn't get the taste out. Plus a tankful of water weighs a lot. So, bottled. I've also got a portable propane camp stove for cooking but also for heating the cabin, because the electric heater also doesn't work and, a week into September, it's getting cold at night.

I go back up and steer while chewing sausage. The extreme engine roar is a constant I can somehow ignore, or even erase, the brain being such a wonderful filter. Or engine of denial. I look back at Gabriola, which I can now blot out by holding a hand a foot in front of my face. This boat is supposed to cruise at eighteen but I'm taking it slow, ten or eleven, and it overheats only a little. It will take longer to get across—this *sea*—and into sheltered water, but so far all is flat. Sleek as lip gloss.

I'm glad they renamed this body of water the Salish Sea. My father would have approved. He wasn't at all racist toward First Nations people, not like he was with Asians. He would have liked saying it aloud, slowly, timing it with a comma to savour it—"the Salish, Sea." It would have become an expression. "So here we are, on the Salish, Sea." The politicians who wrote the change into law used a brilliant manoeuvre and silenced most critics by retaining the European names: it's still the straits of Georgia and Juan de Fuca and Haro, but all combined it's the Salish Sea. An official sea, taking its place with the Aegean, Dead and Black. How can you not like that? Apparently some don't. Personally, I'd rather the name connect to the people who lived here for thousands of years, as opposed to some wiggy bepowdered personage of the British or Spanish court, who never even saw the place.

Over the mist—I won't call it fog, because fog is dangerous—I can now see another small mountain, over what would be Sechelt. I aim for a spot directly between it and Texada. The compass reads exactly northwest. It feels good to use landforms rather than the compass as a guide, because even a compass feels like technology. I will be very disappointed, not to mention scared, if that mist becomes real fog and I have to use my GPS, which is newfangled indeed. It would be too weird, though technically I could do it, to actually roar along blind.

I think I see the Merry Island lighthouse, but that would be impossible.

I put the sausage stub in the cooler and eat some mini-carrots as a chaser. I do some stretches, first removing my stained sweater. Beautiful mirrored sea or not, I see I've grown impatient with the changelessness, and the engine drone. Plowing forward and never a change—in the sky not a bird or a cloud; on the mirror, not a wave or a stick—the trip has too quickly taken on a treadmill quality. I think of the term *limbo*. I realize I've been daydreaming about chores involving firewood. I see I've unconsciously nudged the throttle up, and hit fourteen knots.

That minor god—I'll call him Hubris—who gives us what we deserve, must have heard my inner whining about changelessness and perfect glass, because suddenly the mirror changes to ripples, then to small waves. From the northwest, which can't be right. What an amazing thing adrenalin is. Unable to resist, I edge the throttle forward a bit more. I want sheltered water.

I flick on the radio to the coast guard channel, for updates on the *Continuous Marine Report.* I've been waiting for wind. That is, *dreading* it. Dread is old panic that had its edges sanded off and settled, long-term, in your gut.

All week and into this morning today's forecast remained unchanged: winds five to fifteen knots from the southeast. Which was excellent. Even if it blew a consistent fifteen the waves would be no more than two, three feet, tops, and coming from the southeast they'd be at my back, in effect pushing me. But these waves are from the northwest, totally unpredicted.

My radio gives up nothing but static.

I was an idiot to attempt this trip in a boat with no radio, with a wonky engine, with so many broken things. How stupid was my romantic notion that, because I was revisiting my teenage days I'd recapture their spirit by being unprepared, devil-may-care, a young guy jumping in his shitty car with iffy brakes, going camping with nothing but a can of beans and a blanket. I'm way too old to be on high alert like this, jaw clenched, radio hissing at me as I eye these waves. Which are still, really, only ripples. *But they are from the northwest.*

I won't turn back. I reckon I'm maybe halfway across anyway. I also know this fear isn't just about waves and wind. Beneath it a more sober eye knows this is a voyage to my past, upriver—I'll say it—to my personal heart of darkness. I'm going to see my father at his worst. I'm going to visit myself when I was always alone, a hermit, actually, busy worrying but never deciding. I'll remember exactly what my sixteen-year-old mind felt like. And then discover myself too suddenly sixty. I will feel the hell of time. A life almost gone now. Though I can't hear myself over the engine and radio static, I whisper, only minimally sardonic: *"The horror."* And I crank up the throttle again.

Hubris has been watching and hearing all of this. Not only have those northwest ripples become genuine waves but the needle on the temperature gauge is climbing as fast as the second hand on a clock.

———

Egmont. When we moved from Winnipeg to Vancouver we brought our sixteen-foot lake boat and trolled with it a few times for coho. We learned that the big chinook salmon—often called springs— were caught by moochers. Mooching was what real fishermen did. As we trolled past, chugging smoke and dragging hardware, they sat at anchor, still as buddhas, with daintier, more sporting rods. Later, at the cleaning table, they worked through their tub of impossibly big salmon. My dad and I agreed we had to try it. It felt like a pact. I was thirteen.

One Friday when he got home we hooked up the lake boat and trailed it to Horseshoe Bay to catch the ferry to Langdale. We were heading for a place called Egmont, where some Sears guys had rented cabins. My dad called it "rough" and "middle of nowhere," which sounded great. The farther from civilization, the better the fishing. The whole ferry trip I vibrated. I paced.

During a lapse in the rain we ventured out on deck to watch the water go by. This was the ferry trip where, looking up open-mouthed at the seagulls gliding just overhead, I caught a gob of white on my tongue. I spat and spat and raced to the water fountain inside, and now knew that seagull shit and anchovies taste identical.

It was also a trip where my dad passed on some fishing lore. On the back deck Dad pointed down into the white, churning water getting hammered by a propeller the size of a car.

"It'd be great to throw a line out," he said. "Salmon follow ferries because the prop chops up all the herring."

Staring into the roiling water, I pictured hungry salmon snapping up fresh chunks of herring. I pictured a boat nosing into that wash, catching endless salmon. But I was beginning to suspect some of my dad's lore. I figured that herring must be awfully stupid to just sit there and get cut up by a monstrous prop they can hear coming a mile away.

"But," I said, adding wistfully, not as a challenge, "why don't boats follow the ferry and fish in the wake?"

He didn't hesitate long. "They aren't allowed to. It's a law."

I came to assess other of my father's lore. Some collapsed under the merest bit of logic. When we mooched for salmon, often the rod tip flicked with what looked like a bite but then nothing more would happen. We'd reel up and the bait, a live herring, would be unmarked, frisky and fine. "Slapped it with his tail," is what Dad would always say. It's what salmon did when they weren't very hungry. When I was young this didn't seem like bad lore to me at all. On TV I'd seen killer whales whap the water surface to stun prey. Dinosaurs swung mighty tails to inflict fatal damage. Why wouldn't a salmon? Well, because it couldn't. No more than a human, underwater, could slap someone with a garbage-can lid. A fish "slapping" a tail would simply propel itself, away. It's what fish tails do, they propel.

When I was thirteen I impressed my dad with my use of logic. Our first Vancouver summer we moored our lake boat out in Indian Arm, and I was rowing us out to it in our dinghy. My dad said something about how clean the water was, and how clearly you could see the oar moving through it. I corrected him. An oar doesn't really move through the water, I told him, an oar stands still and the boat moves, which is of course the whole point of rowing. He looked at me a moment, then said, "Hmm, I guess that's right." Resisting my even more obnoxious side, I didn't explain that a fish tail is similar to an oar in this regard, and that when a fish tail moves, the fish goes somewhere else, and no slapping takes place.

After disembarking in Langdale, and passing through Gibsons, where *The Beachcombers* would soon begin shooting, we began a long and winding drive. The narrow road dipped into gullies and hugged corners of rock. Rain began to fall hard. No signs of civilization. Wipers and defrost on max, my dad bent forward squinting for Egmont Road. We crawled along. He cracked beer. We came to another ferry terminal, one for Powell River. We doubled back. At one in the morning, finding a wide enough shoulder, he pulled off and announced that we were sleeping here. The rain was relentless. Its pummel is what put me to sleep there in the back seat. I don't know if my dad slept, six-five, bent up in the front. I heard beers open, and the door thunk when he got out to pee.

In the morning we saw we were not a mile from Egmont Road. Nearing the marina, my dad told me not to tell anyone he'd got lost and we'd slept beside the road. We found the cabin we were sharing with two other men. They were executives like him. At Sears, officers didn't mix with foot soldiers. But my dad was the Burnaby general manager, so the highest up the ladder here. He woke his cronies with funny insults about sleeping the day away. They put on coffee and bacon. My dad cracked a beer. He offered beer to the others and a short, stubby guy took one, though he didn't want it.

I wanted to fish. I couldn't comprehend the sight of our boat just sitting there on its trailer. I went down to the dock and eyed the dirty insides of boats, catching wafts of fish blood and bait. Most boats were small like ours, because Egmont was sheltered, at the centre of four fjords coming together. Eventually I calmed and took in the scene, the vista of waterways walled by mountains. Across the channel, a few cabins reachable only by boat. Two uninhabited islands. Around a corner the dull roar of what sounded like Niagara

Falls—I didn't know about the Skookumchuck yet. What struck me most was the wilderness. Beyond, where the fjords met, no man-made structures on any shore. Clear-cuts patched some mountain-sides, but otherwise there was nothing. At my feet the water sped past swift as a river and looked dangerous for it. The marina and clearing for the cabins looked like a fresh gouge in the forest. This was a place where bears would walk past, casually hunting human refuse. Above, hanging against the blue, an eagle. I heard the trill of another somewhere behind me. Seals basked on the rocks off one of the islands. Graceful as a struggling sausage, a seal got itself into the water.

And Egmont was legendary for salmon. Already, I knew I'd be back.

Breakfast over, we launched the boat and visited the little tackle shop on the dock. My dad poked around the packs of lures and hooks on the wall. He asked the hippyish counter guy if they had any mooching hookups.

"Didn't have time to tie up my own," he added.

The guy gave him an odd look, then flicked a finger at the packs of mooching hookups my dad had just been poking through. My dad tried to hide his embarrassment. The guy's ponytail didn't help.

Dad had been a troller all his life. He showed me how he'd jerk his foot to give his lure "pizzazz" when it was wrapped around his foot. He said a big salmon hurt. He'd also trolled bucktail flies—long, ragged lures made from the white hairs of a deer's tail that tended to float, so you could see a salmon's explosive strike. Trolling had its advantages. You covered territory and found fish instead of waiting for fish to find you. Moving through water made the lure twist and flash and act "sexy." When a fish struck a trolled lure it tended to hook itself. All you really had to do was reel it in. If it was a marlin or huge salmon, that could take some doing—the "sport" part—but the main work was done. Some people call trolling "meat fishing."

And trolling had a downside. The big salmon, the springs, were often deep, often two hundred feet. A trolled lure cruises up near the surface. Unless you tie huge weights to your line and use big broompole rods to handle all the drag, you can't get down deep while trolling. But that's what trollers did, they trolled with stout rods and big weights. The weights, plus the flasher, a shiny chunk of metal the size of a flattened loaf of bread, was a heavy load even without a fish on the end. If a three-pound coho hit, it didn't feel like much had changed. Meat fishing.

Mooching, you got right down to the bottom. Also, it was harder to do and used lighter gear, attractive features to the salmon angler who valued the sport more than the meat.

Here are the directions my dad and I got from the ponytail guy at the dock:

First, buy some live herring. You need a big container of some sort to keep them alive. You find the "hole," or the place where the salmon are. You anchor, but since you don't have one, you can drift in that bay across there (he hooked a thumb in a general direction through the open door) out of the current. Use a four-ounce weight. Use these hookups here (he tapped those on the wall), or tie up two treble hooks four inches apart, with a six-foot leader. Wet your hands so the herring won't lose scales when you handle it. Hook one hook through the nostrils, the other through the upper back. Send your bait down till you hit bottom, then come up ten cranks *fast* or you'll get a rock cod. That's it. If your line suddenly goes slack, that's a strike. They hit from below and come up with it. Reel like mad, and when you catch up and feel the fish, hit it hard to set the hooks. Then the fun starts.

We headed for the little bay. From our cabin we'd borrowed a plastic garbage can for the dozen herring, which, before we were even across the channel, started going belly up. My dad stuck his hand in the water and tickled it for five seconds, saying that should do the trick, but it didn't, and a minute later half were dead. Back at the dock we learned we had to bucket in fresh, oxygenated water every ten minutes or so.

Lines out, hushed with anticipation, we sat drifting. We sat there and sat there, our baits ten cranks up from the bottom. We wondered if we were doing it right or wasting our time. We sat, drifting, not talking much. We had trolling gear in the boat just in case. We could see other boats out there over the reef, including the Sears guys, trolling happily away. A distant net came out, a salmon landed, but we could see it was small, a coho. We weren't interested in that. We wanted to catch the big springs, we wanted to be moochers. We didn't say as much, not aloud, but we both felt the same and we knew it.

Then my dad noticed, rather casually, that his line was completely slack. This either meant we'd drifted in shallower and his sinker was lying on bottom, or—

"That guy," I said, "didn't that guy say something about line going slack?"

My dad quickly started reeling. Not like mad, not at first, but then he noticed that, even after reeling up twenty feet, forty feet, more, his line was still slack. My line wasn't slack, meaning, we weren't in shallower water. Something was going on. He started reeling like mad. Doing so, he'd feel a momentary weight on the line, and then it would be slack again. He reeled and reeled. He looked over at me and shrugged. Two hundred feet was lots of line. He reeled some more.

Suddenly he'd reeled all the way up. Beside the boat, we saw, our neck hairs standing up in unison, a salmon, a spring salmon, a chinook, that weighed thirty, forty pounds. It was just sort of hanging there, sculling, its back wide as a pig's.

"Get—Bill? Get the—"

I grabbed the net. I tentatively reached it out toward the monster. The salmon flicked its tail, my dad's rod instantly bent double, the leader snapped, his rod whipped back, hit him in the face, then pointed straight at the sky, at rest.

That was our one bite. Back at the dock we described our adventure to a guy gutting his two twenty-five-pounders at the cleaning table. He went back on his heels to chuckle professionally, and said, not looking at us, "They don't come in *that* easy."

The size of that fish, two feet from the boat. Its black-speckled green back, so wide and almost frightening for its obvious power. We wanted nothing but to try mooching again.

———

And we did. I did much more so, especially after living up there for months at a time. Mooching became a kind of meditation. You sit quietly. You focus on your rod tip. You are watching for a wiggle, then for the rod to perfectly straighten out. A strike.

But mostly you're just sitting there. Your rod tip is a figure in a field—you are also aware of the surroundings. Shimmers. Waves. Distorted reflections of sky and mountains. There's so much going on. The shining black ball of a seal's head. No, it's a bobbing log. You watch the rod tip. Mountains, ten shades of purple, depending on their distance. The comic sounds of seabirds. Wavelets tickle-slapping the hull. Drone of a distant tug, or trawler, or seaplane. You watch the tip. Occasionally, almost as entertainment, you reel up to check your bait. Refreshed by activity, you sit and watch the tip again.

Mooching tests the patience of some. Friends would stretch and yawn too often, or talk non-stop, or pace the deck as if measuring the size of a jail cell. Or they'd get into the beer a little too early.

I was happy to meditate like that all day. So was my father. It even made him slow down on the beer. Dawn to dusk. Fish or no fish.

Watching the rod tip. We never acknowledged this thing we had in common. I know now how rare it is.

———

The move to Vancouver was a step up for my father, who became by turns the manager of the Burnaby, then downtown, then Richmond stores.

He liked the word *executive*. He especially liked it when the word was applied to a style of house or car or boat. Whenever he said it, pronouncing it the American way, "ex*e*cative," he seemed to be listening to himself say it, the Mukilteo boy amazed to find himself where he was.

But if my dad was looking for respect and admiration from his boys, he had the wrong job. He also had the wrong boys. More than that, he had the wrong era. We came of age in the sixties, an age of glaring contradictions, one where young, long-haired guys lived in their parents' comfy suburban houses yet nodded sagely to read that private property was theft. I remember once shaking my head at our big pool, before plunging in. One day I'd be achieving enlightenment in a cave somewhere, or squatting in a forest shack. I owned a copy of *Edible Plants of the Pacific Northwest*. Once I actually did dig up and suck a licorice fern root. And more than once I forced some dandelions into my patient parents' salad.

My dad may have been a corporate executive, but to me he was a middleman. A profiteer who bought goods from their honest creators, paying them as little as possible, then selling said goods to the pubic, charging as much as he could. He was a retailer. His skill? Buying cheap and selling dear.

Just as bad, the goods he sold were crappy. That's what my brother and I deemed Sears merchandise. It didn't matter that their hardware, appliances and furniture were famously excellent. Sears was crap because the only thing it sold that mattered to us was, of course, our clothes. As family of a Sears execative, we got twenty-five percent off everything, so we'd grown up in Sears clothes. Actually, I didn't mind so much. But my older brother had a sense of what good clothes actually looked like. Also he'd entered adolescence, clothes were a life-and-death matter, and he was very clear on Sears clothes. When I hit adolescence myself, I too came to see how all the shoes were tainted with that embossed stamp, or shiny buckle; how the shirts all had a strange emblem on the chest, very much not the alligator or polo player. Worst of all, Sears jeans had *corrugated stretch fabric at the beltline*.

They were tragic, Sears jeans. This was the global dawning of the age of jeans. Hippies wore them, jocks wore them, so did loggers, and teachers soon wore them too. The northern hemisphere's legs were now encased in blue jeans, and only two brands were allowed, Lee and Levi's. (GWGs were okay for work, or if you lived a hundred miles from a city.) Lee jeans were slightly hipper than Levi's. This was the understanding among the coolest young people, though nothing was ever articulated, not in actual words, because that would have been un-Lee. It was like belonging to the quietest secret society ever, one that had no rules and stood for nothing except the most subtle refinement. Anyway, in the era I'm talking about, both Lee and Levi's jeans cost $19.98, everywhere.

Sears had neither Lee nor Levi's jeans. They stocked only their "exclusive" brand, called *Tee-Kays*. *Tee-Kays* jeans had bright orange thread in its stitch-work, as opposed to the dull yellow thread used in real jeans. The fabric itself had a suspicious sheen. Like real jeans there was a red tag on the butt pocket, but it was twice as large and shouted *Tee-Kays*. So your adolescent bum, which had to look perfect or you felt suicidal, shouted *Tee-Kays* down every high school hallway. Worse, these jeans did not fade with washing—with each wash they looked even shinier.

My parents saw nothing wrong with this. *Tee-Kays* were perfectly good jeans. And here are *two* pairs for you, because they're only seven dollars!

More than once I asked my dad why Sears had no Lee or Levi's jeans. Or even GWGs. Nearing adolescence, I'd become an obnoxious little lawyer almost overnight.

"Every other store has them. Why doesn't Sears?"

"We have our own brands."

"But everybody in the world buys Lees or Levi's."

He smiled wisely. "There's something called a 'markup,' Bill, and—"

"I know what a 'markup' is. Stores with good jeans have a markup too. They make a profit too. But they sell good jeans."

"Our buyers get the best merchandise they can."

"Are you saying they can't *find* good jeans?"

"We sell a lot of our jeans. Someone out there thinks that—"

"Every day I go to a school that's full of jeans, but only one pair of *Tee-Kays*. A good buyer would go there and see for himself."

"Jeans all look the same."

"Dad? I get *laughed at*."

At this point I was a lawyer appealing to cheap emotion. I never actually got laughed at. That would have been un-Lee. And I rarely wore my *Tee-Kays* anyway.

I'd earn $19.98 and once a year go downtown and buy my own. My mother thought that in doing so I insulted Sears, and by extension my father, but she couldn't mistake the sincerity revealed in doing enough odd, dirty jobs to earn twenty bucks, a lot in those days. A pack of cigarettes was fifty cents and a gallon of gas even less.

Though I scorned Sears and my father's uncool middleman function, he was, after all, the boss. He was store manager, with hundreds of employees under him. He was six-five, and handsome, and women employees blushed calling him Mr. Gaston when he called them

Shirley or Karen. He made the most money and had the biggest office. Every now and then my scorn was trumped by a throat-swelling pride. When he became manager of the new store downtown, with its revolving restaurant on top, I was especially proud because, when I was with a girl, anywhere in the city I could look up and casually flick a finger at my dad's spinning building.

One day early in his new downtown job I went to see him at work to get a key for something. Also I wanted to see his new digs. I was in jeans, real ones, faded and ripped, and long hair, and grubby T-shirt, and I asked a painted lady at the cosmetics counter where the executive offices were. As I headed up to the third floor I was joined on the elevator by a young stud. I knew he was security by the way he watched me hard without actually looking. On purpose when I exited the elevator I picked up my pace toward the offices. He stayed by my elbow; I wore a little smile. When I turned a corner and headed to the name R.A. GASTON embossed on a bronze door label, he grabbed my arm with a hand in such a way that I couldn't mistake the power, and disdain, attached to it.

"Can I help you find something?" he asked.

I admit I enjoyed watching the clean-cut muscleman change as he learned I was his boss's son. Suddenly kowtowing and, truth be told, afraid. And I liked the way my dad's pretty private secretary sucked up to me. But I also liked how my hair and rough clothes—and Lee jeans—violated my dad's dark, wood-panelled office. It was 1970, but in Sears-land it was still the fifties.

The secretary leapt up, very pleased for my father because his son had come to visit. She knocked on his door and poked her head in, said something hushed and exited, then opened the door wide and ushered me forth.

My dad sat behind his somewhat vast desk. I caught him in the act of either hanging up the phone or straightening it. He looked up and smiled.

"Well!" he said.

"The new office, eh?"

"My new digs." He glanced around, as if hunting for something of interest to point out. But there was nothing, really. It was big, elegant, but empty. Even his desk was clean of paper, except for a small notepad. Of course this was before computers.

One wall was glass, though, with a fantastic view of Burrard Inlet, Grouse Mountain, and the North Shore waterfront, with its dry docks and bright yellow sulphur mound. I pointed my chin at it.

"Nice," I said.

How happy he was to see me, how proud and even a little nervous that I'd taken an interest and was seeing him in his daily element. He had great posture and sat tall. He was confident here, and he enjoyed being confident. He'd be a good, kind and even generous boss, but he would tower over people who came in here. He enjoyed respect, I knew.

He picked up the phone, and in a boss voice—deeper and more deliberate than his dad voice—asked Shirley to bring in some coffees and doughnuts.

"Six," he said, to Shirley's question. "He's a growing boy," he said in response to another, smiling. "Very well," he said imperiously, and hung up.

I couldn't take any of it seriously, and not because I was an anticapitalist suburban hippie. It was because I'd seen him on Sunday, pissed as a newt by noon but pretending not to be, blatting on his trombone. I saw him singing "Roll Over Mabel" at dinner, and in bed by seven o'clock, making those sighing noises as he drifted off. A suit, boss voice, luxury office and a high-heeled secretary trotting in coffee and doughnuts—it didn't fool me for a second.

———

If my dad was in his element in his office, he also was on the water. The west coast was his home and he knew it well—the tides, the weather, the fishing holes. He could play a big fish, graceful in the struggle. A boat felt natural, you could see it in his legs. In either world, business or fishing, he knew what to do. Fishing was more fun, because there was less at stake and he could relax. I have such a clear image of my father sitting relaxed and confident, beer between his legs, holding a rod. Implacable calm.

I also have clear memories of him being surprised while in a boat. His face.

Once we were fishing mid-morning on a cold, overcast day, the water a mirror. The high mountains surrounding Egmont are black on overcast days, and if reflected in glassy water the entire world is black and grey. We were sitting out there in the twelve-foot aluminum car-top, fully exposed to the elements, like two frogs riding a stick. He had a windbreaker on, and I had a sweater. Big dark clouds rolled up above the mountains. No other boats around.

We saw that over near the Skookumchuck Rapids, about a mile away, it was raining, raining heavily. We also saw that it was coming our way, probably at the speed of the clouds overhead. Several things were odd. One, over the dull roar of the rapids was a sharper roar of that rain hitting the water. Two, because the sea was like a mirror, you could see the rain chew it up as it hit, big raindrops bouncing back a foot high, and this line of chewed, wild water ate up the mirror as it raced toward us. The rain was so heavy, you couldn't see through it. Here, all was calm, mirror-like, silent—and there a deafening wall of water was coming at maybe thirty miles an hour.

Our world was going to change, violently, in ten seconds. My dad turned to me. His eyes were eager. It wasn't a look that worried about us getting wet and tossed. It was a look that wanted my agreement that this approaching wall of water was the weirdest thing we'd ever seen.

The wall hit, we were caught in water and roar, and we were instantly drenched. As if to match the tumult, we roared and shouted. At the second or third thunderclap we madly reeled in our lines, no words needed.

Later that day when we were going over the details and I called it a "curtain of water," my dad twigged to that. "Curtain of water," he said, nodding. Favourite expressions he'd pronounce as though in quotation marks. "That's what it was, a 'curtain of water.'" Over the years, whenever the subject of Egmont came up, he'd say, "Remember that 'curtain of water'?" In his eyes, that same look, seeking my agreement that that had been the craziest thing ever.

In Egmont there were other things we marvelled at, that cloud shaped just like Jesus on the cross, or that empty, ghostly sailboat adrift. Or the summer of black helicopters; or unidentifiable noises coming out of shoreline woods; or once, way out in deep water, a sudden mound of bubbles erupting next to the boat.

Or the time that might be the closest I'll get to seeing a sea monster, what I refer to as the giant worm. Because that's what it was, a giant worm. We were mooching in a bay past Egmont Point, the water clear and calm, and I happened to look down. Not a foot from the boat, and maybe three feet deep, I saw the wiggling and thrashing of, well, a giant worm. It was thick and as wide around as a human leg, and it was salami-coloured, with a fringe of soft spikes along both sides of it, like an ordinary sand worm. It wasn't a severed octopus arm. It was maybe four feet long and had probably been longer—it looked recently severed, hence the thrashing. Little shreds of it, possibly innards, were coming out both ends, which didn't taper but looked sawn or more likely bitten off. I called Dad over, he exclaimed "Holy cow!" as it gradually sank from sight, still thrashing. Neither of us knew what the hell it was and I still don't. How big was the whole animal? What had brought it to the surface? What had bitten it apart? I've since searched images online and found nothing at all like it.

Another surprise had to do with bald eagles. One sad by-product of mooching was that you often couldn't avoid catching rockfish. They're voracious and often you couldn't avoid getting one on, which was a huge annoyance, as you now had to reel it up two hundred feet, unhook it while avoiding its moderately poisonous spines, then rebait and get back down again. The sad part was that when you threw back the bottom-dwelling rockfish it could only float, the result of its swim bladder having expanded due to the change in pressure. The inflated bladder often protruded out its mouth like a grotesque pink condom. And the rockfish was now a floater, and doomed.

It was a shock the first time a released rockfish floated away from the boat and—*whap*—a small explosion, and a bald eagle bearing it away. Egmont's shoreline slopes were home to plenty of eagles and it didn't take us long to learn that a floating rockfish got picked off as soon as it drifted twenty feet away from the boat—twenty feet appeared to be the eagles' comfort zone. It's a beautiful sight, a big-shouldered bald eagle diving a half-mile away, to cruise at speed three feet off the water, extend its talons and—*whap*—grab the fish and bear it up, the weight of the rockfish slowing the eagle not much at all, and you can see its power as it beats the air and climbs with its two pounds of flapping meat. All this from twenty feet away.

We turned this into a neat little trick when first-timers fished with us. The inevitable rockfish got caught. I complained while unhooking it, pointed out the nasty spines and described the pain of getting stung, threw it about twenty feet away, and out the corner of my eye watched a distant white head drop from a snag. Timing it, not looking up, my dad would announce in his odd falsetto, "Hello," and *whap*, out of nowhere the eagle exploded on the fish and scared the shit out of our guest, who would regard my dad as some kind of strange nature wizard, at least until he'd seen the trick four or five times. Another thing my dad and I shared is that we both liked to kick a dead horse.

I'll describe one other surprise we shared. It's easily the strangest thing I've seen. And the most memorable.

I was seventeen and my dad and I were fishing Egmont in the aluminum car-topper. It was too perfect a night to quit early, though it was time and we needed to eat. The light had that rich, early evening quality. Not a cloud in the sky. Then, so fast we could only flinch, about six feet off the water a glowing ball shot by at speed, missing us by mere feet. Volleyball-sized, glowing with the brightness of fire, but not the sun, it had a metallic sheen, the gloss of a liquid bubble. It flew without sound, and curved gracefully as it disappeared around a distant point. That's how it was exactly. We both yelped and turned as it flew past but then it was gone. We shouted versions of *"What the hell was that?"* and tried describing it to each other in amazed babble. We'd both seen the identical thing. I raved that UFOs maybe could be small, maybe we'd seen a UFO. My dad had no theories, he was just amazed. We spent all evening perplexed, shaking our heads at each other, until, well into the hard stuff, he lost the thread of what we were supposed to be amazed about. But for years I'd bring it up and he'd automatically shake his head and wonder aloud, "Yeah, what was that thing?"

A decade later, I was visiting. We sat down to some steaks he'd grilled pretty much raw, or "rare, like you like them," he said. I never liked them rare. Egmont came up, and I mentioned it again, that ball that shot by us. He looked at me and nodded. It was clear he didn't know what I was talking about.

The strangest, most memorable thing we'd ever seen? Something I still saw so clearly? Gone. Giant worm, swooping eagles, curtain of water? Forgotten. Most painful, what I could also still see clearly was us meeting eyes. His, imploring. *Isn't this great? What we're seeing? You and me?*

# FOUR

*Good fathers make good sons.*
—ANONYMOUS

Halfway across, engine overheating badly, radio hissing static, and wind coming up from an unpredicted direction, I do something unpredictable. I relax.

Ease back the throttle. So this trip will take longer. But isn't the idea to enjoy it? White-knuckle fretting is the opposite of that. Images of imminent drowning are hallucinations—these small waves I could manage with a canoe. Pushing the engine is destroying it, and if I do that my problems will be real. Standing rigid, drenched with sweat in the midday heat, I had become the very picture of non-enjoyment.

I decide to perversely *double* relax. I throttle back to trolling speed, which is about like walking. If I'm heading into a tidal current, I might be making no headway at all. I might be going backwards. So be it.

As if by magic, the radio suddenly comes through loud and clear. Maybe engine vibration jiggled a loose wire. Who knows. And it's Audrey's soothing, undeniably sexy voice.

*Halibut Bank? Six. Race Rocks? Two. Victoria Gonzales? Two.*

What will she tell me about where I'm going? It almost doesn't matter.

Even forty years after that rough trip to Egmont on *Cormorant*, the more I contemplated this solo voyage, the more my gut clenched whenever the wind came up, even sitting inside the cabin. Gazing out the window at tossing treetops I'd phone and listen once more to the Canadian Coast Guard *Continuous Marine Report*. I'd hear that in north Georgia Strait (that is, in the direction of Egmont) a southeast wind was blowing at twenty-one knots. Clench. I'd hear about Haro Strait and Howe Sound and Juan de Fuca, and soon the "automated lighthouse and ocean buoy reports" came on and Audrey would tell me how bad it was out there really.

"Audrey" is my name for the woman who voices these reports. She sounds live, but each time she says "barometric pressure" it does sound the same. Each time she says "two" her pronunciation is identical, a chaste sexiness to it. "Six" is always playfully saucy. Maybe she's pre-recorded, who knows, who cares—the point is, I would marry the woman who owns this voice. It's elegant, but there's carnal knowledge in it. Let me upgrade that to carnal wisdom.

I have no idea why "Audrey." I don't even like the name, though it suggests a kind of farm-healthy vixen. Of course there was Audrey Hepburn, though my Audrey is more substantial, less gamine. Anyway, she's Audrey, and I can all too easily picture my dad, head titled at the radio, listening. He'd whistle softly, briefly catch your eye, and say something like, "That's some kinda *poon*tang." I bet he would have listened to Audrey a lot too.

Here she is now, continuing her automated buoy report, from

Sooke northward, and next is Merry Island, which I am approaching, unseen in the mist.

*Merry Island? Winds calm.*

She actually pronounces the *l* in calm, and it's beyond sexy. And not just because it means no waves.

I think of my father whenever the reports mention Merry Island. It's a place we cruised by several times, one of those bald-rock-with-red-and-white-manned-lighthouse islands, and my dad never saw it without saying, "That sure looks fishy." Sometimes he'd just do his sexy whistle. It did look the epitome of "marine," with the bare rocks jutting blackly and dramatically from the water, hence the need for a light. There were wheeling gulls, and it looked like a place you'd wear sou'westers, and where you might drown. It makes sense such a place feels fishy: a land mass interrupting a sea current is a place where sea life is also interrupted, and congregates. Such places are special.

With the slower speed, and maybe because of the skipper's more easygoing mood, *Sylvan's* engine temperature has dropped to the healthy range. And as if by magic, I make out through the thinning mist the red tip on the white Merry Island lighthouse. I'm almost across the Salish Sea.

Here are the island's bleak crags, and forest beyond. It's a bigger island than I remember. In fact, I have to admit I don't recognize it at all. Maybe it's the light, or time of day. But, no wheeling gulls. Seeing it today, my dad might not have said, "Sure looks fishy." It wouldn't have earned his sexy whistle.

I'm ready to head toward Secret Cove when an idea strikes. We regretted never trying out such a fishy place, so why don't I rectify that? I'm in no hurry. Feeling my dad at my side nodding, I decide to throw out a hook and give it a go. Though reportedly there aren't salmon in this part of the strait anymore.

I pop *Sylvan* into neutral and go below for two rods, planning what lures to use. What depth to try. I'm already excited. I grab the downriggers, screw them onto their mounts. I hook up two fifteen-pound cannonballs to the cables. I consider lure sizes, colours, and choose a three-inch Bob Marley spoon for one side and a two-inch Irish Cream for the other. The depth sounder reads 180 feet, and the chart shows this to be a ridge that drops off into the real deeps. Perfect.

———

The first time I trolled with downriggers, I hadn't fished for salmon in many years. All I knew about downriggers was that commercial trawlers used them—winches and big cannonball weights—to get their lures down deep.

Then, a few years ago, a friend of a friend called and said he'd heard I liked fishing. Each August, Willem trailed his seventeen-foot boat from Vancouver to Port Renfrew on the west coast of Vancouver Island, where he rented a cabin and fished every day. Friends joined him but occasionally he needed someone to plug a gap in the schedule. That was me. I'd heard about "Rennie," legendary salmon hot spot, and when I showed up at his cabin door at six in the morning I didn't tell him I hadn't slept at all. I didn't want him to know he had a sleep-deprived maniac on his hands, nor did I want to admit, not even to myself, how excited I was.

Port Renfrew is wonderful. The first time Willem took me out of the bay and around the corner into the open Pacific, I fell in love. Wilderness still rules there, or at least thinks it does. Earlier there that summer, at a dock up a tidal slough, a guy was calmly cleaning his salmon on board his boat and saw a black bear enter the slough and start swimming in his direction. When it drew near he threw a fish head and various guts at it. The bear reached the boat and leapt over the outboard engine and transom and got the guy in a classic bear hug, biting down on his shoulder. Other fishermen charged down the dock to his rescue—one drove a gaff into the bear, another whanged at its head with a hammer. The bear held its hug, and bite. Finally an old-timer reached in with his fillet knife and slit the bear's throat, whereupon it gradually bled out and collapsed, thump, to the deck.

Willem and I spotted our own black bear as we left the bay. Then when we turned the corner into the open Pacific, here were brown pelicans in V-formations skimming the swells, and chaotic swarms of seabirds diving into schools of baitfish. In the first hour we saw orcas, then a grey whale, and dolphins played near our bow. Rennie was rich with wildlife. Japan, Willem pointed out, lay somewhere over there.

Willem taught me a new way of fishing. The electric downrigger and its cannonball took your bait to the desired depth in seconds. If a fish hit, a release clip freed your line from the cannonball and you played the fish on your rod, unencumbered—brilliant. I'd never seen a more accomplished fisherman, and I tried filing away lures, colours, speeds, techniques. A year later I would see him limit out effortlessly on sockeye, a species of salmon my dad had told me weren't caught by sport fishermen because they took neither bait nor lure. Willem had a tackle box of lures exclusively for sockeye.

Port Renfrew was scary, and so was Willem. Huge ocean swells are the norm, and I've mentioned his seventeen-foot boat. On maps, this section of coast is identified as the Graveyard of the Pacific. The Pacific is the planet's biggest ocean, and if this one spot was officially its graveyard, and our boat half the size of a lifeboat, a wind chicken like me remains on high alert. Willem was built like me, which is to say burly, only he was also taller, so more burliness in total. Working on a small boat, bent over, moving here and there, his ass was sort of everywhere. That first hour the weather baby in me couldn't shake what looked like a fatal combination: big ass of Willem, small boat, Graveyard of the Pacific.

It didn't help that a story preceded our meeting, about him "turtling" his boat while halibut fishing. In all fairness, halibut fishing is extra-tricky, because it involves anchoring with a fancy release mechanism. In a squall, Willem's didn't release, and the boat flipped. That was Willem's version. Another version, from Willem's fishing partner that day, is that Willem leaned too far the wrong way and his big ass took them down. Apparently the two old friends were not speaking.

But that first day I survived Rennie and learned how to troll with downriggers. We each got a chinook, one high-teens and the other low-twenties. I hadn't fought a big salmon in decades, and thrilled to the screaming reel as the fish tore out line. As my fish lay on its side, freshly dead, I did a calculation and realized it had been twenty-five years. That fish at my feet looked . . . good. All muscle, a beautiful silver slab, its scales tessellating prisms of light. I could smell it. An unnamed emotion welled, the smell working on my memory like a powerful forgotten song. The black lips, rimmed with little needle teeth. The huge, bright, now sightless eye. The fish looked like a fine predator that had just been beaten by a better one. Mostly, it looked so familiar. It felt like standing before a house I'd grown up in.

Rennie was a taste of what it used to be like all up and down the B.C. coast and isn't now. The bristling wildness reminded me of the Egmont I saw at thirteen.

And the kind of wildness my dad would have known and loved as a child and as a young man. How much did he love it? One piece of hard evidence is his choice of honeymoon spots, where he took my mother—they went "goeyduck hunting" on a wilderness beach on the Olympic Peninsula. True, they didn't have much money between them for hotels or trips, and it is possible that "goeyduck hunting" was a euphemism I truly don't want to know about. They may not have left their tent much, and I don't want to know about that either. But it would have been absolutely wild, and I think it's safe to say that, if given half a chance, a young man will take the woman he loves to the place he loves.

———

As I troll around Merry Island a few boats pass by on their way to somewhere else, but no one stops to wet a line and show me where the local hot spot might be. Not that there's a hot spot anymore. Though I can hear echoes of my dad's whistle, it doesn't look fishy. Still no birds, which likely means no baitfish. One reason the fishery in this entire area died is because the Department of Fisheries allowed the herring to be fished out, letting a relatively small fleet of commercial fishermen get rich selling herring roe to Japan. There were other idiocies, but apparently Fisheries fumbled this biggest, simplest one: if a species has nothing to eat, it disappears.

If I do catch a salmon, I wonder what it will be. Back in my fridge on Gabriola is a plastic bucket full of my last catch, which I soaked in my special brine all night before smoking it over alder wood in the electric smoker I inherited from my father. It was a marbled chinook—its flesh a swirl of red and light pink, patterned not unlike marbled rye bread—and it had been on its way to the Columbia River, back to the hatchery from which it came. It was an American fish.

My dad and I never knew what river or stream our salmon were returning to. We did hear rumours of commercial fishermen wiping out entire runs, so thorough was their technique now. Poetic as it is that salmon, after roaming sometimes thousands of miles at sea, return to spawn in their very birth stream, this also dooms them: it's the *only* stream they can enter. So, if allowed to, any commercial captain worth his salt would go to a river mouth as the run schools there, waiting for the rainfall will that let them swim upriver. Easy pickings for the nets of a seiner, and so efficient that salmon in many streams are now extinct. *Extinct* is the proper word because, over millennia, each run has become, in subtle ways, a distinct species. In any case, these rumours cast a shadow over what my dad and I were doing. Taking even a few fish, were we hurting a run that was already a feeble remnant? Though we never spoke of it, I knew it bothered him too.

Here off Merry, still nothing. I wish I was anchored and mooching like in the old days, sitting in one spot, no motor noise. But there's no live herring for sale anymore, and trolling is all anyone does now.

A true expert would know what to do, would read the chart and know where to troll based on the tidal flow and bottom contour. An expert calculates how time and the moon moves water and baitfish around, and how salmon act in that mix. I remember what that's like, putting all those pieces together, and the joy when experience plus intuition equals a strike.

I'm still learning the finer points of trolling. On the dock I'll ask anyone with bloody hands what's been going on the last day or so. Most will happily share what they know. Some won't, and I suspect they act secretive because it's what pro guides often do, so it makes them look pro too. The most obnoxious of these are the ones who, cleaning a salmon and asked where they caught it, jerk their head in the direction of the ocean and say, "Out there." If I weren't sort of a Buddhist, and if I knew how to fight, and had enough money to cover the lawsuit, and the guy wasn't holding a knife, I would be tempted to throw a punch.

Pretty as it is, Merry Island is proving a bust. I try a glow-white hoochie, and a green-gold Coyote spoon. I try depths from 75 to 130. I resist urges to pull the gear and zoom over to Thormanby Island, the reef I remember there. The grass is always greener.

Salmon hunting has infinite variables beyond the most basic question: Is there a salmon within a mile of this spot? Let's assume there is. What needs considering? First, depth. Even ten feet makes a difference. One hundred feet deep in algae-rich water, from what distance can a salmon see your flasher? Let's say it's seen the flasher, and approaches. Now there's the colour and size of the lure, which must resemble (or "match the hatch" in fly-fishing lingo) what the fish is feeding on today. There's the lure's action—it should look wounded, and make my father whistle. The lure can't smell of gas or soap, salmon having nostrils that lead them a thousand miles back to home water. The length of leader between flasher and lure affects the action, as does the leader's pound-test thickness. The boat speed affects the flasher's action, which affects the lure's. The tide's speed, and direction, in combination with the boat's speed, and direction, complicates things in a way that takes a blackboard to illustrate. There's the time of the bite, which is connected to the tide change, and phase of moon, and which way the tide is moving over the reef. All of these things are vital. Get one wrong, you won't get a bite. Get them all right, you still might not get a bite. There might not be a salmon within a mile of your boat.

Because of the fine poetic pieces written about it, I was once led to believe that fly-fishing is the only artful fishing. At the risk of Roderick Haig-Brown rolling in his grave, I'll offer that trolling for salmon is artful as well. True, trollers burn gas, make noise, and drag cannonballs. But it's not just about fooling a finicky fish. It's the finding them. Flyfishers can often see them there in the small pool, rising to feed. Salmon hunters have to toss a little hook into an ocean.

Despite two hours and zero bites here at Merry Island, it's a gorgeous late afternoon, the wind hasn't tormented me, and I remind myself that I am on a pilgrimage and in no hurry. No need to reach Egmont tonight. I can anchor and spend the night in Secret Cove, another old haunt.

It's easiest just to keep fishing. I put on a spoon I've never tried, called Party Boy. Metallic gold with purple and green polka dots, it looks cheaply careless, a cartoon version of a party animal, and nothing like what a salmon might eat. I've heard it can work well. Maybe a salmon just wants to kill it.

———

When I was eighteen and yearned for Egmont, I packed the aluminum car-top with a tent, cooler, sleeping bag, and fishing gear. I launched in North Vancouver and proceeded to motor through Burrard Inlet, dodging ships and the rapids of the First and Second Narrows Bridges. Then out under Lions Gate and across the wide mouth of Howe Sound. I gassed up at Gibsons Landing, continued along the Sunshine Coast, past Sechelt, Halfmoon Bay, Merry Island, Secret Cove, Pender Harbour, gassed up at Irvines Landing, continued up Agamemnon Channel, turned the corner toward the Skookumchuck Rapids, and tied up at the Egmont government dock, smiling. I'd driven eighty miles up the coast in a tiny tin boat.

I humped my gear to Vera's. Vera was a shy and eerily gentle First Nations elder who stood 6½ feet tall. Her campground had no sign. Near Vera's house was a cleared area for camper vans and such, and hidden well in the trees was a natural clearing. My iron-poled canvas tent took a while to set up. I duct-taped the most obvious holes. When I left at summer's end I was in a hurry and didn't take the tent down, thinking I'd be back that fall for more fishing. I never did make it back to the campsite. Knowing Vera and her ways, I'm betting that, forty years later, there stands a skeleton of iron poles hung with ghostly rags of canvas flipping in the breeze, medium-sized trees growing up through it.

Friends came to fish and party (though *party* wasn't a verb yet), but for the most part I was alone. My friends thought I was a little weird. Not just for going off alone to fish, but simply for being alone by choice. I could see that most people didn't like being alone, or not for long. Nor did they like the *appearance* of being alone. I'd always been perfectly happy to eat by myself in restaurants, so long as I had a newspaper to read. I don't know if it's anything to brag about, but I liked my own company. Fishing alone I was as happy as can be. I remember an "aptitude test" we took in Grade 4. After pages of questions and ticking multiple-choice answers, which were tabulated by some sort of primitive early computer, I got a note saying that Billy Gaston was well-suited for a career as (a) a Priest or (b) a Forest Ranger. Even then, something in my character leaned toward the solitary and the patiently watchful. (Also the judgmental and sanctimonious, but so be it.)

I fished every day. I ate when I wanted. I read books. A half-mile up the road was a lake with lens-like water and a string of chained logs, wide as desks, a long swimming float. You could soap up unobserved. Aside from the marina, with its small café, Egmont had a store for coffee, newspapers, and smokes. I ate lots of fish.

For boat gas and pocket money I had a deal with an older gent, Bev, who with his wife Helen ran the café. Bev paid me a dollar a pound for fresh salmon and two bucks for a big ling cod, which he used for his famous fish and chips. Salmon wasn't on the menu. He froze it whole and sold it to American fishermen who'd been skunked but wanted to return home looking otherwise. It was a fine deal for everybody. I ate in their café, paying them with money they'd just paid me. Helen made the best clam chowder I've had to this day. She said it was the Devon cream.

Fishing, I came back in when I had my limit, or sensed no further action coming. It was a sense I learned to trust. The day itself felt not so much dead as empty, like a soulless afternoon breeze, and I can't explain it any better than that. If when playing cards, you think you can feel what it's like to be on a roll, and then what it's like not to be on that roll anymore—it feels just like that.

There was ego involved. Egmont was hard to fish. It was less than a mile from the Skookumchuck Narrows—the largest saltwater rapids in North America—a saltwater river with standing waves and whirlpools that could suck down a cabin cruiser. Being so close to this torrent, Egmont was very tidal itself, and on the fishing grounds the tide ran at five or six knots, the speed of a moderate river, or a sailing yacht when it's hauling ass. Even experienced fishermen needed to learn some very specific things or catch very little. Once you knew what to do you could be a star at the cleaning table, slicing up your twenty-pound lunkers (you were allowed four per day back then) while the empty-handed stood white-knuckling their beers, trying not to watch you. Some persisted in thinking it was just luck and tomorrow would be different. Others would swallow their pride and ask questions. I never minded being helpful, standing there, knife zipping along a backbone rather professionally now, way younger than them and feeling pretty good about myself.

Midsummer my dad arrived for two weeks, renting a cabin at the marina. I moved out of my tent, happy for a bed and a shower, and my dad footing the bill for decent food. The idea in the air was that I had been waiting for him to come and take me fishing. I was happy to see him, but it soon became clear who was taking whom.

We fished from the little twelve-foot tinny, a couple of sessions a day. It was me suggesting where to anchor and what time of day to try. He joked about me being his guide, especially when I baited his hooks with the live herring—I'd learned how to do it cleanly, not losing a scale, while he tended to be slow and a little rough. He'd whap my feet with a magazine to get me out of bed, saying "C'mon let's get out there, sun's up," and I'd tell him the bite was forty-five minutes later today, and explain again about the pattern of the moon and tide. And when the bite came on as predicted, he called me lucky, but I could see he was impressed. Around this time his old fishing lore began to take a real beating. I was pretty obnoxious. Salmon swatting herring with their tails? I'd roll my eyes and shake my head. "*What*," he'd say. Or, on a dead evening he'd suggest that we stick it out for the night bite, and again he'd see the eyes roll.

"*What.*"

"There's no night bite."

"The night bite. It's when the big ones come out."

There's a definite bite at daybreak—it's maybe a case of hungry fish finally being able to see their food. But, dusk was when the big ones come out? That sounded like romantic crap Captain Ahab would've hissed at you with one eye closed.

"There's no night bite. It's all tide. It changes every day."

He looked defeated. But he saw that we were catching more than most other boats out there. He didn't ask how I knew to tie the leaders at seven feet instead of five, or all the rest of it. I didn't tell him about my friend Ray. Also staying at Vera's, Ray was even more addicted to fishing than I was. When mooching fell off, he showed me how to strip-cast the shallows with Buzz Bombs, and sometimes we were the only ones at the dock with salmon. Wealthy Americans, here for the fishing trip of their lives, were visibly angry with us.

My dad angered me too, at the cleaning table. When we came in, my job was to clean the salmon so it could be bagged for freezing, and his job was to head up to the cabin and really get into the booze. The switch from beer to hard stuff was always obvious. He'd wander back down to the dock to watch me finish up and be too drunk too fast to be explained by the can in his fist. After admiring our fish too loudly, he'd ask if anyone was from Vancouver, or some other clumsy attempt to open a door to bragging even more clumsily about his son the hockey player. At this point I was playing Junior for the Vancouver Centennials, and though I was okay I wasn't the Bobby Orr he made me out to be. But that's the nature of fathers talking about sons—hard facts are stretched and gilded, not unlike in a good fish story.

So when, at the cleaning table, apropos of nothing, my dad told them, "Vancouver Centennials? This guy plays for them—this guy right here," I could see in the faces of the other fish cleaners that they knew all about fathers. I saw them humour him, or mock him to his face from behind his back, so to speak, because their jibes flew over his head. When I joined them with a smirk I felt like a traitor. Mostly, I kept my head down.

One night, halfway into his two-week visit, knife moving fast, hands bloody up to the wrists, I did something I'd never done before. He came down drunker than usual, staggering. He put a hand out to steady himself on a piling, and cleared his throat. He watched a bit, and then, trying to brag, could say only,

"Va'couver Cen'ials."

One or two fishermen looked up, briefly curious.

"*Don't,*" I said.

He said, louder, "Va'couver Cenn'ials. *This* guy."

I yelled at him to shut up. I yelled it clearly. He didn't seem to hear me. I worked faster, not filleting, but crudely gutting and beheading.

"Look at him!" he said, gesturing at me with a flap of his long, long arm.

"There he is," said one of the fishermen, head down, working on his fish, too bored by boorishness to smile.

I hustled away, bags of fish dangling, banging my legs. A father bragging about his kid was only a hair's breadth removed from bragging about himself. And just as ugly. Uglier. But a contradiction was so confusing it kept me in a kind of mute shock: How could I hate someone whose only drunken crime was to be so proud of me that they couldn't hold it in?

———

No matter what his two sons did with their lives, what made their father most proud was any success in sports. For both me and my brother, hockey was life's main passion until the wave of sex, drugs and rock 'n' roll hit and swept us to another beach entirely. Still, despite some long hair and telltale bags under our eyes, we both played junior, and university, and briefly for a living in Europe. I don't know if the love of hockey had more to do with growing up in Winnipeg, or with Dad.

Not the hockey part, the athlete part. My dad never skated in his life, and as a boy I cringed at the thought of him trying it. Six foot five, with thin ankles . . . it would have been ugly. Anyway, basketball was his game.

When we moved, a hoop went up in the driveway. Or he'd favour buying a house if it had a hoop already—such a thing was exactly what would open his wallet, and force my mother to force reason on him.

Growing up I was proud watching him take hook shots—his specialty—or sink free throws the old-fashioned way, from between the legs. Back then on TV only a few freaks (always tall centres) still threw underhand. One was Wilt Chamberlain, and out on the driveway Dad would often preface his underhand attempt with a boyish shout, "Wilt the Stilt!" Like Wilt, about half went in.

Dad was also proud of his basketball days. I don't know when he came into possession of the newspaper clipping, perhaps when his mother died, but when we moved to Vancouver, a framed newspaper article appeared on the new TV-room wall, its headline "Gaston Makes All-American," with a pretty cool picture of my young dad launching one of those hook shots. The article was from the Everett paper. It had been poorly handled, cut in half then taped crookedly back together, and not prettied up before being mounted.

"Gaston Makes All-American" hung on the wall surrounded by less ragged family honours—my parents' degrees, my mother's realtor award, a picture of me sporting graduation robes and a moustache so gapped and wispy I wonder how I ever lost my virginity.

My mother hated that "Gaston Makes All-American." Once, when I was busy watching bad TV and she was dusting the room, she said, more to herself than to me, "I'd sure love to get rid of that."

She stood with hands on hips, glaring. She had her cleaning outfit on, which looked very fifties: tights, apron, a kerchief, and old-school glasses. She looked a bit like a bespectacled Mary Tyler Moore, minus the bubbling humour.

"Why?" I said. She waved it away and dusted the other accomplishments. I thought maybe she hated it because it was badly cut out and looked raggedy. I suggested it was a huge deal to make All-American. Could she imagine, I asked, being one of the top ten college basketball players in the entire— She interrupted me, saying, under her breath, and not looking at me, knowing she was betraying him, "Oh it wasn't even the real thing."

I asked what she meant. She told me it was an all-American team composed of "veterans of foreign wars." I knew my dad had played for Gonzaga, then joined the U.S. Navy to fight the Japanese, and then played for Washington State when he came back. So his "All-American" team was made up only of guys returned from World War II? Sure, I guess that tarnished it a little, but if you figured that virtually all able-bodied men went off to that war, it was probably harder to make his all-American team than one composed of the 4-F guys who'd stayed behind. This was my thinking, but I didn't have that comeback ready for my mother.

She tapped the article too hard with her duster on her way out. "And he hangs it right here."

I considered it something to be proud of. I still do. Some men would display such a laurel and some wouldn't. It was cool to be that good at basketball. It might be cooler if you don't hang it on the wall.

But I loved watching him throw hoops. He was also great to play catch with. He liked playing "loose"—that is, all relaxed and gangly like Wilt the Stilt. Before throwing hoops, even a free throw, he'd often announce to himself instructively, "Loosey-goosey," and flap and waggle his limbs, flicking tension from fingers and toes. Playing catch, his long, long limbs just dangled. He'd pitch, and follow through forever. So graceful for a tall man. You could throw him one twenty feet wide and watch that long body fly jointlessly across the gap and snag it. Stretching for a ball like that, he looked so comfortable in his body. Happy.

He taught my brother how to throw a good curve. It was always, "Hey Pal, wanna throw the ball?" He made a big thing about his special glove too. In those days it was hard to find an adult lefty's glove, maybe because those were also the days they'd only just stopped forcing lefties to be righties, in school. I don't know how he escaped that ignominy.

Though tall he was an all-round athlete—in high school football a wide receiver, and he ran high hurdles in university track. But as a child I'd never seen him run, other than a few steps to grab a wayward ball. How bizarre it was the first and only time I saw him sprint. I was ten. We were at a Sears summer picnic, one of several I went to over the years. There were races for kids and adults, mostly of the three-legged and potato-sack kind. But that year they had a sprint for adults, sixty yards. I recall my mom being embarrassed at his decision to race, her quiet, "Oh Bob."

Maybe she'd seen him run before.

The starter's pistol snapped and eight Sears employees took off. That storky junior exec out in front had a frightening style. His head bobbed forward with each stride, like a pigeon's, arms cocked up like a dinosaur's. His feet splayed wide, almost so his right foot pointed at the spectators on that side and his left foot at the other. He was a strange bird, but he won. Years later I watched my daughter Lise, and son Vaughn, sprint for the first time. Lise was fast for her age, even holding a city sprint record for a while. I'm not saying her style was as ugly as my dad's, but you could see the resemblance. She didn't bob her head, though. It was Vaughn who inherited that. Nature.

Dad loved that my brother and I were good athletes and went far in hockey, but what he really wanted were basketball players. In Winnipeg, hockey rinks everywhere, that wasn't what he was getting. Also, I ended up barely six feet, and my brother an inch shy of even that. My dad watched me play a couple of games in Grade 8, and that was painful enough to keep him away until he was pretty much forced to come when, in Toronto, my Don Mills Junior High team was playing for the championship. A good jumper, I was centre. I was a so-so passer, and that was it for basketball skill. The Etobicoke centre was six-four, but we had a trick play at the opening jump ball. I'd surprise the guy with my vertical leap, plus put some hockey shoulder into him and whap the ball forward to our only good player, a small guard who suspiciously already lingered halfway to their basket. This play worked only once per game. It worked that championship game too, though we lost 60–20, and the jump-ball whap was my only assist. I just wasn't very good. My dad didn't have much to say about the game and I think he would have preferred not witnessing it, final proof that fatherhood and genes only travel so far.

———

Despite my promise to leave my brother out, I will bring him in for a small cameo. I was thirteen, my brother a year-and-a-bit older. It wasn't like he was Dad's favourite but he was the first-born. And he had already taken the teenage path of ignoring his parents, which had the effect of making my dad seek him out more and, basically speaking, suck up to him.

One afternoon when Dad got home I asked him if he wanted to shoot baskets and he said he was too tired. I wandered downstairs to my bedroom, with its window opening directly under the driveway hoop. Not five minutes later my brother got home, my dad met him outside, and from my window I heard this:

"Hey, Pal, wanna shoot some hoops?"

"Okay."

Then the sounds of a bouncing ball, curses, Dad's playful, "Wilt the Stilt!" and the ball hitting the rim. I could see their fast, happy legs through my window.

I fell onto my bed and bawled into my pillow. I was too old for that. But I was really bent out of shape. Forgive me an amateur psychologist's moment, but it was a case of being bent *into* shape. A bank of emotions, a personality, and in some ways a future is shaped by these mother- and father-sized dollops of giving or withholding.

When I think of that day my dad rejected me for my brother, or other times he bent me *into* shape when he let me down or embarrassed me, or the one time he got physical—a hesitant shove to aim a whining child back to bed—I only have to think about my dad's own childhood, the one I've recently learned about, and my self-pity vanishes. I try to picture what he went through and I can't begin to. I think of him being bent into shape by violence, and abandonment. I'm amazed he went through what he did and yet ended up a successful man, a proud father, with a marriage that lasted fifty years, and by all reports an all-round decent guy. I'm also amazed at the bitterness, the grudge I held for decades.

But isn't that what kids do?

———

There were other factors.

Like so many WASP families of the era, our collective failure shone brightest at festive occasions. When I was child and focused on presents and food, Christmas was good. But it began to grow steadily hellish. Even at the time, I knew *expectations* were to blame. We were supposed to feel joyous and warm; the fact that we didn't made it feel worse. Though we sat quietly and polite around the table, there was a sense of inner anguish and flailing.

Santa Claus was the Sears catalogue. The fall edition, or the *Wish Book,* had idyllic Christmas scenes on its cover. I'd go through it, make up my wish list and give it to my mother. If I wanted something not in the Sears catalogue, my wish would not be coming true. I could expand my range of possibility by using the summer catalogue too. The business of drawing up a wish list got more and more practical the older I got. By the time I was a teenager, my wish list, which might include clothes, hockey gear, maybe fishing stuff, looked like this:

Summer Cat.
p. 31  A. large, blue          #004 639
p. 119  C.                         #001 552

Wishbook Cat.
p. 57 G. large, tan            #201 177
p. 233 A.                          #201 523
p. 239 C. large, black        #203 201

Things got even more practical when my mother set our individual spending limit. Now I had to put in the prices too, and tally them so they didn't go over. I also had to factor in the discount, so if my limit was $100, I could go up to $132, which after the discount was applied, actually totalled $99. I handed over my list, my mother phoned it in, and a day later my dad picked it up, wrapped, to bring home. The only surprises would be if the catalogue people screwed up on the colour, and my black sweater turned out green.

Sometimes my mother slipped up. Instead of asking me if I'd done my wish list, she'd tell me I had only four more days "to put in your order."

Things were even more coldly calculated when I bought presents for my parents. It would begin with my mother asking me if I'd shopped for my father yet, knowing I hadn't.

"You don't have much time," she'd add.

"What should I get him," I'd say.

"*Maybe* he wants an extra-large grey cashmere cardigan sweater. They're on sale till Saturday."

I'd go to Sears and charge the sweater to my dad's own card, and wait while it was wrapped. Likewise, my father would tell me what my mother wanted, usually Chanel No. 5. Sometimes my mother, doing all the wish lists at once, would herself call it in, my gift to her that I didn't yet know about.

Christmas morning we'd open our gifts, one at a time so everyone could watch, uttering sounds of delight and surprise. It wasn't unusual for my mother to unwrap then thank me for my gift to her, one she'd thought of, ordered, and put under the tree herself. Seeing my gift to her for the first time, I was the only one surprised. No—my dad was surprised too. He didn't care about gifts at all, and that sweater was her idea to begin with. Sometimes it looked like he actually liked what he got.

"Thanks, Pal," he'd say to me, lifting the sweater out of its box, shaking it out in front of him. His smile was mischievous, a bit of a wink in it, acknowledging how little either of us had to do with this sweater at all.

Birthdays were comic in the way that bleak Ingmar Bergman films were comic. It became a family tradition to celebrate birthdays in restaurants, and these evenings were masterpieces. The comic formula was, the more my dad drank, the less my mom did, so to speak. That is, the louder he got, the more she clenched up in silence. She never actually drank. But sometimes we really wished she did, despite the evidence—there in the shape of my father—of what drinking did to you.

Depending on whose birthday, there might be others along instead of just the four of us, adding to the comedy. My brother or I might bring a date or, later, a wife, though we tried to avoid this. A frequent guest was my mother's bridge partner Doris—who I enjoyed talking to, especially after I'd read Malcolm Lowry, because Doris had been friends with the author and his wife Margerie.

We tried nice restaurants, one being The Savoury, a high-end place right in Deep Cove. We stopped going after the food went downhill, which was code for us being tired of my dad invading the kitchen to thank the grandly mustachioed Wolfgang, foisting a double brandy on the chef and not leaving. All smiles, Wolfgang would usher him out, declining the brandy, which meant that my dad got to drink Wolfgang's too, which was likely the plan all along. Dad would always have the prawns and scallops in *sauce pernod*, exclaiming as though he'd never had them before and, if he'd been gulping rather than sipping the wine, over his food make effete little noises and finger gestures that I think were supposed to be European. Two double brandies would come and he'd announce, "I have to thank Wolfgang."

I've been ignoring my mother's role in the comedy. I'm not blaming her; she had the hardest row to hoe. She was an upright, somewhat regal woman, and attractive in the way a female banking executive can be attractive. (She was apparently also attractive in the other way—nauseatingly, one teenaged friend confessed to having a crush on her.) In any case she was very proper. She abhorred a scene, especially one involving her husband. So she got more colourful during these birthdays.

Let's say it was my birthday. The Savoury. I had a date along, who I already felt sorry for. My gut was tight. No one was speaking at this point, due to my father's most recent loud question, "Where are her McGuffins?" when my small-breasted friend had gone off to the washroom. "There's nothing to hang on to!" The meal was over but we were waiting. My scheduled individual birthday-cake surprise hadn't arrived yet. My father forgot what we were waiting for, and he was overdue for his visit to Wolfgang in any event, so up he got. My mother knew complaint was useless. She already had her coat on, car keys in her fist, and a tight smile. Her chair was angled out into the room, ready for instant launch.

Near the kitchen, heads turned at the sound of my father's booming laugh. As if propelled by the noise, a waiter shot out bearing a tart, its single candle aflutter. Tableside, depositing my surprise, he mumbled, "For the birthday boy." He didn't appear to like us. I guessed his stomach was clenched too, and I wondered what my dad had quipped at him.

Without looking at me, my mother slid a white envelope—my birthday present—across the table.

"You didn't put in your order this year," she said, "so it's just money."

I wished my default wish, world peace, and blew out the candle. Beside me I could feel a young woman losing any desire she may have had to be a part of this particular gene pool.

The more restaurants we birthdayed through, the more my dad drank, and the more clenched my mother became. When someone came for the drink order, she'd interrupt whoever was being asked first to order a coffee, black. She ordered instructively; there were options other than alcohol. It got so that she would angle her chair so it faced the drink person's imminent approach, and depending how the night went she might keep this angle for her exit launch. She also took to ordering her meal from the drink person, despite being politely informed that our server would be along shortly. When she insisted, he would pause, take in the look on her face, spin, and go fetch the server. She would come and my mother would order her meal. We might have opened our menus by now, though not my dad, who was craning his neck, itching for the drink guy to come back.

During these years of birthdays my mother was driven furious by appetizers. We always ordered them, she never did, and she'd sit watching us eat our salad or oysters or, my dad's favourite, any kind of bisque. "Lobster, *bisque*," he would announce, liking the word. Not that he'd hurry to finish his bisque, because at this point any food was a threat to his buzz. "Appetizers" was that period of time my dad spent getting drunker while Mom waited helplessly for food. She couldn't hear the word without freezing. "Appetizers" came to drive her crazy in a way that even Dad stopping drinking couldn't fix.

We started going to Chinese restaurants for birthdays the year my dad went on the wagon because many were not licensed to serve alcohol. My mother chose the restaurant based on this feature and my dad nodded soberly. Later, my dad drinking again, he soberly insisted we keep doing Chinese, as if this were somehow still a noble thing and as if we didn't notice that his favourite spot was now licensed. In any case, "appetizers"—my mother couldn't get it through her head that spring rolls and potstickers and hot and sour soup were not appetizers but simply what you ordered as part of a Chinese meal, the dishes coming out as they were prepared. But because she perceived those first dishes as official appetizers she refused to eat them, angling her chair toward the door while the rest of us spun the lazy susan and helped ourselves. One time, my dad drunk-in-advance, she was furious-in-advance, and angled her chair at the first poor woman who approached, one whose English didn't extend beyond menu items and the information "Spicy" and "Is coming soon."

"Coffee, black, and I—"

"No coffee. Tea? Chinese tea?"

"No. And, will you make sure, that *the rest of the meal*, is brought *at the same time*, as the *appetizers*?"

"You wan' appetizer?" She tapped the menu instructively.

"I want, the *rest of the meal*, brought, *at the same time*, as the *appetizers*."

The waitress leaned in and pointed more instructively to the menu. All of us at the table were into a good stomach clench now, and my father wasn't the only one craning his neck for a drink guy.

I recall gentle Doris putting a hand on Mom's arm and saying that this was not how the Chinese did things. And that she'd heard this place was supposed to be fabulous. And that next time we'd know to bring a thermos of coffee. And my mother—laughed. It tickled her funny bone, this notion of bringing your own coffee to a restaurant. My mother could change gears in a second. It seems she could simply decide to be girlish and friendly and, all of a sudden, she was.

One night at someone's birthday something happened to Doris that made me hate my father. At the end of the night he was drunk but coherent, and as usual my mother drove. We were dropping Doris off, and I was in the back with her. We had just pulled into her driveway when Doris said, very quietly, that she didn't feel very— She lost consciousness. Her head fell against the window. I smelled the rising tang of excrement. My mother said, "Oh dear, Doris said this has been happening." My dad and I got out. Doris came to and, her arms over our shoulders, we got her up her front steps and almost through her front door when she fainted again. "Oh my, she's soiled herself," said my mother, who smelled it now. We got Doris into a chair as she came round again, and my mother helped her to the bathroom, fetched her robe, and for ten minutes Doris insisted that she was fine now, please don't call the ambulance. My mom finally agreed, but made Doris promise to phone her in ten minutes, and then again, or an ambulance would be on its way pronto.

As we were leaving, approaching the car, my dad leaned my way and snickered knowingly. He met my eyes and rolled his.

"What?"

"She was faking," he whispered, more of a snort.

"What do you mean, faking? Why would she fake that?"

"She was faking." He shook his head. "She likes the attention."

"*How* do you fake that?"

I knew Doris as well as he did. She was more alert, kind, and normal than any of us. She could be plain-spoken about hard things, and I know she'd more than once asked my dad about his drinking. Which would make her his enemy. If anything, she didn't like attention, not at all. So what he had just said was not only mean-spirited, it was so stupid as to be insane. Who would deliberately shit their dress clothes to attract attention? It was impossible. And the way he'd suggested it, like he was somehow in the know? He disgusted me from all directions.

I did eventually find reason to forgive him, but not yet. For years this night would fester, until after he was dead.

———

Enough celebrations. Except, Christmas Eve. The idea perpetrated by movies and TV was that Christmas Eve was prime time for warmth and joy, as family gathered to talk and pass treats and laugh, and the TV wasn't on.

Some people believed the movies and TV.

Guilt made me stop by, taking a break from the carousing that had become the real tradition. I once took mescaline and went to midnight Mass with a pack of friends, none of us Catholic. There were always boisterous parties at friends' houses. But first I would drop in at home. A fire would be going in the fireplace, the one time that year. My mom would be in the kitchen, playing solitaire, my dad in the living room listening to the dreaded Jimmy Rogers record, a series of mournful carols played only on Christmas Eve. Partly because of the era, I viewed my father as a man who'd been duped by the American dream. He had dutifully acquired everything—career, wife, house, car, swimming pool, two sons, tail-wagging dog—and, having amassed it, following the game plan, he could not understand why he felt empty.

If my dad was in fair shape I'd hang out for a while, crack some festive nuts, talk about the Canucks. My mom might join us. If he was in bad shape my visit was short and my mom stayed in the kitchen snapping cards. Once I caught my dad slurring to himself, wondering where everybody was. To this day, Christmas Eve is the most depressing time of the year. When I hear certain carols, my God. When I hear the "Chestnuts roasting on an open fire" dirge, a ghost wails inside me.

It was on a particularly bad Christmas Eve, right after my dad ghosted off to bed, that my mother, eating festive nuts non-stop, told me, trying to apologize for his many sins,

"Your father never had a father, so he never learned how to be one."

One Christmas Eve a few years ago, when all four of my children still lived at home, the two boys had gone off to their respective parties and it saddened me. I had to remind myself that the last thing I wanted was for them to feel guilty about not staying home tonight with dear old Dad, but I was still sad.

Christmas music played in the living room. I nursed a beer in the kitchen and did dishes. The Pogues' "Fairytale of New York" came on and our oldest, Lise, did a spontaneous dance with Lilli, ten years younger. I spied on them through the kitchen door. I began breathing hard as my body swelled with a kind of grief. It had been a fun dinner, everyone here, happy and healthy. I'd had at most a glass or two of wine. Watching Lise and Lilli dance, I burst into tears. I hunched over, unable to stop sobbing, joy colliding with a sadness I held deep in my body, my crying the hot blend of both. What's odd is—or maybe it just shows that my family knows me well—nobody asked me what I was crying about.

# FIVE

*It is a wise father that knows his own child.*
—SHAKESPEARE

Reeling in the lines I resist zooming to Egmont right now, in the coming dark. I decide instead to take time, take in these waters I haven't seen in so long. I'll find Secret Cove and pull in for the night.

It's well named. I almost miss the entrance, despite scanning with binoculars. A wind has come up and, funnelled by hills and this narrow channel, built some decent waves. I bounce as I scope the shoreline and a safe harbour feels necessary. I think I've missed the entrance and wonder if my memory of this area can be trusted at all. But, over a rock outcrop, the tip of a sailboat mast. Then another mast, and there's the cove's entrance, a black artery of water behind a bald yellow rock.

I putt in, excited. There's the government dock, red-railed as all government docks are. It's where I tied up for the night, exhausted and giddy with a sense of safety, after the first voyage of *Cormorant* through that soul-shaping storm. The dock is more than full; boats are doubled up. I putt in a little deeper. A few more houses are nestled in behind the trees, and more private docks, but the years haven't choked the cove with development. There's the marina with its fish-cleaning table, the same arc lamp hanging over it, under which my dad once watched me clean salmon while dozens of dogfish—small sharks—waited for tossed guts, cruising tilted on their sides, one eye looking up at the single glaring light, in hopes of food raining down from the sky. I was fifteen, sixteen.

This being a sheltered cove, I'm guessing it's safe to anchor. I haven't spent a night afloat at anchor since the *Cormorant* days. Only the rarest of storm winds could make the boat drag anchor in the night, and I'm confident a wind that strong would wake me in time to get the motor started before *Sylvan* crashed into rocks or other boats. I putt to a little-inhabited side of the bay that sits sheltered behind a ridge. Grabbing hand-over-hand on *Sylvan*'s side railings, very aware that I'm sixty, I make my way to the bow, where the anchor is stowed inside a small hatch. I've used it only once, when Lilli suddenly decided she wanted to go swimming.

There's something soothing about putting an anchor out. First the heavy splash, then the chain rattles along its length, then the rope slides quietly and fast until the anchor hits bottom. I let out another fifty feet of slack line that floats on the surface. When the boat drifts and tightens against the anchor it feels like a good set. It feels like safety, and ease, in the pit of my stomach. I can daydream, I can eat, I can fall asleep and not worry about this damn boat. Sailors of old disliked "riding at anchor." Anchoring meant you were in the shallows, and near a reef or rocks, and storms could come up, and anchors drag, and then those rocks were fatal, because no one in those days knew how to swim. It's funny, in a frightening way, that those sailors who couldn't swim a stroke felt way safest in the deepest water possible.

I double-knot the anchor rope to the cleat, look up and survey the pretty cove, all in shadow now because of the hills and their tall trees. I take a deep breath, suddenly exhausted, though it's still not sundown. It's hard work keeping control of a boat all day, even sitting, your inner core adjusting to every tiny motion of every wave. It's exhausting having to worry about wind, and time.

And I'm hungry. I consider what I have on hand: the sausage I already gnawed on for lunch, and some crackers and cheddar, some dried figs and apricots. But I have a crab trap, and two cans of tuna cat food for bait. It takes just a minute to set up. I have no idea whether Secret Cove has crab or not, and no floats are out indicating other traps, but this means nothing. Incredible as it seems, people who live in crab-rich waters can get sick of crab, tired of the catching, cooking, cracking, and the finicky business of picking meat out. In both Hong Kong and Toronto's Chinatown they call the Dungeness crab around here "Vancouver crab," and it's known as one of the premier crabs in the world. It's a little less sweet than king crab, but a richer flavour. Nothing on the East Coast compares. I love it, and I'm fine with the fuss of eating it—it makes me eat more slowly.

I heave the trap over the side and it sinks out of sight, dragging its yellow rope behind. I am already eager to pull it back up to check it. I love this part of the world.

———

One of my favourite meals I enjoyed with my dad was an illegal and guilty one. Salmon fishing leaves innocent victims.

We're anchored, waiting for the bite. In our hurry to get fishing we've had nothing but coffee this morning and we're hungry. Then one rod gets a little bite, but it disappears, then a little bite, then mysteriously nothing, and so on, and it's time to check the bait. There on the hook is a little salmon, a grilse, maybe a pound. If we were trout fishing we'd be happy. But this was a nuisance fish, a waste of a live herring, and also the waste of a salmon, because grilse are delicate, and any hook in the throat or gill is fatal. And this grilse—hungry, stupidly fearless—is gill-hooked.

After unhooking a mortally wounded little salmon you can do one of two things. You can throw it back to die, as the law demands, or you can heat up the bacon grease in the frying pan, quarter a lemon, and prepare to eat the evidence.

Throwing it back makes no sense. In fact it's crueller, since a bleeding death is slower than your bonker. Eating it, you can give the dead creature the respect it is due—by deeply appreciating its taste. You slice off head and tail, pull out the guts, scoop its backbone liver with a teaspoon. The pan is now medium-high hot. Don't bother skinning and scaling. Lay it in on one side of the pan, hear it sizzle. Open a can of beans 'n' molasses (not tomato sauce). Besides salt, lemon is the only mandatory seasoning. (Well, if you're that sort of person, some fresh aioli is also perfect with grilse.)

After five minutes you flip it so it lands on the empty side of the pan. The cooked skin has stuck to the pan and stayed behind, all according to plan. The other side will also stick, and voila, you will have a perfectly skinned fish. Another five minutes does it. Test by lifting the extruding stub of backbone with a fork. The instant it lifts cleanly, leaving all flesh behind, means boneless perfection. One minute too soon or too late means less than perfect, but still splendid. Lift the fish out, one half per plate, onto a lumpy swamp of beans. Spray with lemon, be liberal with salt. (Salt after lemon, or you spray the salt away.)

Fork into a meal so good that, if a reel goes off, you'll simply keep eating. It's young salmon ten minutes out of icy water. It tastes like an impossible blend of tenderness and strength. Not many words will be spoken. Thoughts have stopped, too. Like sex and a few other things, it can't be described, so I'll stop trying.

———

Except, my dad's smoked salmon. Sears sold electric smokers so of course he had one, and every couple months he'd do up a batch. His brine recipes included garlic, demerara sugar, bay leaves, peppercorns, and red chilies he grew himself. I remember how some Christmas Eves weren't so bad—gobbling up lots of smoked salmon, once impressing a girlfriend with it.

I inherited the smoker when he died, and when I use it I think of him. I try to duplicate his brine recipes, in which you soak the chunks of fish overnight, and I picture him stooping to load the smoker with the little pan of wood chips, bought at Canadian Tire. (Alder is best; it's what the Coast Salish used.) When it's done and I brag about it to my kids, I sound pretty much like he did.

The first time I hauled that old smoker out of the basement after catching those Port Renfrew salmon with Willem, I burned our house down. Not down, but almost down. It was a coin toss as to whether it was a teardown or repair job.

No one was hurt, so I can josh about it. What happened was, smoking my lovely, expertly brined salmon out on the sundeck, I disposed of each batch of charred, spent wood chips by dumping them into a big plastic planter full of dirt. The planter happened to be sitting against the cedar-siding wall of the house. When dumping the black, dead chips, I saw no smoke, no embers. Even at midnight, when in darkness I dumped the last spent chips and brought the finished salmon inside, I saw no embers, no living coal.

At dawn the paper boy saw our outer wall ablaze. His pounding on our front door made the dog bark, and Dede, who went to see, screamed "Fire! Fire!" in a voice I never want to hear again. Somehow I ended up on the sundeck with the garden hose. The wall I faced was on fire, as was the deck floor and also the corrugated plastic roof, which dripped with that sizzling-drip sound beloved by toy-burning children. Connor stood beside me throwing dishpans of water up into the burning roof. We were both in our underwear. Connor's date, a young lady we never did see again, stood in the kitchen looking hung-over, wrapped in a sheet.

My hose put out the wall and floor and Connor's thrown pots took care of what was left of the plastic roof. Dede, who was down on the street by now, has a favourite story to tell. Just as the first fire truck pulled up, there I was in my underwear yelling, "It's out! We did it!" From the street she could see the whole roof on fire, and billowing smoke so thick it engulfed the next two houses on that side. Anyway, the good firefighters with their burn suits, oxygen tanks, axes and hoses managed to put out the fire. Who knew dirt can burn?

Someone heaved Dad's old smoker off the deck and it bounced into the backyard. I pounded out a couple of the bigger dents and—good as new. Now Dede always asks me how I'm disposing of the spent wood chips and I always tell her I am wisely dumping them into a bucket of water. I haven't told her how, though the chips are black and dead-looking, they smoke and sizzle loudly when they hit the water, as if to say, *We only look dead!* making me feel stupid all over again. And I remember, only now, the sound of the spent chips sizzling as my dad dumped them into his own bucket of water. I remember the bucket was white, exactly the white of his hair.

———

My dad had special regard for meat. I don't know if this had to do with an impoverished childhood or if it was his generation. But whenever he came up to fish, he'd do a grocery shop, a couple of bags' worth, and in the bags would be little else but meat. Steaks, hamburger, chicken, maybe a small ham, some breakfast sausages, a garlic coil, a package or two of sliced lunch meat. That, and a couple of cans of beans, a hunk of sharp cheddar, and loaf of bread. (This sharp cheese he called "old fort," not knowing the *fort* was legally required and French for "strong"; he thought it had something to do with a cheese favoured by pioneers and soldiers.) We'd stuff the meat into *Cormorant's* icebox, scrunching up my lettuce and milk and whatever else I had in there.

I was usually the cook or, in any case, the one who asked first about dinner that night. Drinking, he could easily not get around to thinking about dinner at all. But at the tail end of a day's fishing, I'd broach the subject.

"So," I'd say, rod in hand, looking into a sunset, "what you feel like eating?"

"Maybe the steaks?" The breathless emphasis he gave the last word suggested a rare treat, like we hadn't had steak once a week since I could remember.

I asked what he thought we should have with the steaks. I was just as interested in the spaghetti, or mashed potatoes.

"I don't know. Hamburger?"

Or chicken, or sausages. To this day, I don't know if he was joking. He did eat things besides meat; he ate whatever well-balanced meal my mother put in front of him. It might just be that he lacked imagination, or didn't care, especially on a fishing trip. But it was more than that. Here we were surrounded by the best seafood in the world—we could buy live spot prawns beside the road for a buck a pound—but fish just wasn't the same. He'd eaten fish all his life.

Meat meant something to him. It meant he wasn't poor. So if you could afford it, and especially when you were on vacation and fishing, you celebrated with not just the best meat, but two kinds of meat. If I'd let him, he might've gone for three kinds, meat and more meat, meat on top of meat, meat inside of meat. His regard for meat made me picture him, a fourteen-year-old beanpole, standing silently in the school lunch line while his mother pincers up meat from a steaming bin, and flops him extra. That is, before she got fired for doing it.

Dede and I have a long-running joke. We eat meat of some kind maybe two or three times a week, and if one of us asks what we should have with the chicken, the other will say "hamburger," in a matter-of-fact way. The kids don't know where it's from, nor do they find it funny.

————

My dad's loud regard for meat, and food of any kind, was odd in another way. Part of the show, funny but also not, was that we all knew he couldn't taste anything on his plate. Not a thing. Visiting Wolfgang to praise his scallops in Pernod? My dad could have eaten a shoe in Pernod and not tasted the difference.

He had polyps in his throat that were surgically removed every five years when they began to impede his breathing. From what I could tell, he could taste a bit for a year afterward, but then increasingly not much at all for the next four. He never spoke of it but every five years he'd be nervous and distracted and we'd know that the operation—day surgery, local anesthetic—was soon. He once made a kind of formal announcement about a condition he had, called polyps, which every five years—etc. I don't know how he could think I didn't already know all this. Not only had he made his announcement, but his polyps, or more exactly his inability to taste, was a hard thing to hide, though he kept trying. It was as if an inability to taste was unmanly. A man was supposed to tuck into his steak with gusto and proclaim it one fine cut of meat, God, he could taste the Alberta grass in it. My dad would proclaim with what I think was his favourite word. He'd tuck into his steak and begin nodding. The word often came out garbled and wet because he'd be chewing and the meat would be tough:

"*Succulent.*"

Once I was visiting from the Maritimes with my two oldest children, who had never come west before, and the trip was a big deal to me. Dad had decided to barbecue some halibut. He'd probably instructed Mom to buy it, which was the first mistake. Hyper-organized and excited about our visit, Mom no doubt zipped out and bought it that same day they discussed it, "to have everything ready." I found it in the meat drawer when I rifled through their fridge two minutes after arriving, rifling through their fridge being my favourite lifelong pastime. The best-before date was two days before yesterday, and in any case a best-before date for fish is ridiculous, as the only thing to do with store-bought fish is to find what's freshest, smell it, buy it, bring it right home and cook it.

I suggested to my dad that maybe this halibut should get itself cooked sooner rather than later. It was a big expensive chunk. He said, "No, your mother is cooking chicken tonight," and pointed to the oven from whence the chicken smell was issuing, and I knew that, inside, were two side-by-side, sadly unspiced chickens well on the road to being roasted dry. Then my dad uttered, like a jovial, exacting chef, that he "wanted to let the halibut get just right." He wasn't joking. And here, six minutes into my cross-country visit, I witnessed my father's ability to lie, be in denial, and go temporarily insane all in one go: he *knew* fish was best fresh, but he *believed*, while saying it, that it was good to age it "just right." He was only three or four beers in but nothing he said could be trusted.

It all instantly came back. My stomach was hard, icy. I chuckled as if he'd made a joke. My kids were downstairs getting set up in the spare bedroom, and I went right down to them to see that they were safe.

When we ate the barbecued halibut two days later it was badly fishy, but edible in the sense that it didn't taste like we'd get sick from it and I didn't want to insult my dad. My mother was very capable of not tasting something she didn't want to taste. My kids gently pushed theirs away and filled up on the many treats their grandmother was only too happy to step and fetch.

The killer was that, after I forked into the first bite, I saw the halibut was basically raw inside. Not just stinky, but uncooked. The hot barbecue ticking mere feet away, it wasn't a big deal to flap something back on.

"It's a bit rare in the middle," I told him, standing up.

"Whaddya *mean?*" he asked, like this was not only a first, but an impossibility. Fifty times, a hundred times, here on this deck, I'd cut into a raw steak and taken it back to the grill. Chatting and watching him work the tongs, I would have suggested that maybe he should cut into one steak and check it before taking them all off the grill. I'd add that that was what I always did, *had* to do, because how else could you tell? Despite years of evidence to the contrary, he believed he possessed an impeccable sense of steak timing. He simply knew they were perfect. Sometimes they were, by accident. Usually they were too rare, or overcooked. He always called them perfect, and actually would not see the blue meat you pointed at, an inch from his face. He would deny the blood running down his own chin. And he wouldn't, or couldn't, remember to cut into one next time.

"It's a bit undercooked, here, in the middle." I paused in front of him and pointed to the grey, translucent halibut flesh.

"It's fine," he said. "Mine's perfect."

"It's also a bit off," I said, sticking the knife in deeper, tired of this particular dance, "so I want to make sure it's cooked."

"Whaddya mean?" He looked genuinely hurt. "Mine's great."

He actually believed his was. The thing was, he hadn't even touched his yet. When he was into the beer, he was never hungry and, until my mother pestered him enough, he'd sit cracking jokes and nudging his food.

It was a perfect little storm. My glowering judgment. His beery haze, and his pride, and his polyps.

But he wouldn't admit to his polyps either. And the less he could taste, the louder he'd proclaim about the food, this equation telling me how close the next operation was: louder praise equalled deader taste buds meant surgery soon. Once, tired of the game and feeling cruel, after hearing again how succulent his steak was I asked him how his polyps were doing, knowing the surgery was that year. He looked panicked for a moment, unsure of what I knew about them.

"Polyps?" He made a dismissive fart noise and waved his hand. "Long gone."

Drinking, he'd say anything. Anything.

———

I wait the ten minutes. It's probably more like seven. Pulling up the crab trap, hand-over-hand, I think I can feel extra weight to it. No, I can't tell. No, it's definitely heavier. Now in the clear black water I can see its faint boxy outline. Now I see some colour—beige, some red. Definitely something in there, something big.

A small rock crab and a big sunstar, one of those soft, slimy, twelve-legged beasts. They apparently like tuna cat food.

I pull the dripping cage over the side and drop it on deck. I draw the crab out—by pinching its smallest foot—and plop it back in the drink. Now I wrestle the sunstar. How did it squeeze through that little door? I yank and pull, trying not to hurt it, though I doubt it possesses a central nervous system. I see no pores but water gushes out with my squeezing and wets me to the elbow. I eventually pull it free and heave it, *kabloosh*, and down it goes. I throw the trap out again, but from the opposite side of the boat this time, as if that will matter. Sunstar and trap will both meet again, ten feet apart, on the bottom.

———

I was fifteen and here in Secret Cove leaning on that balcony railing right up there through those Douglas firs. I see no sign. It used to be the Jolly Roger Resort.

Beside me leaned Randall, a young executive, maybe thirty. He was quietly furious. It was dark out on the deck but electric light, cigar smoke, and the drunken shouts and laughter of a poker game blasted from an open door.

"*Listen* to that," Randall hissed.

He was angry, he told me, that he didn't have a deep booming voice and people paid attention to deep booming voices. Nor did he like to drink, he hissed further, leaning with me there on the rail, a careful five or six feet apart. I felt like quipping, "But maybe drinking will give you a deep booming voice," because I didn't like him. Randall seemed like the junior exec who took golf lessons so he could impress the boss if he ever did get invited. I could somehow tell that he didn't like fishing, which is why everyone was here.

It was a little creepy, an underling of my father's, twice my age, confiding this stuff to me. It was the Age of Aquarius, and I was a fan of intimate, bare-your-soul talking, but not with him. It was also odd that he was Randall, not Randy.

"And the *smoke*," Randall said, disgusted. The poker players had been chomping on cigars all evening. I had just finished a cigarette and flicked it off the deck, but I don't think he noticed much about me.

Another eruption of laughter after a punchline from my dad. The laughter didn't stop. I looked in through the door and someone had Dad in a headlock from behind, tilting him back in his chair, at which point my dad brought his hand to his lap and mimed masturbating his two-footer, and everyone bellowed again. I gathered he was winning at cards and had just successfully bluffed somebody.

"*Listen* to that," hissed Randall. It was weird because the man with the most booming voice, the hardest drinker, and the winner of the popularity contest inside, was my father. And Randall knew this.

"And he's *big*. I'm not *big*." It was true. This was getting bizarre, this man's whimpering, futile malice, and me standing right there.

"*It's not fair!*" he hissed, spectacularly petulant. He looked in danger of losing it. He'd had a few and maybe this was why he didn't like drinking: Who would, if it so easily flipped a switch and revealed an inner weasel?

I knew that if Randall ever climbed the ladder and became boss, he'd be a mean one. If his sibilant rant there on the deck affected me in any way, it was to make me proud of my dad, who wasn't a mean boss at all. It made me proud of his height, his deep booming voice, his racy punchlines, and that he was winning the popularity contest. His loudness seemed somehow generous.

When my dad was drinking he could be charming, drunken charm being different from the more subtle, sober variety. Drunken charm is full-veined and brash and is rarely perceived as charm unless you are drinking too. He was in there singing "Roll Over Mabel" and people were laughing, not clenching. There's the rub, the rub known by anyone who's suffered a loud drunk while sober themselves.

My dad was good at parties if the booze was flowing. He tended not to drink himself under the table when there were people around. So maybe it's strange, and in some way sad, that I never once sat down and got drunk with him. Occasionally we did pass like ships in the night when in my late teens I'd come home after having had a few. One such time he caught me downstairs in the rec room smoking hash.

"So you smoke that stuff, eh?" His smirk was both sly and wary.

I exhaled, and shrugged.

I offered him some and he sat beside me on the couch. On TV, Abbott and Costello were doing their thing with the sound off. My dad wasn't great at sucking the expensive smoke through the hollow ballpoint pen, but he did get some in. We sat for a while, snorting quietly at the TV, embarrassed to be sitting there saying nothing, and when I asked him what he thought of it he claimed to feel nothing. He seemed to me radically more sober, but I didn't say so.

Another time on the same couch I sobered him up with tequila, which he'd also never tried. I told him it was "weird" booze, almost like a drug, and after a couple of shots he indeed grew sloppily somehow more serious, and with a long pause and gaze into the middle distance he said, "You're not kidding."

But usually I wouldn't come home till the wee hours, after he was long in bed. Or sometimes at one of our horrendous restaurant birthdays I'd have a beer with him, both as pre-drinking for my post-dinner carousing as well as to survive the dinner itself. But I never just sat down and cracked a bunch of beers with him. Even when on a fishing trip. I know this made him sad.

It mostly just felt natural not to drink with him. It wasn't strategy. My not accepting a beer felt instinctive. On a gut level, to drink felt like encouragement. I suppose the word is *enabling*.

But he would drink whether I did or not. Saying no to the "Wanna beer, Pal?" felt like punishment. It heightened his guilt, which is exactly what I wanted. In some ways it might have been better if I'd got parallel shit-faced and cancelled his stupidity by joining it. Maybe if I got absolutely balls-out drunk and sloppy, showed him what it looked like, maybe it would scare him straight, or at least make him worry about his son.

Anyway, he was nothing but good stupid fun, drinking. He was nothing but amiable. I liked how he got a little twisted, with his little rhymes, his jokes, his hauling out the trombone and blatting on it until my mother made him stop. After hanging out with my drinking dad for even a short while, my friends would exclaim what a great guy he was.

But I was caught in a trap. He'd begin his lonely party of one, I'd hear his first beer hiss open, my gut would clench and my spirit grow ice. Sometimes this ice brought me closer to my mother, because now I was in her territory. I'd hear him cough to mask the sound of snapping open a can. He coughed by habit now, every time he opened a can, not aware of it anymore, and with every cough I'd weather a deeper blast of cold.

———

.

I haul up the trap again. Its weight is suspiciously familiar. Still no crabs, but there's the big sunstar. I heft it over the gunnel and onto the deck, slimy water everywhere. It has to be the same one. And I'm not too surprised. It isn't like a sunstar has either brains or will. It probably can't learn. I wrestle it out of the trap again, not trying quite as hard to avoid hurting it, angry at it, which makes me its intellectual equal. This creature is probably more like a magnet, one with an automatic attraction to meat. I'm tempted to throw it and the trap down a third time and see if I'm right, but I'm too hungry. And the sun is going down. And it's cold enough to need a sweater. I heave the gushy star over again and go below to raid my cooler for the rest of that sausage and some old fort cheese. I can't stop myself.

For some reason, the few talks my dad and I had about his drinking happened while driving together in the car. This was early on, before it got really bad and talking about it no longer made any sense whatsoever. But when I was in my teens we often found ourselves driving, just the two of us, to or from another fishing expedition.

I was fifteen, and we were just past Sechelt to begin the climb toward Secret Cove when he said something that I have long chewed on, it being tough food for thought. I don't remember exactly what question of mine prompted it, probably something friendly about beer in general, seeing as he was driving with a can of Black Label tucked between his legs.

What he said was: "After six of these, I feel juuuust right."

I remember he said six. I can still hear his sensuously prolonged and spiritually fulfilled tone of voice saying "just." I also remember being instantly curious about not only my dad, but about life, and being human. Why didn't we feel "just right" all the time? What was in us that ordinarily felt "just wrong"? Why would alcohol make people feel better than they *naturally* felt? After over forty years I don't know that I've found the answers, but maybe I've made progress with the questions themselves.

It was a second drive, the following year, when the subject came up again. Maybe I felt emboldened by our talk the previous year, or maybe I just didn't want him drinking this early in the day. I broached the subject halfway to Egmont. He had just reached back and grabbed a first can. He nestled it into his crotch and waited for a straight stretch and lull in the traffic before cracking it.

"You don't need that," I said. It sounded like a line from TV.

There followed ten seconds of intense silence. Then in a voice I'd never heard before, one barely under control, he said, "Don't ever talk to me about my drinking."

I didn't, not that trip, or for a while thereafter. He didn't speak for some miles, and he didn't lighten up until we reached the resort, and his buddies, who also never walked from one place to another without a beer in hand. I got the feeling as he climbed out of the car that him feeling just right also had something to do with getting away from me.

A third time we talked about it in a car took place on the way back from an Egmont trip a few years later still. He'd been at it pretty heavily, mostly hard stuff now. All week, the V-berth in the bow of *Cormorant* had thundered with his snores and the groans and whimpers of his dreaming. I was driving. He'd dosed his coffee that morning and kept at it, having me stop at gas stations en route, staying in the car during the ferry crossing, and the usual ploys for sneaking a shot. When we disembarked the ferry he casually asked that I pull into the liquor store near our house so he could pick up something. A mile or two closer he mentioned it again, just in case I hadn't heard. And again, when we were a minute away. He sounded more and more nervous, because I still hadn't responded, from the land of ice. Finally, when we rounded the corner and came into sight of the strip mall:

"Hey, could you zip into the parking lot, Pal? I just wanna go grab something."

I drove past the mall, turned down the street to our place.

"If you want it that badly you should probably go up and get it yourself."

I'd been in a frosty clench ever since he tipped the vodka into his coffee. I'd never done anything remotely like this before. Never such a comment. Never taken such a stand.

I parked the car in the garage and we just sat there. He shoved me his wallet.

"Hey, well, how about going up to the liquor store and getting me a fifth of Smirnoff's?"

He called a twenty-sixer a fifth. It was American. Fifth of a gallon? He'd been living in Canada almost twenty years.

"Nope," I said. "I hate it when you drink, so I don't want to buy it for you."

"What do *you* care if I drink?"

"*What do you mean, what do I care?*" It felt great to shout. "I care because it wrecks your life. I hate watching it. I care because—" It just came. "—I love you. What do you mean, *what do I care?*"

It also felt great to say "I love you," and it was easier while mad and giving him hell. It was a first. And I would love to say this was a huge step in our father–son relationship, a grand opening up. It wasn't. Even as the magic words outrageously escaped my mouth for the first time in my life, I knew he wouldn't remember. And this was what let me say it.

That's where we were now. When we were together, it no longer mattered what happened, or what we said. Our best shared moments, a pig-backed salmon, a swooping eagle, giant worm, curtain of water, he forgot all of it. But now he was forgetting everything as it happened, everything was gone by the next day. That was the worst. Because sometimes we did get real, and talk. Even about his drinking. Even about him forgetting everything because of his drinking. Even declarations of love. All heartfelt words—ceased to matter. Why talk at all? Why visit him?

I'm not sure if my dad ever knew, for certain, how many children I had.

But there in the car I'd said it. For a moment at least, he felt it. He looked overwhelmed, but that passed, like it all did. Though maybe this time I'd left a good scar.

As if caught red-handed, he mumbled stuff. Then grew antsy, overwhelmed now by something else. He'd be heading up to the liquor store himself as soon as I left, no matter what more got said in the car. He might try to drive rather than walk the uphill half-mile. So I said okay. He made a lame promise about drinking less and going back to only beer. Maybe he would remember something about this—maybe there'd be a new wariness in my presence and more hiding his drinking. So, yes, maybe I'd left a scar.

I held out my hand for money. He said, "Don't tell your mother."

———

I like to think that I want my kids to talk to me about my drinking. They've grown up seeing me drive to the party and their mother drive home. It's not nearly the problem it was in my dad's life, but there have been over-the-top times. I've described to them two patterns alcoholism can take, one being the daily drinker and the other the binger, and I've said that I seem to have a bit of the latter. That, even now, at sixty, sometimes I feel like keeping it going at the dinner party, pouring myself more wine after everyone else has shifted to the tea or coffee. Something in me, call it a magnet, it's that stupid, just wants more. Some brainless momentum has found traction, driven by the ruse that all will be better—will be juuuust right—if more wine goes down the neck. Rarely these days, but sometimes common sense goes to bed and it's a private party.

I can talk about this to my children as easily as I am doing right here. My dad was much more bound by the ropes of addiction. So bound up that he couldn't or wouldn't see the ropes or admit to them, even though people kept finding him tied up and toppled. Even on the rare times he did admit to them, he didn't know where the ropes were, exactly, or that there were knots.

I've warned my children about our family history. And that addictive behaviour is inherited. I've explained that our kind can fall prey not just to alcohol and drugs, but to food, to video games, to porn, to social media, to any habit that puts a buffer between you and the hard light of life. I've marvelled aloud about how even the worst, nightmarish behaviour—the hard-core alcoholism, spousal violence, sexual abuse, everything—can somehow loop and repeat itself, parent to child, even though the child has seen that particular hell and "knows better."

I don't know how much they've listened. They don't seem worried about me. I guess despite a few times being a stupefied fool in their presence, I haven't done anything vile or lasting in their eyes. Nor do they seem worried about themselves. I do, when I suspect one of them has been hitting the bong more than just on weekends, or if another looks too hungover too often. I pause to remember how much I drank at that age, and I'm not sure if this helps.

# SIX

*I cannot think of any need in childhood as strong as
the need for a father's protection.*
—SIGMUND FREUD

*When I was a boy of fourteen, my father was so ignorant I could
hardly stand to have the old man around. But when I got to be twenty-one,
I was astonished at how much the old man had learned in seven years.*
—MARK TWAIN

Waking from my first night aboard *Sylvan* I rock foot-to-foot and light the camp stove as much for its warming blue flame as to make coffee, and its hiss is a promise of heat. It's not quite sunrise. I didn't sleep well, pleading all night with the thin, hard cushions of *Sylvan's* V-berth.

Sipping coffee on deck I come to, empty-headed in the good way. It's a perfect morning on the water. The mirror surface reflects a colour that sits impossibly at a cusp between pink and blue. There's nothing else like it. It's so powerfully quieting. I'm slowed down. Problems feel distant, transparent, like their existence might even be questionable. If sunset is French-horn melancholy, sunrise is a barely heard melody that things might go well today.

Somebody's rooster goes off, so much louder out here on the water. I don't know the physics of this. I realize it's this rooster that first woke me up. Two, three lines of smoke rise in the shoreline trees, so others are awake. Secret Cove is tiny as coves go and it feels like a community where everyone would be aware of everyone else at all times. I wonder if I'm being watched. There's my futile yellow line hanging over the side. I left the crab trap in all night. I'll haul it up soon, free the dumb sea star.

It's easy to feel my father here beside me because he would have loved exactly this, keeping still on this deck in this moment that has become even more silent in the rooster's wake.

———

Water might be medicine. It certainly was an opiate of one old navy man. He seemed happiest at his Deep Cove, North Vancouver house, where he lived for his last thirty years. It's also where he fell into his worst drinking, and that contradiction doesn't appear to be uncommon. In Deep Cove he had a beautiful view of Indian Arm, a fjord bordered by mountains, the highest of which were snow-capped half the year.

If he was home by himself, which he usually was, depending on the weather you'd find him in the living room, or out on the deck, or under it, three vantage points for gazing at the water. Under the deck he was closest to his stash in the storeroom beneath the stairs. In one sense, since he was going to drink anyway, he was lucky to have such a beautiful spot to do it. He had hazel eyes, a strong nose and chin, and high cheekbones—there were rumours that his side of the family had Navaho blood. He was a handsome man. I can picture that long-distance gaze of his with ease. It wasn't just a quiet nobility, it was a stubborn nobility, the gaze of someone who had known war and was still in one.

On Gabriola, to get my fix of water I don't need the ocean. Our humble pond seems to have the effect that I'd always imagined of waterfront property. Any time I sit beside it feels like time well used. Without seeking it I ease into a tranquility. Up from the city, I need two or three days to lose the internal jitters and gain the openness, or vacancy, really, that knows how to appreciate still water. Maybe I'm easily entertained, a kind of eager village idiot, but the pond does become an endless dramatic spectacle. A turtle might rise out of the depths to hang suspended, watching me watch it back. The other day, in reeds a foot from my knee, I noticed a dragonfly, my favourite insect, then I noticed three others, each a different kind: one bright red, one with a fluorescent white tail, one the big iridescent blue kind, and one, equally big, with blue-and-white-striped wings. I'd never seen the red kind before. Red as lipstick.

I watch for new fish to rise, of course, and this is the biggest treat. Sometimes, and it's always a surprise, mink cruise the pond's edge, hugging the bank. Despite their cuteness they're of the weasel family, and even these smallest weasels have a fearsome, electric energy. Twice now I've seen snakes swim, and one of them bumped into a floating turtle! They both looked unsure of what to do. Different birds call from the overhanging forest, and when I hear an unfamiliar one it's like a new foreign language. Especially in the evenings, ravens trade one-liners in clucks, hoots, screams, and *doink-doink-doinks*. In summer, vultures circle thirty, forty feet above and, higher up, eagles soar a steadier course. Around dusk, a barred owl might glide past not ten feet from my head—too big a bird to be so silent.

I haven't seen an otter for a few months now. Nor have I smelled any scat. I'm happy that a few frogs seem to be surviving the summer. They're a brownish-pink kind, and once I saw a pale yellow one.

The entertainment can be the pond itself. Artful patterns of breeze cross its surface. When the water is mirror-calm, foliage on the opposite bank is reflected but upside down—and now it's easy to see no pond at all. Sometimes I seem to stop having thoughts. I'm just a quiet part of things, a pair of eyes, nothing special, nowhere as vital as that aspen, its bloom of tremulous hissing leaves.

Sometimes it gets seriously dramatic. A frozen deer I dragged to the middle of the yard (as instructed by the animal control people) for eagles and ravens to see and dispose of, was gone the next morning. I found it intact a hundred yards into the woods. What besides a cougar could, or would, drag a dead deer? Once, above the pond in a cedar snag, an osprey came in from its ocean hunting ground to perch. It spied some of our fish, its head jerking lustily. Hair-raising, its sudden dive—folding into a trident, then arrowhead, to slice completely underwater. It came up empty-taloned, but I wouldn't have begrudged this bird a fish.

One day this spring I sat in a chair on the pond-side deck, quietly alert for fish, thinking I was alone with my beer, when footsteps clunked behind me. I spun to see a large buck, front hooves on the deck so he could get at some red petunias in a pot. We shared a look, then he blithely resumed munching. Though deer often wander through to nibble grass or crunch fallen apples, they trot off if I appear. This one had no fear, and big sharp horns.

"Hey, big guy," I said clearly.

He lifted his head to chew and watch me, unblinking.

"Got some nice ol' *buck*-horns on ya there."

I don't know why I was talking like Sarah Palin. He took a step closer, but only so he could reach another scarlet flower. The buck was five, six feet away. I could *smell* him. I was careful to make no sudden movement. In his bearing was a knowledge of those antlers. Prime bucks seem to enjoy that they look a little dangerous, almost edging into the carnivorous realm. For whatever reason, I wished that it was my dad I could whisper to, "You believe this?"

One weekend morning I caught him under his deck, chair pointed at the water as always, so excited that he forgot to hide his drink. It was a phase where he'd declared that he was only drinking beer, because that wasn't really drinking, but what looked like a vodka and orange sat on the cement beside his chair. He was standing, pointing, binoculars against his leg.

He stabbed. "There it is," he whispered, like he might scare it away. "It's the damndest thing. It just *stands* there."

I saw now what he was looking at, a large soaring bird.

"That an eagle?" I asked. Not many eagles visited Deep Cove. But an eagle wouldn't garner this kind of excitement unless my dad had really lost it.

He brought the binoculars up again, searched, lowered them and pointed. "There! Look at him! What is that!"

The bird had stopped soaring and flapped to achieve a stationary hover, like he *was* standing there. A huge bird, white with black markings.

We were speechless, watching that bird hang in mid-air. And then it dove, fast as sight. Neither of us had seen an osprey before.

———

It seems I can take only so much morning stillness, because before I know it I'm pulling up the crab trap. I release my sunstar buddy, then go down to fire up more coffee. I snap off a couple of bananas. As if to accompany my breakfast, some faint music wafts from behind the shoreline trees. Jazzy riffs of synthesized, delicate horns that gain volume. I cock my head and try to recognize it but I don't.

Back on deck I sit with my coffee and second banana. Nature plus music is a different kind of beauty if the music fits. If it's respectful. This is okay. I'll just sit here and take my time. "No hurry" being the mantra of this trip. My dad's not going anywhere, after all.

As if to mock both me and peacefulness in general, Stompin' Tom Connor's' "Hockey Song" comes blasting from a different thicket of trees and a different, possibly competing, possibly pissed-off stereo. Beyond the song's loud yokel joy it feels aggressive. Someone put it on for a reason. I recall that it's Saturday morning, so last night was Friday night, and I wonder if this is some sort of payback, or early morning resumption of hostilities. Hippies versus football fans. Hatfields and McCoys trading potshots across the cove. It's funny, but also sad, and I wouldn't want to live here. It's time to go. I put down my coffee and banana and do a few geriatric stretches as preparation for pulling up *Sylvan*'s anchor.

What's also funny, and a little coincidental, is that the late Stompin' Tom always reminds me of my dad. Not the music, which my dad would have chuckled at but disparaged—they looked a lot alike, especially the bright, steely eyes, with something a bit Asian to them. Another man my dad resembled, John Wayne, had those eyes too, a certain squinty kind of hurt in them for all to see. Stompin' Tom, of course, had a famously painful upbringing. A prodigious drinker and chain-smoker. He hitchhiked around Canada, homeless, from age thirteen to twenty-six. I can imagine my father and Stompin' sharing an appraising look if they met in a bar.

When *Sylvan* roars to life it feels like I've entered Secret Cove's musical fray, my engine's contribution the loudest and ugliest. As it warms up I haul anchor, hand-over-hand, and I don't know if it's my imagination when I hear Stompin' Tom go up a notch as someone puts on "Sudbury Saturday Night." I turn on the GPS and sonar, and as the boys'er gettin' stinko I tap the throttle, give it a bit of gas, and the engine sounds in perfect tune. It's good to be going somewhere again. I can easily make Egmont by this afternoon. Or I can stop and fish some old haunts. Or I can drift aimlessly, lie on my back, and stare into the sky. What will I do? I force myself to try to actually understand that I'm in no hurry. Why is that so difficult?

————

Music was important to my father. He played trombone in his high school band (I have no evidence, but I bet there were jokes about his adolescent bone rack and its resemblance to this long, skinny instrument, and I wouldn't be surprised if that's why he was assigned it in the first place) and he continued the trombone in college. For as long as I can remember he owned one, stored in a black case cushioned inside with blue velvet. In North Van he kept it in a closet off the rec room and almost never played it. For one, my mother hated "the noise," but mostly it's just not a good instrument to play solo. A few times I caught him blaring along to a big band record, trying a long note, or short riff, and mostly getting it right. Only when I tried to play it did I see how hard it was to get a smooth sound, and even harder to hit a note, the trombone's slider having nothing like frets or keys to do that work. Like the violin, a trombone requires an ear, one thing I didn't inherit from him.

We always had the best stereo Sears sold, and in the sixties and seventies our living room had a wooden stereo cabinet the size of a couch. When he was sober my father played classical. Beethoven, Tchaikovsky, and Bach. Handel. Some Wagner, though I think he felt guilty about that. One week aboard *Cormorant*, the single time my dad was on the wagon during his visits, we listened to *Russian*

*Easter Overture* again and again, while mooching at anchor, no other boat around.

He loved playing things again and again. Like an infatuated teenager. I believe I would still recognize every note to every Beethoven symphony—though I wouldn't know its number, or even that it was Beethoven. He would play his music loud unless my mother was home. She told me once that she found classical music "so depressing."

When he was drinking, he played swing. Big band jazz. Benny Goodman. Gene Krupa. Tommy Dorsey. Glenn Miller. These tunes would have been the background to his first beer, his first kiss. He went to war with big band music. "String of Pearls." "In the Mood." In a way, I grew up to big band too. I knew a ton of songs.

I'd arrive home, and if I heard big band from the driveway, he was drinking. It also meant my mother was out selling real estate, being extra-helpful with clients, taking time, literally going the extra mile. It was chicken-and-egg with them: he'd drink because she was out, and she was out because he was drinking.

He wouldn't hear me come in but when he saw me he'd leap up. Forever an athlete, he could be well into it but still graceful and fleet of foot.

"Ya gotta hear this!" he'd yell, and I could hardly hear him. He'd hop to the stereo to turn it up even more so I could better appreciate it.

"I could hear it from the driveway," I'd say, not overly friendly, and in any case unheard.

*"Listen to this!"* he'd yell, the song pounding out louder. He'd always act like he was playing me something new, though it was always something I'd heard before. I'd stand dutifully beside him, a smile propping one side of my face, and wait it out. I can smell him, his two strong lords: tobacco, and beer. At some point he'd punch my shoulder and yell, *"Sex music!"*

If I was in a bad mood I might conduct, slashing and stabbing my hand with each beat of the crescendo—meaning either I was psychic, or I knew this song really well.

Or I'd come home to loud music and go to the kitchen and my dad wouldn't know I was there. I'd hear him listening to something over and over, sometimes just one small part of a song, lifting the needle and placing it, addicted to certain riffs. Songs from the musical *South Pacific*, or *Victory at Sea*. Or they would be from stuff my brother and I listened to. Harmonies in Emerson, Lake & Palmer's "Lucky Man" entranced him. Certain Moody Blues parts, and Beach Boys too. Much later, for its maudlin but kooky bass melody, the soundtrack to *Twin Peaks*. But usually it was harmony, and in a minor key. Sad music. One sweet riff, over and over and over and over.

———

Back out in Malaspina Strait I take in surrounding landforms that seemed unfamiliar yesterday but don't today. I recognize the smell here! And that particular way those clouds are torn ragged as they drag against Texada Island's high mountain spine. Added up, I spent four or five years in and around these waters. To the north I can see the mouth of Agamemnon Channel. Even at a gentle cruise, Egmont's only a few hours away. I could troll, I could fish all the way to Egmont and still make it by dark.

Instead, I edge the throttle forward, gain some speed. Pender Harbour, about a half-hour ahead. I lived there a full year, renting a tiny cabin and finishing my first book. There are lots of places to anchor. There's a pub at the head of the harbour, in Garden Bay. Out here in the strait, I could fish. What's my hurry? What should I do?

Quarry Bay takes a half-hour to reach. It's glassy calm and almost hot. After throwing out the anchor I unfold a deck chair and prepare for a sit, to mull things over, sort some gathering memories. After moving the boat from our base in Egmont, my dad and I mooched exactly here a half-dozen times. It's beautiful. I'm a hundred yards offshore, and just past that bald rock and scatter of arbutus is an old quarry, where well over a century ago they cut blocks of limestone to barge to San Francisco to build an opera house. It's strange to imagine chunks of Quarry Bay grown old and weathered in a glamorous stone building down south when, sitting in *Sylvan* and looking north, south, east and west, I see no man-made structures. Not a one. Nothing here is in a hurry at all, including me.

———

My father—the six-five ex-navy man and all-American athlete with a brush cut, the successful executive who looked like John Wayne—was frightened by authority of any kind. Any boss, coach, or cop. Any mechanic who knew some words that he didn't.

It feels strange to recount my dad's more subtle weak points, his less admirable qualities. Honestly, it feels foul. Who am I to be telling them, and why? It's one thing to speak ill of the dead, and another when it's your father, one you loved and continue to, and who has no say in the matter as his stained laundry is hung out in front of strangers.

A friend recently described how, as a young child, he watched as his perfect, all-knowing father was surprised and hoisted from behind by a boisterous friend. His father didn't like it and tried to run, legs cycling in the air helplessly. My friend remembers being frightened. And how, from then on, something between him and his father was different.

The fall from grace. When the flaws, even if they're small, suddenly outshine the virtues, even if they're huge. It's the hero not just falling down, but getting muddy, never to be unsoiled. It's the cracking of the illusion and the cracking hurts, both because you've been fooled and because you no longer feel absolutely safe. It also hurts because it feels like your dad could do things differently if he only knew how. Could *be* different, if you could only deliver unto him the right, all-knowing advice. Which, of course, you possess.

What I can say is that his fall from grace would have looked different to me had I known then what I know now. Back then, though I knew about his impoverished background, I had no clue about the bigger things. But even had I known the whole truth of his early life, I wonder if I'd have forgiven him at the time. The scornful adolescent being one of the more rigidly intolerant of life forms.

Here's one. We're on *Cormorant*, anchored right here at Quarry Bay with a few scattered boats. I'm nineteen. We spot a Fisheries boat a distance away heading in our general direction. Fishing is dead slow, so we have four lines out though we're allowed only two. It's a new rule, one they might not be enforcing yet. But to be on the safe side we decide to reel two up, fast. We turn our backs to the Fisheries boat, hiding the rods in case binoculars are trained on us, and my dad looks scared. We get the lines up and, breaking the two-piece rods down, walk the evidence into the cabin. The boat's getting closer. I mention that if they come aboard and check, it'll be easily determined that these rods and reels are wet. My dad doesn't like this information. He's in the cabin, fretting. The boat's maybe fifty feet away when it turns, veering off somewhere else. Maybe they saw us stow the rods and are satisfied with that. Twenty seconds go by. My dad, head down and pale, suddenly launches himself out of the cabin and announces, loudly and jovially, "How you *doin'* today?" The Fisheries boat is one hundred yards distant now, and shrinking.

Seeing my father petrified by a Fisheries boat, so scared that he would announce rehearsed lines into vacant air, unable even to look up to see where the boat was or wasn't, did something to me. This display of weakness—a "fear of authority" spasm I couldn't get used to—made my gut churn. I couldn't see why my father, a looming figure on all counts, lost his mind at the approach of a couple of minor bureaucrats wearing green-and-yellow jackets. If they had pulled alongside, we might have had to suffer a warning, or at the very worst a fine, but you don't throw your own balls into the ocean just because someone has a bit of power over you. You don't speak a whole sentence without daring a glance up to see if someone's actually there. You don't do any of this when you're somebody's father.

One night a few years earlier I was speeding home through the Burrard Reserve and happened to catch up with and tail my dad's car, also on the way home. To him I was just a pair of lights in his rearview, but he instantly started going slower, then dead slow, then took the corners of the suburban streets at a crawl. I knew he thought I was a cop. He slowed even more as I took every corner he did. I guessed he'd had a few, hence the panic. Doing all of five miles an hour when I tailed him into the driveway, he parked, leapt out, and strode toward the cop in pursuit. He was already talking, and trying to smile. Only when I turned off my headlights did he see it was me. I got out, chuckling and puzzled, and he swore, and breathed deep, and told me he thought I was a cop. I couldn't bring myself to say, "So?" Because he was stone sober. So why the fear? I didn't pry. I let my regard for him take a dip. Even at sixteen I seemed to be more suave, more cool in the world, than my dad. It's not that you want your father to be a Viking, or a criminal, but you certainly don't want him to be a timid little victim. Actually, criminal would be better than victim. Viking would be better still.

Intolerant adolescents have not a lot of insight. I certainly didn't. I don't think I once figured out, let alone wondered about, how my father's past might have shaped his future, and made him the man I was seeing.

Maybe this was because, when my dad was drunk, and he got lifted from behind by life, his feet cycling in the air, I just got used to it.

He'd never remember the times he embarrassed himself in front of me. When I found a freshly killed vodka bottle carefully hidden in the freezer. A night outside the bar in Pender Harbour when I helped him up out of a puddle and, back on the boat, found him some clean pants. None of this appeared to register. The next day if I called him on stuff, which early on I sometimes did, he'd deny all knowledge. I don't know if it was good old dead-brain-cell forgetfulness, or denial, the pain of remembering working like an eraser.

I almost wish I could forget or deny the worst thing I've done drunk, as witnessed by a child of mine. It's only natural that I've fallen from grace with each of my four children, but one fall was way too quick. I reveal it not so much to whip myself with a chain, but to take a step toward exonerating my father.

I was at a party, a "wine and cheese," wherein all guests brought a favourite wine, and a favourite cheese, all this to spark interesting conversation like, "Well, the South African sun is harsh in spring, so this pinot is more like a *shiraz!*" It was the kind of scenario that made me want to guzzle beer and loudly crave some Kraft slices. But I met James, who would become a friend.

The hosts had kids, so three of ours were there too, and at eleven Dede left with young Vaughn and toddler Lilli, giving me brow-knit instructions to tarry not long, bring Connor when his movie ended, and . . . was I okay to drive? I verged on drunk but hid it. We lived five suburban blocks away. What could go wrong?

What went wrong is, two young studs came in with a bag of weed. Now, the weed of bygone days was long gone but we old-timers could still forget that a joint was no longer just a joint. And the young punks, maybe sixteen, unfurled their bag with an arrogance that needed some adult remonstration. They asked superciliously if "anyone"—James and I being the only ones there—had any papers. James said, "The fuck needs papers," and turned an apple into a bong in about seven seconds. The two old cowboy dopers were going to win this one.

We smoked and smoked, cooling our throats with beer mugs of shiraz. The kitchen lights got too bright. Though our heads were twice the size and still growing, we cowboys demanded more and more, implying that if the punks put their bag away they were chicken. Eventually the phone rang, Dede reminding me that Connor had that game tomorrow and where was I?

Understanding from my pounding heart and vast unmanageable head that a challenge was upon me, I ushered my sleepy child and we climbed into the car. I was getting more deranged by the second and trying neither to giggle nor talk, because nothing would come out right. The car got started, the doors got closed and seat belts clicked, the road started to move under us, and things weren't so bad. I was a good stoned driver, slow. A block from home though, BANG, a curb came out and got me. I crept, five miles an hour, the last block, one hand over an eye so I could see, unable to answer Connor's frightened questions. Some jabble came out when I tried. I think it was the inability to put three words together that scared him more than anything. He was eleven.

My relationship with Connor was beautiful. My first son, with all that that means. In his early years he was pudgy, which made him all the more lovable. Words didn't come easily to him. But he was born sardonic, and with an old soul. In Fredericton, I drove him to hockey games, tightening his little skates, and then to soccer, to witness his precocious eye for the passing game. We'd talk strategy after, joke about that thug on the other team. We loved the same food, and over-ate in exactly the same way and for the same reasons. If I travelled, he was disturbed the whole time. Once during a vacation on PEI, when

Dede and I arranged a sitter and a night out, one of our first ever, Connor demanded that he be asleep before we were allowed to leave the cabin. I lay with him on the bed and he stuck a finger into my back, so that if I moved he'd wake up. He and I were so close. I was his trusted ally. Bigger, stronger, able to answer most questions, and wise enough to admit not knowing all.

Hitting the curb, unable to talk. Connor, in the back seat, crying. He was too old to cry like that. No, he wasn't too old to cry like that. Because he saw me. He saw he wasn't safe anymore, and never had been.

Incensed at my state, Dede installed me in a chair in the living room. We speak of that night still. I had failed many levels of trust. To drive one of our children, like that. What I remember, and will never forget, is me swaddled in a blanket, tilting in a living-room chair, trying to apologize but unable to make sense, and Connor crying as he's led away, not able to take his eyes off me. I'll never forget that face, because it's still his face.

If I'd had a brain at the time I would have been crying too. I knew I was in some way dead to him because I know how my dad had died too, a bunch of times. And when you're dead, you're dead. The hero part anyway. Maybe it's partly a good thing, to give them the hard information. But it's so sad, no matter how you see it. I wanted my dad to be my hero. I wanted to stay a hero to my boy. I didn't want it to be less than that. Or let it get so sadly complicated.

It's so sadly complicated that fathers and sons can't even talk about it.

———

But of course it was always going to be complicated. Here's the next time I took Connor fishing, two years after I fell from grace. There was that first time on the Nashwaak River, anchored in the rowboat,

Connor too small to know what was going on. The next time was in the Saint John River, his dad swooning to the long-forgotten smell of sunfish. This third time, though, was a real time.

After we moved to Victoria we splurged on a cottage for a week each summer, up in Qualicum Bay, renting it from our dentist. It was right on the sandy beach, and with all the trimmings. A fridge next to the hot tub, just for beer. We dug clams a stone's throw away, our dog Blackjack ran free—and we came every summer, that kind of familiarity a great thing for kids. Best yet, there was a boat! A fourteen-foot aluminum with a forty-horse that pushed it fast enough to ski and tube behind. It was really quite the system, launching the boat. The beach at low tide went famously out for a half-mile, which meant safe wading for toddlers, but how do you deal with a boat? Our good dentist's boat sat on a wheeled trailer, which was harnessed to an endless cable wound on a huge drum powered by an electric motor, which made launching easy.

Connor was thirteen, the age I first fished Egmont and loved everything about it. Two years older, Lise was eager to come fishing and helpful in all ways, which is her nature. Vaughn was too young and hyper to be in a cramped boat with swinging hooks. As we made lunches and packed bait, Lise was properly in awe of my tales of past fishing exploits right out there in Georgia Strait, excited about what we might catch—huge ling cod, spiny rockfish, flounder, shark. There was a very real chance of salmon, I intoned, meeting their eyes. Lise's went wide. Connor's didn't. He hadn't been listening. Lise and I waited for him to finish his video game.

Lise and I packed the boat, rolled it down to water's edge and launched it. Connor made his appearance. Up to the elbows he wore bright yellow dishwashing gloves. Squinched onto his head, a green rubber beach ball we'd busted playing soccer the night before. He looked like a throb-head alien from *Mars Attacks!*

In Connor's defence, he wasn't simply mocking and deconstructing his dad's passion for fishing, though that was part of it. He also had a reluctance to get his hands dirty, especially slimy. But mostly he's a funny fellow, dry yet colourful at the same time, if that's possible.

For a few miles we zoomed as fast as I dared, then set the anchor in the lee of a bald rock covered with California sea lions, which we could smell. Lise's awe grew; Connor, very aware of his beach-ball hat, asked what movie was on tap tonight. I baited both rods, sent them down, and in minutes we got into a double-header of big ling cod. Both kids got theirs up after a five-minute battle. Lise's ten-pounder twice peeled out line on a run. I netted them and bonked them both dead. Lise was amazed that I knew this exotic world. Connor drummed rhythms on his thighs with those gloved fingers, wanting nothing but to pull anchor so he could go fast again, and also to get away from this fishing business he knew I wanted him to like as much as I did.

———

I recently read the Keith Richards' book *Life*, and it has a section on his relationship with his father. He'd grown up afraid of his father's disapproval and, despite his becoming a world-famous rock star, the well-publicized addiction and scrapes with the law made him too ashamed to get in touch with his dad for twenty years. When he finally did, his father called him a "bugger" then of course instantly forgave him, became his drinking buddy and accompanied him on tour, flying in a plane for the first time and with Brooke Shields on his knee. We non–rock stars can't hope for tidbits so great, but it's the kind of reconciliation that rings true, or at least hits our wishful thinking's bull's eye. Especially the "drinking buddy" part. Actually, maybe the "buddy" is enough.

Keith also has good things to say about being a buddy. He says that friendship is all about distance, that is, the lack of it. It's about cutting through distance. He says it has nothing to do with being a nice guy or an asshole, and that all of his best friends are assholes but there's no distance between them. In other words, it's about intimacy.

That might be a good way to look at fatherhood too. How close can you get? How intimate? It goes both ways, of course. From what I can gather, sometimes it's the dad who won't, or can't, break through, and sometimes it's the child. Usually it's an awkward mix of both. Maybe sometimes two people simply and literally *can't* see eye to eye. Some people just weren't built to get close, it seems, or even to get along. Even at the best of times, given the pressure and baggage we all bring to this relationship, it's hard. But it's also hard to say if it's anyone's fault.

When I was approaching adulthood, my mother would repeat a version of her line "Your father never had a father, so he never learned how to be one," to cover up one of Dad's screw-ups or his latest clumsy attempt to woo my brother or me.

Even then it struck me as false, that there was a particular way to "be one." As per some manual of fatherhood. Since taking on the role myself I do see that there are basic principles one might adhere to—don't just try to be their friend, try to be a role model, and set boundaries—but to tell the truth I have my doubts whether any of those, or any principles you can think of, always hold. Maybe there's a single one: love unreservedly and show it.

But even that can have its soft spots, especially with certain kids. All kids, like all fathers, being different—being unique, in fact. So maybe the smart father stays alert and ready to respond to the unique child who emerges. And be ready for the child to change, because they will. I think most modern fathers do this. If you have more than one, aside from setting some rules that apply to all, like being fair—if Bobby gets your old car, then Billy gets your points for a ticket to Europe—most fathers naturally do engage in unique relationships with each of their unique children. You have to if you're going to get close at all. It's like any love affair. All women aren't remotely the same, so why would your kids be? But some fathers still seem to think they are, though maybe such men suffer an inability to relate at all, to anybody, not just their own children. Some people remain islands. Sad and tense rock formations unto themselves. Sometimes with beer in hand.

My father would have given me anything. Unreserved love can have its weak side. It was my mother who set the limits, behind the scenes. If it hadn't been for her, I have no doubt I could have approached my dad at any time, asked for a thousand dollars, and got it. Love was part of that, but there was also the guilt of the drinking man and the hope that redemption can be bought. It was also probable he knew of nothing better to do with his money than give it to the likes of me.

I'm not saying that my father's display of love was all weakness and calculated hope. The love, the unquestioning, indescribable love was there. It's more the day-to-day I'm on about, the way love gets expressed. Some parents, especially dads I think, throw money or favours at their kids because they don't know how else to express the big urge inside. It's awkward and embarrassing for everyone.

But we get over it. When I was nineteen, I got over my dad buying me a twenty-six-foot Tollycraft after I'd casually mentioned that having a nice boat, for instance a twenty-six-foot Tollycraft, would be great. Suddenly, here I was, living in natural paradise on a quality cabin cruiser all summer long, pretending to run a charter business, drinking my face off with friends who came up for a few days, and otherwise fishing each day and, at night, typing down some earnest fiction. I could plead in my defence that budding writers need to take advantage of everything they can to aid an improbable career. But, basically, my dad bought a boat because I said I wanted one. While it's true that he also wanted one, a nice big one, a reward for being an executive, it was also a contrivance—here's the warm, awkward part—that guaranteed we would keep fishing together. But it was an extravagance that floored my penny-pinching mother. I can only imagine how my dad convinced her.

———

I didn't understand why my father was a liar.

Some lies I did understand. Anyone who knew him saw that my father was gentle, timid even, and his attempts at a gruff, macho front just came with the territory. Maybe it's changed and maybe it hasn't, but in my father's day men had to act a certain way. Especially if you were an ex-jock, with a basso profundo voice, fought in a world war, and were now a corporate executive with an ocean view and in-ground pool. Socially, the more you could be like John Wayne, the better.

I can't imagine, not for a second, my dad hitting anyone. I can't even imagine him telling someone to shut up. Or butting into a lineup. He was a gentle man. But, going for the John Wayne, he tried not to be.

Fairly often, after some beer, staring straight at the TV screen, Dad would report to me grimly as soon as I came in the room, "I had to *fire* this guy today." He'd add some detail, like what the guy had been guilty of—some form of theft, or serial incompetence. He was a "poor bastard," but also a "stupid bastard," because he had a young family to support.

His line "I had to *fire* this guy today" always had the same complexity to it. The tough way he said *fire* was a kind of bragging to his son that he had power and wasn't afraid to use it. But there was also the head-shaking regret, the sadness for the poor bastard. There was also a tone of self-pity, that I should feel sorry for him for having to carry out the execution. And also, clearly articulated in the tone, was the suggestion that now he had good reason for getting drunk. It also suggested, bizarrely, that not only did this getting drunk have a special cause, but also that it was a rare event.

One year, during my time at UBC, he was transferred, going from manager of the downtown store to manager of the Richmond store. Ostensibly to avoid the forty-minute commute from Deep Cove to Richmond, he rented an apartment across the street from the Sears mall. He went home weekends, but during the week ate frozen dinners and watched TV on his own, and stayed separated from Mom, and I still wonder if it wasn't in fact an actual separation. In any case, it was no surprise that, not having to hide it from anyone, his drinking climbed several notches that year.

I was in his apartment for the day, using it to write an essay in peace, but I was also answering my mother's encouragement to visit him there. She must have known something was up. He came in way too early from work that afternoon with a bottle of Scotch, and he told me what just happened. He was shaky, though there might have been another reason for that. He told me how, just an hour ago, there'd been a *boom* in the Sears public washroom and how he, as store manager, had been called upon to investigate. He said he went in just as police arrived, and he witnessed the blasted and blood-soaked bathroom stall, a headless body slumped there, a newly purchased Sears shotgun smoking on the floor.

Telling me this, shaking, he poured a big tumbler of Scotch, saying how badly he needed a drink. He was visibly excited, both by what he'd witnessed and also by the prospect of a damned good reason to drink and a guilt-free bout of it ahead of him. He asked me if I wanted one, but I had to drive. There was no way I was hanging around. He'd be gentle, but he'd be instantly maudlin, and soon stupid, and it always hurt to watch him get so stupid, so fast. Though I didn't have this insight at the time, it also hurt because, when he got drunk, he abandoned me, escaping to his private swirling world.

Anyway, it didn't dawn till years later that he probably made up the entire suicide story. That bottle of Scotch had become a daily fixture for him in Richmond, as had the early exit from work, and he'd had all day to think up a good drinking excuse to tell the nuisance son who'd invaded his hidey-hole.

I came to see that the more animated the story and more excited the telling, the more likely it was a rehearsed lie. Once when I was thirty, and popped home to say hi, my dad came up from downstairs to find me and started raving in his John Wayne vengeance voice about some hit-and-run accident in the shopping centre parking lot. He'd come out of the store (with the butter, or bread, or whatever other reason he'd had to go buy his two-four of beer) to see his side mirror bent and with "goddamned white paint on it, it must have been a goddamned white car. *God damn it.* Goddamn *hit-and-run driver.*" I asked him if it was badly damaged and he said, "Well there's *white* all over it. It must have been a goddamned white car, I know that much." He was moderately drunk, but so over-the-top and emphasizing all the wrong things that I knew he was lying. Later, on my way out, I inspected his car mirror. It was a bit askew, with some white paint on it. I knew right away what had really happened, and checked out the garage. There on the garage door frame at precisely the right height was a fresh gouge along the white paint. He'd been ashamed, or possibly had driven drunk, and had come up with a flailing, macho story. *If I ever find that guy!* I wouldn't have noticed, otherwise.

He entered a phase where he drank and lied more. Some of his sudden utterances were so bizarre I was glad that I was freed from believing them even for a moment. They would take the form of official announcements, often while staring at the TV, often in the John Wayne voice: He had a brain tumour and six months to live. His wife was cheating on him. He had tried to save a shipmate from jumping over the railing at sea but the guy had slipped through his hands.

They were the crudest grabs for sympathy, and mostly they just got me mad and made me bugger off. I don't want to add more examples and shove my father's memory deeper into the ditch. I mention any of it only because, knowing what I now know about him, I find it incomprehensible that in those pathetic bids for sympathy he never simply told me the truth about his past, one word of which would have won him all the sympathy he could ever want. It is crushingly sad that he never just told me about himself.

Nor did I see his lying as something he'd learned to do in his younger life, to survive. I see that only now. If I asked him even a simple question, the truth didn't automatically occur to him as the answer that was necessary, or even desirable. If I was to ask him what a camshaft did, or if our house had ever been painted yellow, or if he'd ever seen a man die, his eyes first flashed wariness of the question, and then a calculation of what the best, not the actual, answer might be. He often said, "Whaddya mean?" as a way to buy time. It was never "I don't know." For long stretches of his life, my dad said whatever he hoped might get him through one moment and on to the next.

Sometimes I saw the size of his fantasy life. One time, I was living across town and I dropped by in the middle of a party. These were rare, and eventually stopped altogether after the friends had fallen away, or my mother didn't want to see her husband act out in public anymore. I arrived to music, lots of laughter, even some dancing. I was in the kitchen going through the fridge when my dad leaned into the room and said something to me. He was sweaty from dancing, and looked to be having a great time, not drunk but effervescent with the first half-dozen. Just right. Popping his fingers, moving with the music. Big band.

"I bet you haven't seen your old man drunk before!" He punched my shoulder, did a little dance move.

I froze. He wasn't making a joke. He wasn't being brilliantly ironic. Here was a man I'd caught chugging vodka from the bottle, just in the door from work, car keys still in his hand. A man I'd seen on Saturday afternoons passed out on the couch, open-mouthed snoring. Someone I'd spent countless hours with at dinners, fishing, in front of the TV, driving him to the liquor store, hanging out by the pool, while he was drunk but—apparently—thinking he was successfully pretending not to be.

What floored me was a brilliant irony of another order: this was maybe the most sober, at this time of night, that I'd seen him in a while.

I pretty much wrote my father off that night. Such a decision isn't exactly conscious, but more something that happens in the body. Constant disappointment becomes a kind of disgust. Eventually a big switch turns off a big light.

It's hard to see clearly when disgust turns that light off. But I did sort of understand it wasn't my dad who was lying, not really. It was the alcohol that befriended him, then tricked him, and finally got the best of him. Alcohol can weaken and then rob a person of inner strengths. It robbed him of nobility, which I believe he had. It made him insane. Alcohol can make a husk of a saint.

But there was something I didn't know. How, *why*, did alcohol conquer him? Lots of people drank. I did, I got right out of my mind sometimes. But it hadn't conquered me. It hadn't made me insane.

What I didn't know was what had hurt my father, and what had shaped him, before the alcohol, which he took to like medicine.

———

There was another time, and another kind of lie, but I liked it more than I hated it.

Sixteen, I'd hitched from Vancouver to Toronto to see friends, and then a month later I hitched back, reaching Vancouver late in the evening. I called home from near the Exhibition grounds, hoping for a ride, since buses didn't go to Deep Cove. Relieved and excited, my mom said she'd be right there.

With the last of my money I bought a Filet-O-Fish and was wolfing it out on Hastings Street when our car pulled up to the curb and the trunk popped. I hoisted my pack. But my dad bolted from the passenger door and reached me in a few strides. He wasn't staggering but he was drunk. He blocked my way, reached across the gap with a straight arm and grabbed my shoulder. His eyes were glassy but clear, and he smiled in a kind of wonderment, like I was some kind of magical being, like it had been years, not a month.

He said, "Just let me look at you."

We were blocking the sidewalk and stayed planted there, as traffic rushed by in the smell of the harbour, me with fishburger in one hand and pack in the other, my father drunk enough to allow himself to do this, a hand on my shoulder, eyeing me up and down, that little smile of wonder. But not really seeing me.

He gave my shoulder another shake.

"Just let me look at you."

# SEVEN

*When a father gives to his son, both laugh;*
*When a son gives to his father, both cry.*
—WILLIAM SHAKESPEARE

I decide to leave the calm reverie of Quarry Bay and troll the shore of Nelson Island, named for you-know-who, all the way to the mouth of Agamemnon Channel, at which point I will haul the gear, turn left and head north to Egmont. But it'll be fun to try trolling in a place I only mooched in silence, decades ago.

I'm restless to move, having been put off by a sour memory of my very last charter on *Cormorant*, which took place right here at Quarry Bay. My customer was an ex-pro athlete, I won't say who, and it was booked months in advance, a father's favour to his daughter, who I was dating. We were no longer dating when the charter came to pass, which was awkward, because the father hinted broadly, more than once, not only that he was on my scruffy boat solely because of his daughter, but also that his last fishing trips had been up in "the Charlottes," where salmon under thirty pounds got thrown back and the last boat he patronized served daiquiris and canapés. It wouldn't have helped to explain that I was still fond of his daughter and that it was she who had dumped me. It only got worse as the trip progressed. There was a monstrous coho run and non-stop action across the strait at Sangster Island, and he probably knew this, but my engine had issues and I didn't want to risk the crossing. So we stayed close, here at Quarry Bay. We did get some coho, stragglers and mavericks from the main horde, but only two and they weren't large. The day was sweltering, conversation stilted, I had on offer neither daiquiris nor canapés, and it's sad that a memory like this can survive underwater for thirty-five years and surface to ruin this beauty.

I get the anchor up and am in the process of fastening the down-riggers—excited to get fishing again, picturing what lures to use, the ghost-glow hoochie or a Kitchen Sink spoon—when two jet fighters hardly miss Texada's peak as they fly right at me, and by the time I get my head up to look they are already over and gone, all but their blood-boiling roar.

They don't fit. They *still* don't fit. The Comox base is twenty, thirty miles away, nothing to a jet, and I remember how in the seventies, when the whole idea of a Canadian fighter jet was strange, their flyovers were frequent enough, smashing the air barely a hundred feet over your head, the roar trailing two seconds behind. Thrilling, but then a bit depressing. To a long-haired solitary moocher, war in general already seemed unnecessary, and here in pristine nature it seemed only ridiculous.

Once, motoring with my dad not far from here, en route to a hot reef off Lasqueti Island, while crossing Malaspina's famously deep channel we saw a submarine's periscope slice the water. I'd never seen such a thing. It was strangely hard to gauge its distance from us, or its size, or speed, but it seemed to be going twice as fast as we were. I marvelled at how big it was.

"That would be a nuke," my father said.

"You think that's American?"

"Has to be."

"Are they allowed up here?"

He looked at me over the tops of his glasses.

———

My dad fought in the South Pacific with the U.S. Navy, aboard ship where he worked bent over a sonar screen. He told me how nervous he was, confined in a windowless room buried in the heart of the ship, which is exactly where kamikazes aimed their planes, trying to fly straight down a smokestack. Another story about those days was the time he triggered an all-hands-on-deck emergency signal and the blip turned out to be a large sea turtle.

Just two years ago I got a package from Jan, the daughter of my dad's lifelong best friend, Arnie Torgerson, or "Torg," and Torg's wife Ilene. The package contained news of Ilene's passing, along with some letters my dad had written Jan's grandmother—his buddy Torg's mom—during the war. Torg was in the army.

They are brief letters, upbeat but also thoughtful. Their language brings to mind movies starring Jimmy Stewart. He addresses her as Mrs. Torgerson, and one begins with this sentence: *"Just received a swell letter from Arn—he sounds much happier than usual and seems to like the Philippines—I really appreciate your sending me a picture of you and 'Big Torgy'—it was swell of you—you both look well, which is what matters most—I suppose Everett is getting the usual spring showers, where I am the sun seems to be alone, with clouds appearing very rarely."* Other than admiring such a long sentence, and his use of the dash as punctuation,

I learn something about my dad from his sense of the sun being "alone." In the second sentence I learn about a sailor's yearning for land: *"Am getting used to life aboard ship more readily now; actually like it at times, but that land breeze smells pretty darn good whenever we pull into port!"* The third sentence, following a paragraph break, is amazing: *"Well I guess the Germans are making their final stand—you've got to give them credit though, they're holding out longer than anticipated."* In the middle of the letter: *"Maybe next Christmas can find us all celebrating together—I sincerely hope so."* And the last sentence: *"Just received a letter from Mom, and she says that Arn is believed to be behind the lines; that's swell, hope he can stay there for a while, he's done enough."* He signs the letter *"Love, Bob."* The return address on the envelope is:

R.A. Gaston 5 1/c (RDM)

U.S.S. Ostara K.A. 33

"N" Division

F.P.O.

I've gone online and looked up the USS *Ostara*. Scuttled in 1965, it was an "Artemis-class attack cargo ship," named after an asteroid called 343 Ostara. Its service record lists to-and-from voyages to San Diego, Pearl Harbor, Saipan, Haiphon, Guam, as well as Tsingtao, China, and also Yokohama, Japan, which must have been at war's end. I recall my dad mentioning San Diego bars, and some of these foreign ports. He owned a soapstone carving he picked up in China, which now lives on my windowsill. He never mentioned docking in Japan, though he did return with a beaten-up Japanese officer's sword. Once, though, drunk and with a storyteller's look in his eye, after making sure I knew that "Japs" were so evil that their kamikaze planes had just enough fuel to reach the enemy convoy but not fly home, he told me about a Zero aiming at them, out of fuel and gliding, gliding, gliding to crash within just metres of his ship, and how one of the other guys at the railing crapped his pants.

If my dad landed in Japan it must have been after the A-bombs went off. This would have been a unique experience, to say the least. I'm appalled I never thought to ask him about that. Though maybe it's good I didn't. Those two blasts—that history now tends to view in all its complexity, including the possibility that it was humanity's nadir—might have felt like grand, heart-swelling vengeance to those who, like my father, had joined the war the instant the Japanese attacked Pearl Harbor.

In a second letter to Torg's parents is the only reference he makes to the Japanese, who'd bombed his country, interrupted his college and basketball career, and whose kamikaze planes were trying to kill him as he sat amidships sweating and staring at a dark green screen: *"I'm up for a 3rd Class Petty Officer rating—it should come through about April 1st—well, it looks like Germany is about ready to throw in the towel— hope these damn Nips get the same idea—but I doubt it."*

It's strange to read letters from a father just out of his teens, and ten years before I was born. I wonder what Torg's mother meant to my dad. Maybe, in writing to her, especially while at war, he was touching in to a place of imagined stability, safety. But I also wonder why he didn't address the letters to Torg's dad. It does make me warm to see that he apparently got letters from his own mother. Is it odd to feel paternal, and protective, of my own father? I wonder about the truth of one rumour, that my dad didn't write back to his own mother all that much, if ever.

———

Not so many years ago, my mother's blooming dementia often had her talking non-stop about her past, sometimes slightly racy stories about her coming-of-age, stuff no son is disposed to want to hear. Some of it had to do with beaus before my father—but then along came Bob Gaston, tall, a basketball star and dreamboat. My mother made it clear she could have had her pick, and that Bob Gaston was a catch. They both went to Everett High and she was aware of him there but he was two grades above her and they didn't start dating till her college days, after he got back from the war. I got to know these stories of hers well, like how she fainted during their wedding ceremony and "I was the talk of the town—they thought I was pregnant. There's no way in the world I was pregnant!" She spoke to me like I was a reporter getting the exclusive goods.

But one day, as I was stooped, emptying her fridge of long-lapsed "best before" packages of shrimp (I could smell them through the saran) and lunch meat (turning that unique grey-green), and hardly listening to yet another same-old-story, I heard, "My parents loved that he was from such a good family." Not removing my head from the fridge, I interrupted her.

"Dad was from a good family?"

"Well of course he was."

"But what about being poor and fatherless and all that?"

"Well, that happened later. He was from a really good Everett family and everybody thought a Gaston boy was quite the catch."

I sat down across from her at the kitchen table. She snapped the cards of her endless solitaire game.

"How were they a good family? Like, were they wealthy, or—"

"They were just a good family."

"Do you know what his father taught? When he was a university professor?" Being one of these myself, ever since learning this detail I'd been curious to know what his subject area was. Though my grandfather was a drunk and an abandoner, this information might widen him for me. Make him more complicated, in any case.

"Well, I don't think he was a professor. I haven't heard that."

"Oh. I thought he was." It was my mother who had told me this, a year before. It struck me now, and raised a few hairs on my neck, that she may have been conflating the two of us, that is, me and my villainous grandfather Ozro.

The scant details of Dad's known history were hard to keep steady. One of the oft-told and poignant stories—one I've already told in this book—was how tall and painfully thin he was in adolescence, and how his mother, whose part-time job was ladling out food in the high school cafeteria, got fired after being warned not to pile so much on her son's tray. At last she could give her skinny son enough to eat and she couldn't control herself. One changeable detail was whether she got fired just the once, or insinuated her way back into the job and got fired a second time, for the same crime.

I still hadn't learned the secret truth about Ozro, or my dad. The only other familiar, accepted story from the Everett years was that, with no father around, and it being the Depression, sometimes on the last night of the month his mother would pack their scant possessions and in the dark of night steal away, skip out on rent, and find a new flophouse somewhere in the area. I always pictured a rainy night, in winter. My dad bone-skinny, sleepy, fearful, led by the hand, him leading his little sister. The point of the telling was always to stress how poor he had been growing up. Never in his presence, the story was hauled out during discussions of how nice his house was now and what a great view of the water and mountains it had, or how well he'd done in his career. In light of this story, it wasn't hard to respect his success.

He had help. Divine help, of a sort. While still in high school his basketball skills caught the attention of scouts from Saint Martin's College, a tiny Catholic institution. My father was a decent athlete, but he was tall, and—unless you're a genius passer like Steve Nash—basketball is for tall people. In 1940, if you were six-five you were not just a centre but a tall one. In any event, an Everett High School junior caught the attention of a couple of priests. They saw how skinny he was, and for a year sent his mother food money to fatten him up for rebounding battles to come. Graduating high school with average grades and penniless, he received, literally, a full ride to college. Two years later that full ride took him to Gonzaga, a slightly larger but still minuscule college in Spokane, Washington, and one that, even today, punches above its weight in basketball and is often a part of the NCAA March Madness tournament shown on TV.

I once asked him what Gonzaga was like, the Catholic part in particular. He said there were lots of prayers, and church services. He had to take Latin, and retained a few phrases he sometimes used. Apropos of nothing he'd occasionally make a cross in the air and say, *"Dominus, vobiscum."* He'd add, "I like that one."

I asked him nothing else about Gonzaga, and he didn't volunteer anything. Only recently I learned that the school is an odd one in North America, a school founded by Jesuits, who are among the more mystical of orders, as well as historically aggressive in their attempts to convert the world. In their desire to spread their belief to Indigenous people, for instance, they basically settled New France, or what became Canada. They were the ones whose faith was so strong they didn't hesitate to confront hostile tribes about their inferior beliefs, fully expecting to be burned at the stake or disembowelled, or sometimes both. Apparently they could *reason* their way into this degree of sacrifice, as they were famously the most intellectual of orders as well. To top it off, the Jesuits are mendicants, meaning they get along by begging. So it feels somehow fitting that they would give out full-ride scholarships to someone in need. I'm sure his height had lots to with it; in fact, maybe they'd been begging for someone just like him to come along. And maybe his being a basketball star helped save him from the main squeeze of their attempts to convert.

I learned all this online, trying to find out something more about my father's college years other than that he liked the sound of *Dominus vobiscum*. I learned that he played for Gonzaga after Pearl Harbor was attacked, because Gonzaga had put together a kind of national all-star team comprised of basketball-star volunteers that they enrolled in naval officer training. After the war, he transferred to Washington State U to play more basketball and finish a degree. I'm not sure who he was playing for when he got his front tooth knocked out in Madison Square Garden during the Final Four but I think it was Gonzaga—in their archives there's a fine picture of him in uniform with the four others on the starting team, him in the centre, holding a basketball at his navel. The others flank him on either side, a little behind, so that he is the front of a V-formation and closest to the camera, which makes him look taller still. No one is smiling, and their faces are burnished with pride. On the ball is written "Northwest Champs, 1944." Which meant they were heading back east, to March Madness.

He did tell me about the sport itself, the playing part. My dad would eventually watch hockey on TV even when I wasn't with him, because he'd learned to appreciate it from years of watching his sons play, but what he really loved watching, and I liked watching with him, was March Madness. Unlike the NBA with its no-defence, its seven-footers dropping the ball into the hoop with too much ease, these college guys played their hearts out. Skill challenged by desperation is always a worthwhile spectacle. And though my dad went on to play some ball on a senior circuit in Seattle and later in Vancouver, with the Clover Leafs, college was the last serious ball he played. WW II put a dent in his NBA chances, was the sense I got, though he never said this in so many words. There was that "All American" photo on the TV-room wall, but he never once bragged to me about his talent.

So I regret never asking him more. Here's a guy who played in the Final Four, in New York's Madison Square Garden, centring a team from a tiny West Coast school that had heroically beaten all comers so far. Watching March Madness games on TV, once in a while he'd chuckle about how different things were back then, how instead of jump shots you'd take "set shots," not leaving your feet, and of course the underhand free throws, and how dunks were rare back then and almost seen as a kind of cheating. I knew his nickname was Gaspipe, because his old pal Torg still called him that. I knew about the tooth that had been elbowed out, in this very tournament we were watching. And he told me about a clumsy, second-string centre on the team, a six-foot-nine guy called Tiny, whose name mocked not his height but his small feet, which—my dad claimed with a sympathetic snort—made even walking difficult for him. And my dad once played the Harlem Globetrotters, when the Washington Generals, the all-white team that acted as straight man to their skilful clown act, got stuck in transit. He said, "On defence, they told us to 'just stand there.' It was really hard to do." We saw them on TV a few times. When the whistled theme music came on, he'd always say fondly and with a little smile, "Sweet, Georgia, Brown." He also liked to say, "Meadowlark, Lemon," as their clown prince did magic tricks with the ball in front of the tall Washington General who lamely waved his arms, just standing there.

But that's what I know, because I never asked him more.

Which probably is natural. I played a level of hockey maybe about the same as my dad reached in his sport. I played in China and Japan, and in Europe for money. My kids know the general story, though not the details, because they haven't asked. They know mostly that I didn't make it to the NHL. That's about it, and so what? Any athlete worth his salt is too cool to brag, especially to his kids. And any kid worth his salt is too cool to ask. Their lives are way more exciting to them than mine is, which is as it should be. The alert dad stays aware and wary of that age-old trope, the eager codger proclaiming, "When I was your age I . . ." which is less a dispensing of wisdom than a sad grab for attention. As a codger-in-training myself, I've seen eyes glaze over. I'm no dummy, and neither was my father. We learn to clam up.

Except maybe after a few beer. You know it's a sad grab even as you begin. You feel the urge well up and burst your dam of good sense, and you blab anyway. You know it will take a bit of colour, maybe some exaggeration, maybe even outright invention, to cut through their glaze. You might make a habit of lying, and perhaps you learn to lie with ease. You might even become a fiction writer.

———

I start my troll, still disturbed by the fighter jets, the current state of the political world so lunatic and vertiginous these days that Canadian warplanes might actually *be* warplanes, training for something imminent and dire. Again, this thought really does not fit this place.

I have a three-inch Pink Sink lure on the port side, fifty-five feet down, and on the starboard side a UV Glo-White Ghost Shrimp hoochie, at a hundred. At trolling speed, I believe I can sense the absolute lack of fish underneath the boat. So it feels good to be travelling, which feels like hunting. Which feels like I'm actually doing something, and that there's a purpose in life.

But I'm in no hurry. I'm not. So why do I feel like I am? Is it because, at sixty, I *should* be in a hurry? Because it's now or never? Whatever "it" is.

Every hundred metres brings with it a vivid memory I wouldn't have recalled otherwise. That bald point. That oyster beach tucked away, hidden by hanging trees. That derelict dock. I used to live around here. Spying Daniel Point, behind which is Lee Bay, I remember Jane and her huge barn-coloured house, which must still be there. Maybe I'll cruise by. She had a harrowing story of a storm, and she wasn't the type to tell a story that wasn't true. For kicks she and her fiancé had rowed out from the beach to explore a small island a half-mile out into the strait. The wind came up on the way back and they capsized, and the fiancé drowned. Jane's experience of their struggle was awful and she cried freely while describing it to me. But the strangest thing happened. As Jane verged on drowning herself, she was suddenly hovering in the air outside the closed window of her bedroom, just under the second-storey eave. She was gazing back to the overturned boat, watching her own dwindling struggle. Then she was back in her body, with surprising new strength, and she knew to turn and make for the island, not her beach. And on the island she was later rescued.

Still no bites. There won't be any. *Sylvan* rounds a bend and there across the channel is the A-Frame, a tiny bay that's actually the outfall from Ruby Lake and in rainy months spouts a decent waterfall. The A-Frame used to be famous for big fish, a strain of forty-, forty-five-pounders coming through in early fall. It's where a tiny man with an immense beard, who I thought of as "the leprechaun," would fish evenings, proudly rowing an old dory all the way from Irvines Landing and then all the way back. And often with a good fish, because he was the A-Frame wizard. Back at Irvines Landing, where I lived on *Cormorant* one summer, the leprechaun loved to stride the marina docks with a salmon almost as big as him hoisted up and balanced on a shoulder. I remember him catching the eye of my dad one night as he passed the cleaning table, with its hissing light and chaos of bugs, this twig man who was barely five feet tall, strutting his load before a giant, who'd been skunked, was into the hard stuff now, and who thankfully only looked away and shook his head.

It's time. Not just because trolling is fruitless. It's time to go. I haul the gear, get the downriggers unscrewed and stowed, take *Sylvan* up to cruising speed and crank the wheel dramatically left, into the mouth of Agamemnon Channel, a narrow fjord that's the final stretch north to Egmont. It's instant wilderness. To both left and right the trees are fresher, more virginal, a little hostile. Shadows look blacker. Both sides of the channel are steeply sloped, with no flat spot for a house nor any reason to build one. There are neither roads in nor any coves to shelter a dock from damaging storms. It wouldn't be hard to find stretches here where no human has walked. Heading north toward nothing but mountains and clouds, it feels a shame to foul this waterway with a gasoline roar.

———

It's the main bonus of being a fishing addict: in order to find good fishing you have to find undefiled places. Not just unpolluted, but pristine. You have to find marine wilderness. Here on the West Coast, wilderness is often at its showroom best. Dad and I routinely fished surrounded by beauty—world-class, divinely tinged beauty. We rarely said a word about it. Typically we found ourselves on mirror-still water, reflecting an orange-purple evening sky and ringed by the black silhouettes of mountains. We sat lightly, in a charged silence. It was a beauty to make you consider a benevolent God. Or, more likely, that you're looking at God, and God is nothing other than this.

"Nice night," one of us might mumble, if the evening had special charm.

You can get used to beauty but not this kind, because its details are the sky, and continuous liquid change. If a breeze came up, even for a wind chicken like me, the patterns on the water could mesmerize. Tesselation. As poet Jan Zwicky puts it, water is the laughter of geometry. You don't necessarily talk about it but you feel it buoying you up. Having an effect. Sometimes it's simple satisfaction, which eases the need to actually catch a fish. Sometimes there's pride, other times gratitude, in knowing most of the world doesn't get to see this stuff. Sometimes it gets intellectual, as you can almost understand that what you're seeing is visual music.

Thinking of this beauty and my father here in it, fishing, I remember that he grew up in exactly this. As a kid, probably he had only to row past a point to be in true wilderness, the coniferous edge of the Salish Sea. This helps me understand why, when he was offered a last big promotion, meaning a final transfer from Vancouver to the head office in Chicago, which as a city is a kind of bigger, taller Winnipeg, he turned it down, effectively pounding the last nails into his career's coffin. I remember him agonizing over it but we knew what his answer would be.

One part of the American dream that doesn't get mentioned is that it can never be allowed to stop. You dream, and if you're able, and lucky, you succeed and reap its rewards—but then your house is never big enough, your job never prestigious enough, your family not loving enough. The American dream is cursed because it cannot stop. The sky is indeed the limit. In turning down that last promotion, my dad found himself in an odd contradiction: he was where he wanted to be, but he was stuck there.

It might be coincidence, but not long after his decision to stay put, to live where he wanted to live, his drinking accelerated. I was twenty-one and living across town when my mom phoned expressing her worry, wanting me to visit more, talk to him more. I did, but if he was just home from work he was edgy and could barely stand talking to me, only wanting to get into a bottle, and if he was already into it I didn't want to be there at all. He'd be friendly and joshing but soon any serious talk would be useless; he'd remember nothing. I couldn't imagine how, unable to remember even the most basic things, he could go to work and do any kind of a good job. I imagined his staff covering for him. And also not covering for him—underneath him were scores of go-getters, other men dreaming the dream.

My mother called once to ask me if she should leave him, wondering if that would shake him up enough to get him to quit drinking. We agreed that, on his present trajectory, her leaving might kill him, or put him on the street. Neither of us could imagine him on the street. For one, my dad wouldn't know where it was or how to get there.

One weekend he was nothing but drunk. Then on the Monday, and the Tuesday, he still hadn't left the house for work. My mother called me, so frantic her voice was wooden. He hadn't gotten dressed in four days, she said.

I drove over. My mother was on the phone in the kitchen, her back to me and all things, talking cheerfully and non-stop with clients and co-workers, her way of coping. I heard my father in the bathroom. He emerged and passed me in the hallway. He looked grey, and shorter, because his shoulders were weirdly up and his head hunched into his chest, vulture-like. He murmured something in a scratchy voice and I caught the word "sick." He went back into the bedroom, towing a hideous waft. He smelled like the poisonous corpse of alcohol.

I got my mother off the phone. She didn't know what to do. She couldn't remember the last time he had eaten. I went outside to the garbage cans and lifted a lid to the sight of a spectacular number of empty Smirnoff bottles. Normally he would hide an empty bottle under a layer of garbage, but he had stopped doing even that. And there was no garbage. It was nothing but vodka bottles.

A second cousin of my father's, Barbara, was head of Alcoholics Anonymous in the Pacific Northwest. I'd heard of her from my mother, who'd mentioned that, over the years, her several encounters with my father hadn't gone well, largely due to her broad hints to him that "she'd be seeing him someday," in her professional capacity. And right she was.

Two more days passed and nothing changed. My mother called Barbara, who drove up from Washington the next day, after asking what exactly he'd been drinking. Lured into her car with a fresh bottle of Smirnoff, my dad went catatonically, still in his pyjamas. Barbara knew who to call and what strings to pull. The detox centre was upscale, located on Vancouver Island. Sears would be paying. Apparently alcoholism was an occupational hazard among their executives.

Families were considered a large part of the rehab process. After a few days my mother joined him to stay at the facility. After a week, so did I, though only for two nights. Despite the country-club exterior, the accommodations were spartan: we weren't there to relax but to learn. First, I was briefed about my father's condition, hearing of his early days in "the rubber room," full of drugs as the most severe detoxing took place, the delirium tremens and the rest of it. He would remember nothing about it, nor about the previous weeks or perhaps months, given the amount he'd been drinking. I sat through a few films and met with a psychologist, who made it clear that the alcoholic's family wasn't *necessarily* the cause of the alcoholism. Apparently the family of an alcoholic had as many problems as the alcoholic himself, minus the actual drinking part. The doctor's gentle suggestion that our family was likely as dysfunctional as a bag of bent roosters was not news to me.

We got together for "family time" around a table on a large communal patio, with other scheduled families, grouped just out of hearing range if no one raised a voice. It was summer, there were plenty of Hawaiian shirts. Gaiety was encouraged—you don't need alcohol to have a party! My dad wore his familiar white pants and powder-blue shirt. I was all jeans, T-shirt, long hair. My mother wore her business attire. Bright colours, a scarf. We didn't match at all. We could have been sitting on the sundeck at home. Still on drugs of some kind, my father was content in a dazed way. He clutched and sipped irresistibly from a fancy mixed-juice drink, on the rocks. All the patients worked on bottomless juice drinks or coffees. Apparently some patients were in for drug addictions, and I tried to discern who they might be, but couldn't. Everyone chain-smoked and looked identically haunted. Detoxing men outnumbered detoxing women about two to one.

My dad was sheepish, not about what he'd done, but because he didn't know *what* he'd done. He had the air of taking everyone's word for it. He also announced something I'd heard from the psychologist.

"Well, they say I'm allergic to booze," he said, eyebrows up, surprised. "I have this *allergy*." He shrugged. So meek the words were hard to hear, he added, "They say that's what it is." He took a quick last pull on his juice, then rattled his ice cubes at the bottom and looked over his shoulder as if for another.

My mother sprang up to get him one. She was falsely cheerful, nervous about the whole business, and embarrassed for the family. I was used to her being more in denial than even my dad was about this unspoken problem of his. But she couldn't hide her relief, her hopeful joy even, that something was finally being done.

My dad and I had some fun playing pickle-ball, a game with wooden paddles and plastic ball that didn't fly far, or fast. Before one serve my dad shook out his hands and wrists and said, "loosey-goosey," and for a minute seemed his old self. I kept to myself that I found much of the psychology bogus. I hoped he didn't read it on my face, because I certainly wanted their remedies to take hold and cure him. I did like that the "allergy" explanation called his disease a disease, and helped ease guilt, which he had in spades, and also the stigma, of which he was petrified. Not all alcoholics lack self-esteem, but it sure looked like my dad did, so I was all for anything that might deflect the pummelling. But to take what was probably a simile—that alcoholism was "like" an allergy—and make it a fact, well, you could see failure in the making. All of these addicts waking up surprised and pleased to have a simple allergy. I heard one proclaim to another, "Some people are allergic to shrimp, we're allergic to a glass of wine!" This was fine, and

I hoped it would help them avoid that glass of wine, but nothing in this approach was acknowledging the main difference: people don't crave shrimp so much that they ruin their lives to get some. One patient, no older than thirty, wore a Hawaiian shirt that couldn't hide his quiet desperation, or a grotesquely bulging liver. His wealthy parents, doing "family time" at a nearby table, looked incapable of even fake smiles. No one said much, and the son was clearly biding his time. I learned he had severe liver disease and his next binge would likely kill him. The look on his face was that of an animal eyeing a hole in its cage. I wondered what he thought about his "allergy."

My skepticism also had to do with just how well I knew my dad. His skepticism was much like mine but taking longer to kick in. For the moment he was parroting a lot of the standard AA instructions, including the belief in a higher power, but it was parroting, and he knew it even in his haze. He'd always been good at saying whatever was needed to get him over rough spots. And I'd learned—I'd been trained—not to believe a word he said.

But, fingers crossed. All that mattered to me, there at the facility, was that he wasn't drunk. He wasn't drunk today. I held to the good and necessary wisdom of one saying, at least: One day at a time.

The most telling experience at the facility had to do with the final film I watched with my parents and about thirty other well-heeled alcoholics and their families, all of us on folding chairs. I was sitting between my mother and father, and as the lights went down my father grabbed my hand, a gesture I'd seen with lots of the patients and loved ones. I liked it. His hand felt big, soft, capable. It felt humble, and full of heart. How long was it since I'd held his hand? Since I was a toddler? I gave his a squeeze, which he returned, and then, to the relief of both of us, he withdrew it.

The reel-to-reel projector began flicking. The narrator introduced the film as a kind of marriage guide, emphasizing how entwined relationships are with addiction. It quickly veered into sex, and then became mostly about the female orgasm, delivered as if shedding light on a mystery.

I was very aware of my mother at one side and my father at the other, both of them hardly breathing. I don't think my mother breathed at all. The visuals showed a squeaky clean couple sitting fully clothed in a loose embrace, trading pecked kisses. The cheerful male narrator explained orgasm as being like a pleasurable sneeze, and that it was brought on by specific stimulation—"oral, genital, or manual"—and that humans were very lucky to have it. But it was sometimes harder for women to experience. It then went into a step-by-step description of how that might be rectified. I became even more aware of my parents as the clitoris was identified as the key to success, the push button in question, and how this button not only wanted but deserved the kind of attention the penis always got.

This of course was good advice. I tried not to be too smug as a baby boomer enjoying the recent sexual revolution and giving any clitoris I was lucky enough to encounter all the attention it deserved and more. It was interesting that unsatisfactory sex was being put forward as an important piece in the puzzle of addiction. But my parents still weren't breathing noticeably. I sneaked a look at some of the middle-aged faces, and they were rapt. There was no rattling of ice cubes in juice drinks. I got the sense that a good number of these people of my parents' age were taking in new information. I had no idea about what might be new for my mother and father, and of course biology made this thought hard for me even to entertain. And maybe they weren't absorbing any of it because I was beside them. But my sense of their reaction was that—and I really hoped I was wrong—this was news to them too. And that they weren't just embarrassed about me. They were terrified watching this film in the presence of each other.

My father had been back home a month when he called to ask if I'd go with him to an AA meeting. In his voice I could hear how hard it was to ask this, and also that it was something he was supposed to ask, as part of the program he was on. He didn't like talking about it, but from my mother I knew he'd been going, twice a week. I even knew where, and who from the Vancouver Island facility was going to that location too. It was in West Van, near the British Properties, so there were corporate executives mixed in with what my mother called "the riff-raff."

In the car my dad apologized for inviting me, and said it was something "the rehab people" told him he was supposed to do. It could be just this once. From his tone of voice I could tell that the AA part of this project was likely doomed, but I was as upbeat and encouraging as possible, and told him I was eager to go, and more than just this once, if he wanted that, or thought it was a good idea.

The meeting took place in a basement room of a rec centre, dim and reeking of old coffee and, I think, potato salad. The setting itself suggested guilt and hiding from public view. Nothing about it felt like pride. Watching my dad go through the ritual greetings, I could see him trying to make it work. When the meeting started we all stood in front of our folding chairs and took the hand of the person to either side, and one was his, and he gave mine a quick squeeze again, of thanks and, I think, hope. He was glad I was here, he was serious, he was even scared. Of course he was scared. Only an idiot wouldn't be scared. The thing is, it seems that some of us adopt the role of idiot fairly easily. But at least for now he had admitted to having a problem, had admitted he was an alcoholic, and he would take this bitter cure.

As people gave their testimonials, warm-up acts for the main speaker, he leaned over on occasion to whisper, "Can't stand this guy." Or nudge my leg, flick his eyes at the talker, and shake his head. He wanted to make sure I didn't think these people were his friends or that he respected them. He sipped coffee constantly, but his hand was steady. He chuckled a few times at the main speaker, one of the AA professionals who made the rounds of meetings and told colourful tales. He was polished and funny, with plenty of "I lapsed on my meetings and fell off the wagon and got my hand around that first cold one at a bar only about a mile from right here—and next thing I knew I was waking up in an airport in Ireland. Thing is, according to my passport, I'd also just been to Spain." Tappa-*boom*. People grinned and nodded knowingly. You could tell some wanted to believe their own blackouts had been as glamorous and funny. None of the unsmiling rougher types, who looked the most freshly beaten up and also the most desperately hopeful—the riff-raff—got up to speak.

On the drive back I was as encouraging as possible. But the writing was on the wall. One thing about AA, at least at that time, was their certainty and insistence that, without them and only them, you were doomed to getting drunk again. I know my dad bristled at exactly this kind of sales pitch, and he might see it as a challenge to prove them wrong.

We chatted about some of the testimonials, skirting the main issue. Some blackouts *are* funny, at least in the telling. He liked a couple of the guys (I noticed they were quiet types like he was; I wondered if, like him, they were loud drunks) and he liked a woman who'd been funniest of all—"She's a nice gal"—and who I learned owned a real estate company. But he couldn't stand most of them. He seemed almost a snob. He didn't like being lumped in with them. They were alcoholics. Failures. Alcoholics were failures. From their faces you could tell that some had fallen off the wagon many times and spent time on the street. To take these people on as his new friends, his new colleagues, his team, was to admit failure. He told me there was another group he'd gone to once, closer to home. He might switch to them.

From the way he apologized to me for these people I could see it would be way easier on him if I wasn't there. He thought I was judging him. If he only knew how relieved and happy I was that he was sober, and that if I had judged him at all tonight it didn't come close, not by light years, to how I judged him on a thousand drunken nights. But of course I didn't say so.

All I said was, "It would be great if you kept going."

Barely making himself heard above the sound of his quiet, executive's car, all he said was, "Why?"

———

I've made drinking sound only dire. And it's old news that it has ruined countless lives. So then why do many of us do it?

Nothing but sincere, George Bernard Shaw called whisky "liquid sunshine." Benjamin Franklin's "Beer is proof that God loves us and wants us to be happy" is one of my favourites. Humanity's oral history is rich with such wisdoms about what's happened since we learned to put yeast and sugar in the same room together and let them have at it.

You might have noticed, out on the patio, maybe halfway through the second glass, how from your middle a warmth spreads out, not unlike a pat of melting butter. Not unlike melted butter with a smile. You're at an outside table with friends, the server has taken your food order and you might have noticed that, though you're gently melting butter, somehow you're also energetic, even effervescent. Your wit, even your flippancy, is received with grins from your companions across from you, and they are also melting pats of butter. Starting your third glass, it might make sense to you that "intoxication" is a word commonly used to describe love or, even more fittingly, infatuation. Not that this third-glass-love is any big deal, because nothing is a big deal, except maybe this perfect summer evening, out on this patio, with friends. One of whom you've always sort of mistrusted, but now, almost through this third glass, you love. You see his love for you come out in a funny old story you'd forgotten, and you also see that what you distrust in him is really just a shy privacy and that you are being invited in. You can even speak of each other's flaws now, not just because *in vino veritas* but also because, as broad and warm as the setting sun, this love holds and rocks hard truth in its arms easily. You might even notice that all truth is, in fact, beauty. Your fourth glass arrives and you want to laugh, and you can, at pretty much everything, and you might notice it's a laughing with, not at. And then, almost too soon, your Greek lamb skewer is placed in front of you, surrounded by the rice, and tomato and cucumber salad, and his chicken arrives, and her fish, and her huge salad, and you love rather than hate it that she's ordered her shaved parmesan on the side.

And you might have asked yourself, now what could be wrong with any of that? It's not drinking that's dire. It's when the infatuation becomes blind, and you stop noticing, and alcohol drinks you. Maybe beer is proof that God loves us, but too much beer is apparently proof of something else. Or, maybe what's dire is something really, really basic. Maybe what's dire is that, if you're anything like me, you always want to feel better than you do right now.

———

When I was seventeen, it was only easy for me to flee his house, stiff with disgust—then go out with friends and get drunk myself. Those were the days you drank till you puked, and when you finally fell into bed you got the whirlies and you clambered up to puke again. Hangovers weren't that bad though, since you were young and in shape. You could go crazy Friday night, then almost as crazy Saturday.

My hypocrisy made complete sense to me. I had reason to drink. All my friends drank. We were young, it was a rite of passage.

I first noticed the pull of addiction when I was twenty-five and living in France for a year. Living alone, I enjoyed an evening routine of cooking a nice meal for myself, something inexpensive but French, and accompanying it with a few glasses of wine, in the proper French manner. I bought the very passable plastic litre jugs of table wine and typically drank half of one. I would get a little mellow, and then I would do the dishes, digest and pick up the bad first novel I was writing.

This routine was a month old when one Sunday evening I was taken by a friend's family to eat at a small rural restaurant. I recall that as the father ordered the meal I was alert to the quantity of wine he was ordering, doing the math of number of people divided by bottles. When he was told by the embarrassed waiter that the establishment had run out of wine, and with nowhere nearby to purchase any, I experienced a tremor of panic. It was small and soon over, but it was real, and came from deep within my body. If I have a root, that's where I felt it. And I understood what it was.

Interesting, I thought. And of course I thought of my dad. My family lineage. To some extent that bone-deep pull was palpable knowledge of my genes.

Thereafter I steered clear of daily routines involving alcohol. Even a summertime ritual of a beer before dinner I've kept a watch on, because I've noticed that, in my case, it can become two beers, then something inside wants it to be three, and dinner can wait. Though it hasn't been hard for me to go through the years like a normal person, having a couple of beers or a glass of wine, really it's been easiest simply not to drink at all.

I doubt I could have become a daily drunk like my father, and his father. Whenever I did or do get drunk, the next day and for several days after that the last thing in the world I want is alcohol of any sort.

I've mentioned that I see two styles of craving, and alcoholism. I think of the day-after-day kind as "horizontal," and the other—the single binge—as "vertical," and it's this second kind I've toyed with, here and there, for much of my life. Nothing's really changed since I was a teenager. No, that's not true, a teenager *plans* on getting drunk. If anything, I plan not to.

My addiction is simple. I have a beer or two, and it feels good, so I have more, the idea being that I'll feel even better. And that's it. At some point in the evening it has become automatic: the arm lifts the hand that brings the beer to the mouth. With no real memory of drinking anything, I am waggling an empty can in my hand. So I get another. Or not.

It's interesting to be aware of a line and then cross or not cross it. A decision to not cross is almost like a "coming to." After two beers, it's easy. Or, I'll be six or seven beers into an evening, at a bar. A server sees the inch remaining in my glass, raises her eyebrows and smiles a question. I ask myself the same question and the answer is, Yes, of course I want another. I'm sort of drunk, and feel fine, juuuust right. But I know that after another I'll feel no finer. I *know* this. I'm staring at a line drawn in the sand of my consciousness. Generally, especially in the last twenty years or so, I won't step over. But sometimes I say, "What the fuck." It's an interesting moment, this "what the fuck," an out-and-out pulse of nihilism. It's vaguely suicidal. It's a moment of choosing to turn out the lights. I'm not sure what it says about me, deep inside. I like to think of myself as an optimist and quite glad, in general, to be awake and alive.

But there have been times when, over the course of an evening, I'm blind to the line and step over with nihilistic verve, and the next day isn't pretty.

I don't mean to overstate. Nights where I fail to toe the line have gotten fewer and fewer over the years. The nights when I literally "lose it"—and do things I sheepishly learn about the next day—have never been more frequent than once or twice a year, and in later life two or three years will go by without a night like that. Often hard liquor is involved. It took a few years to put two and two together, but now I avoid it completely, save for the occasional glass of Scotch after a meal with a Scotch-loving friend. Seeing the Scotch in my hand, Dede will still give me the wide eyes that ask, Are you sure? She's been through the wars, you see. The nights I went missing. The mornings she had to fill me in. She'd be happy not to have to see me like that again.

I've been hanging my father's dirty boxers out on a long clothesline and it's only fair that I hang mine out too and expose myself as I've exposed him, and reveal things about myself that I'm wincingly not proud of. Though I also have funny stories, the kind I can tell with false chagrin and make people laugh, here are some I have never told anyone, not even friends.

It's only fair that I reveal the time, the year I played hockey in Toulon, France, when twice I lost it with Dennis, who played for Briançon. Each team was allowed one playing coach, and when Briançon visited Toulon to play us, we two Canadians got together at my place after the game. Over bottles of wine I erupted with pent-up stories and talked his ear off. The next day he told me how at one point he fell asleep and when he woke up a half-hour later I was still talking. A month after that, Toulon played in Briançon, and after the game I went with Dennis and some of his teammates to a bar at the train station, because I'd be catching one later to Toulon. I poured endless beer down my throat as we ordered jug after jug. People drifted away. I kept insisting on more, not caring that I missed my train, there were lots of trains. Soon it was me and one or two others, no Dennis, and I don't think these others had anything to do with his team. Then, middle of the night, it was only me and lots of empty jugs and a sizable bill to pay. A row ensued with the waiters, because

I had only a scatter of coins left in my pockets. Two big waiters grabbed my arms from behind, and our main waiter, a small, older man, began punching me in the stomach. Mostly, I laughed, twisting my body away from his punches, but sometimes he connected, which made me laugh louder, which made him angrier. In scummy dawn light I snuck onto a train back to Toulon. I remember wanting to die on that train.

Another time, during an old-timers' hockey tournament in Chilliwack, at a teammate's family cottage, I apparently hogged the team sambuca and later I was naked, save for my eyeglasses, dancing around the bonfire on the beach. Everyone was in their forties and fifties, bankers, lawyers, teachers. I was the only one naked, and the only one who doesn't remember what I did. In the morning, their laughter was mostly polite. It was hard to see them through my right lens, which I apparently broke when my face landed on a fire stone.

I haven't done being fair. Here's the most recent one. Tim, an old friend, came out from the Maritimes, and he likes weed. I'll go years without, and I avoid the strong kind. But, proud of B.C. bud, I procured some for Tim. We hit a music bar and, going out to the alley between pints, I forced joint after joint upon him. I quaffed pint after pint of extra-strong Christmas ale. That's all I recall. I tried to break into the Royal B.C. Museum. I was "hilarious." I woke up in a car with a police car beside me, and a beeping flatbed tow truck approaching to scoop me up. A cop banged on the window. The car wasn't running. I had no key. The car was not even mine; I had no idea whose it was. I did not recognize the part of town I was in. After the cop questioned me, and the car's owner came running out of her apartment to see what was going on, there was nothing to charge me with, and the cop called me a cab. We agreed that I was walking home and had climbed into this car to get out of the rain. What I didn't tell him, because I had frightened myself, was that the car, a blue Yaris, looked identical to mine, but mine was parked downtown near the almost-violated museum. *Maybe* I was walking home and hopped into this unlocked car to wait out the rain. More likely, I was deranged enough to think I had magically stumbled upon my car and I hopped in with hopes of driving it.

These were shameful times, times of failure to stop, when I was no longer using alcohol but alcohol was using me, and I could go on. Spilling these secrets does feel like contrition, like exposing my darkness to sunlight. At the same time, something in these stories smacks of the colourful tales that fuel AA meetings. My dad wasn't impressed then, and wouldn't be now.

I think that, though my dad had a cement-hard habit and drank ten times as many barrels of beer in his life than I have in mine, he was a bit of an innocent compared to me. It's odd saying this and I'm not sure what I mean. But I realize that's how I felt even back then, even when I was over for a midday visit and he was passed out on the couch. Maybe, deep down, I suspected that, unlike me, he had a reason.

And one thing remains different between my father and me. He let alcohol take over his life, and I didn't. It could be that the Gastons are learning as they move through the generations—learning from the sins of their fathers. Or more likely it's luck. Whatever the case, compared to his father, mine was not violent. He was a gentleman while sober and a frat boy while drunk, but he didn't abandon his family, not physically. He did disappear, sliding into the darkness of endless bottles where he could no longer see us, nor we him. This is one thing I learned or have been lucky enough not to do, at least not that often.

# EIGHT

*To remember that you're alive*
*visit the cemetery of your father.*
—JIM HARRISON

In the upper reach of Agamemnon Channel the mountains get higher, the channel narrows, and as the world grows darker it also gets more familiar. Egmont's not far now. I speed up. *Sylvan's* heat gauge begins to climb. I keep the throttle forward. I don't know why but I want to zoom into Egmont. It feels good to go fast. Maybe because *Cormorant* was so slow. Hey, I'm back, everyone, and I've got a fast boat this time.

*Sylvan* zooms past the deserted Saltery Bay ferry slip to Powell River, and I'm getting more excited. I can easily picture Egmont, its dark, nestled, sparsely settled ambience, having googled it a few weeks ago. Scanning the gallery of pictures I was shocked how little's changed in forty years. Though no longer bright pink, Bathgate's store perches over the government dock where I moored my aluminum car-top while I stayed at Vera's campground that first summer. The Egmont marina where I lived on *Cormorant* now has a pub, called the Backeddy, where Bev and Helen's little café used to be. (A back eddy in my mind whispers to itself that if it rains, or if I just sort of feel like it, I can properly explore this new pub, having a cozy boat bed just a short stumble down the dock to snore in.)

The tiny old cabins where I first stayed with my father when I was fourteen have been replaced with chic Quonsets. The marina's website waxed ecstatic about the hiking, the kayaking, the scuba diving, the Skookumchuck rapids, the fact that it's the cruisers' gateway to Hotham Sound and Princess Louisa Inlet. There's not one mention of fishing.

I enter the somewhat mystical confluence of four fjords. *Sylvan* zooms through the centre of a cross. And here I am. Egmont Point. Princess Royal Reach, heading north into darkness, no man's land, Deserted Bay, Princess Louisa. I ease *Sylvan* into a graceful, wide, zooming right turn. There, the two unnamed islands, and past that, the small First Nations reserve. And there's the channel, the Gap, where every day I anchored and fished.

Zooming atop this immensity of fast, black water, under circling mountains, the shocking sense in my body is that I never left. I think of my father, easily. He's here too, as I knew he would be.

After he died, we rented a boat to scatter his ashes in view of his house in Deep Cove. Even while letting my father, now the consistency of sand, sift through my fingers into Indian Arm, I was aware that, overboard, the water was seamlessly connected. To Vancouver Harbour, to Georgia Strait, the Pacific, and all other waterways of the planet. I'd had this thought before, but not its feeling.

It does feel like I am visiting the cemetery of my father. In my old junker, roaring too fast and loud. Maybe so he can hear me coming.

The boat lurches with a sudden baritone *thump*—I've hit something underwater. Throttling all the way down I look behind me, expecting a waterlogged stick or small rotten log to surface in the wake. Nothing does, then after a long delay the shiny bowling-ball head of a seal lazily rises and stays there, not typical seal behaviour. I'm some distance from it now. It might be a round root burl, but I think it's a seal.

Cocking an ear engine-ward, I throttle up a tad. It sounds fine. Purring, in fact. And no shudder to the boat. No damage done—to the boat at least.

After forty years I don't want to mark my return to Egmont by killing a seal. But I think I have. Like the eagle battling those herons, it smacks of an omen. I really don't know what to make of this stuff. On the one hand it feels like simple bad luck. On the other it reminds me, in the deeps of my body, that I did an awful lot of killing up here. It was sort of my raison d'être, though I don't like to think of that.

But I've made it. The marina is tucked into a notch in the shore; you wouldn't call it a bay. There just up from the dock is the Backeddy Pub, all cedar and glass. And the new cabins. But the dock's the same—it's the very same! The same dock shack and two gas pumps. The configuration of fingers is the same, and about half full of boats. There's the parking lot, and boat-launch ramp, still the only bit of pavement in sight. The old outhouse in the salal has crumbled into nothing.

*Sylvan* swerves in the famous tide—it's like heading up a river and getting your nose turned this way and that. Aiming for the dock at trolling speed I don't get any closer, so I nudge the throttle.

There's movement in the window of the dock shack but nobody comes out to help me land. Which I'm happy about, despite suddenly becoming aware that I'm sixty, with an artificial hip and a bad shoulder. But it's nice to feel one's competence assumed. And I do it, I dock a twenty-six-foot boat in a river's current, bumping *Sylvan*'s starboard side against the dock and leaping out to grab the boat's rail. I strain mightily, pulling the bow back toward the dock, closer to the dock, against the dock, and tie it.

I catch my breath and look around. On the mountainside across the way there's an immense and ugly new clear-cut, but other than that, the same. I remember how dark it is here in this trench between mountains, which not only makes for a late sunrise and early sunset, it snags and holds these clouds. But I remember occasionally baking in the sun here too, and how I'd walk the road to the lake to soap up and plunge in, my only way to clean myself. I could use a shower now, as a matter of fact. If it's sunny tomorrow, maybe I'll check out that lake.

I look around again. The thing is, even in the light there's a dark feeling here.

The tide rips past my feet, still viscerally frightening as it sucks an ocean of water up to and through the Skookumchuck Narrows, not a mile away. I settle my breathing, tip my head forward, and listen. Faint, but there it is. Roaring.

Only once did my dad and I try fishing there, at slack tide tying our bow rope to some floating kelp bulbs in a shore nook near the edge of the rapids. Watching the whitewater grow with the rising tide, we rode it out. We caught no salmon, but it was thrilling. If our kelp anchor failed, and if in our ensuing panic the engine didn't start, we'd be sucked into the tumult and maybe die. It would be a stupid death, trusting to the strength and underwater clinging power of some seaweed.

The cleaning table sits in the same spot beneath the ramp, but it's been rebuilt. I recall that first Egmont summer, my dad up to fish with me and impressed by how much I'd learned, happy enough that I'd surpassed the teacher, but enjoying it immensely at the cleaning table, beer in hand, fielding the questions of the less fortunate onlookers, their "where" and "how deep" and "what time of day" questions. I gutted and beheaded, listening to him bullshit, his lore. "All morning they were just slapping it with their tail, then they got hungry . . ."

I don't know who first brought up the notion that I should become a salmon guide, but whenever he floated the idea it piqued my pride. We mused on details. I would need a boat. If it was big enough, I could also sleep on it. If he bought said boat, and I began an actual business, he could write off the payments, and moorage, and fuel. And he'd have a place to stay for the two weeks he'd spend up here fishing with me.

He wondered what sort of boat. I said it'd be great to get one like Colly Peacock's.

Though I sometimes saw the legendary guide out with a client, fishing the Gap, I also stumbled on him elsewhere, anchored in a bay or on a secret reef with no other boat for miles around. He could study a chart for bottom structure, add the tidal flow, add the possible arrival of a small run en route to a certain distant river, and know. Colly Peacock's bag of tricks was triple the size of mine. Quadruple. Because he died soon after, we spoke only the once, at the marina, in Bev and Helen's café.

Bev left his cash register to formally introduce us, identifying me as a nice young lad who couldn't seem to get enough fishing, rain or shine. I was proud when Colly Peacock said he'd seen me out there in my tinny. I ate chowder, he had a bottle in a paper bag under the table, celebrating a successful trip; a happy customer was spitting gravel driving up the hill from the parking lot even now. It was barely noon and he'd likely been up since three or four. Round-bodied and red-faced, he wore jeans and jean shirt, a fringed leather vest and a flat-topped leather cowboy hat with a peacock feather in the band. He talked like a storyteller and loud enough for an audience of twenty. He'd only meet my eye after a pause, to add zest to a punchline.

He started in, knowing what I wanted to hear. He described a legendary run of monstrous chinook up in Deserted Bay, genetic freaks, throwbacks to the previous century, which over the past decade he had tried and tried to catch.

"And then last year," he said, and paused, and then looked at me, "I hooked one."

He fought it and fought it. One of its peculiar traits was how it dove straight down, no angle to its run at all, just straight down, *down and down into the deepest reaches of hell, Billy.* He didn't say that, but that was the spirit. In the end he just couldn't hold it, and when he reeled up his slack line the hooks, all three of them, straightened out. I didn't question why steel hooks would all straighten out but the leader not break.

"So this year," he said, and paused, "I've been hunting," then paused even longer, then looked at me, ". . . *hooks.*"

He searched and searched for larger treble hooks, for "ought *fours,*" but—and here he narrowed his eyes, hunched a bit, and whispered confidentially, *"Nobody sells treble hooks large as that."* But then, just last month, he located some, from a mail-order supplier in Florida.

"Do you know what they use 'em for down there, Billy?" Not looking at me.

"Um. No."

He paused, then this time pivoted to look me in the eyes. *"Tarpon."*

In my memory I hear him say *Harrr* at this point, but in reality he didn't. Colly's story continued and I'll ruin it and simply say that these huge steel tarpon hooks were also straightened out by another monstrous Deserted Bay chinook. And I believe Colly Peacock died without ever landing one.

It was the next spring when my father bought *Cormorant,* a Tollycraft just like the one Colly Peacock had. A Tolly is an excellent boat but it did cross my mind more than once that the flamboyant man may have had one because it rhymed with his name.

A Tolly is a quality fibreglass cabin cruiser, wide in beam, heavy and indestructible. Stand-up head, three-burner stove, oven, kitchen sink, table that sat four if you squished. It had an all-chain anchor system, with a heavy-duty winch that could raise or lower the anchor from inside with a simple flip of a switch. You could steer from inside the cabin or up on the flying bridge. It had a huge back deck, or cockpit, for fishing. An eight-foot dinghy folded up against the stern. When my dad took me down to the boat broker in False Creek to sea-test the boat he'd just bought, when I first stepped aboard and it didn't even move to my weight—I knew this was a big and wonderful boat. You could go anywhere in it. *Cormorant*.

And so continued my string of summers at Egmont. I was supposedly running a charter company; my dad didn't mind that I wasn't very aggressive and let the business start up by word of mouth. So at first I enjoyed almost no business. I lived aboard *Cormorant* and fished most days. Friends came up and we fished and partied. I bought a cheap typewriter, orange plastic with a black racing stripe down one side of its cover, and began typing. The first summer aboard *Cormorant* I wrote a bombastic story called "The Forest Path to Malcolm's," written from the point of view of Malcolm Lowry's fictitious bastard son. My mother's best friend Doris, the one who had known Malcolm Lowry and played bridge with his wife Margerie, read the story and liked it. I also began meditating, and got to know intimately the boat's subtle movements, a lack of stability underfoot that very much mirrored life's. But usually I was busy writing, or fishing, or partying.

And my father would join me for two, sometimes three weeks at a stretch. The floor space inside the Tollycraft's cabin was about the size of a large bathroom. He was tall, and getting wider now too, and after a long day's drinking he snored as loudly as most people yell. Lodged up in the V-berth for it seemed like ten solid hours he would snore, and the shape of the V-berth was the cone of a bullhorn, pointing at me, and my shouts at him to shut up were useless. During those two weeks, I would come to believe in all seriousness that I was damn well earning that boat.

I exaggerate. He drank steadily but worked hard—I see that now—to stay under control. In one sense, he was afraid of me, afraid of falling from grace. Or straining our contract. Or afraid I might get honest on him. And on *Cormorant* there was nowhere to hide. He couldn't escape downstairs or under the deck or in blaring music. Each morning I watched him weigh the consequences of having a breakfast beer. I watched him measure his day and pace himself. I saw him use discipline, and I saw that it was tough. There was no passing out. No stumbling. We were on a boat, after all. He kept to a pattern I'd often seen at home: hang on till noon, start slow, only beer, peak after docking for the day, then a bit of a show around the cleaning table and then a late dinner, let the food slow him down and put him out.

One interesting thing aboard *Cormorant*, though, was his constant fastidiousness. Maybe it was a holdover from the navy. I was a slob, but he kept our small quarters "shipshape," a damp cloth always hanging from the oven handle.

And we fished all day because we both loved it.

Expressions, never said sober:
*Your old Sea Father* [himself]
*The sea, oh the sea, oh the great fucking sea!* [sung basso
        profundo, tunelessly]
*Roll over Mabel, it's better on the other side.* [often sung in
        front of your girlfriend]
*Doogans* [cigarettes]
*Birds* [cigarettes]

*Poontang* [sex]

*Squib* [women]

*Squinch* [a woman]

*Keep your tits up!* [a bad pun on rod tip, which must be kept
    pointed up as the salmon runs]

McGuffins [breasts]

*Might as well be drunk as the way I am.* [opening another beer]

*Up his kilt with a geegaw.* [screw him]

*Hon-yock* [a local yokel, or anyone he didn't know
    personally]

*Jap* [Asian]

*Skedaddle.*

*We better beetle.* [in a hurry]

*Someone's all bright-eyed and bushy-tailed.* [accusing you of
    being horny]

*Catty-whompus* [as in, the ball hit him in the catty-whompus]

———

Then, he changed.

After his "vacation" on Vancouver Island, my father arrived in
Egmont sober, and we had an entirely sober visit, the only one aboard
*Cormorant*.

He hadn't had a drink for about a year and you could see it.
Before, he always had his left hand in his pocket, jingling change. He'd
go at the coins like a Greek his worry beads, but way more worried,
waiting for happy hour. He no longer did that. He was steady, and in
his steadiness he was almost cheerful. There was something deeply
peaceful about him.

Though I no longer lived at home, I'd been visiting more, both
to support the new state of affairs but also because now it was easier

to be there. So by summer we were both used to each other in his new mode. It's funny how fast that happens. At first his sobriety was such a trembling and tenuous thing, then before you know it, it's only normal. I'd visit and I'd be amazed to see my parents already bored, or bickering, or sitting there with nothing to talk about, the sober-husband honeymoon already over. Which was good, which was great. It was ordinary. It was life.

That sober summer my new father and I had a couple of adventures of the kind that would've been impossible a year before. The first was with none other than Colly Peacock's legendary Deserted Bay salmon. In Bev's café the now-departed guide had hissed in my direction one last bombastic hint, that there was a place, "twelve mile" (not miles) north up Princess Royal Reach, on the way to Deserted, where you had a shot at that big run. There was a log boom anchored there that floated suspended over a hidden reef. The monstrous salmon would pause in their journey north and hide under the logs, Colly said.

If I wanted to have a crack at one, it had to be mid-August. I had to tie up to the outside of the boom. I had to use the biggest herring I could find, on the biggest treble hooks—Colly chuckled here at the impossibility of finding such hooks—and to fish at ninety feet, and if I got one on, to untie and cast off immediately from the boom and motor a hundred yard (not yards) off, quick as I could, because the fish would instantly go for one of the underwater anchor cables and wrap the line around it and—I see Colly's eyes on me—*part yer thirty-test like sewin' thread.*

My dad and I motored up Princess Royal Reach and found Colly's log boom. My dad didn't remember me telling him about this ancient run of monsters, or for that matter about Colly Peacock, or Colly's Tolly, or any of it. Since it made him sad to be reminded off all he'd forgotten, or actually all he'd missed, I was careful to tell him the story as if I'd just heard it myself. We were following a fresh lead, a hot rumour. And he was keen; there had been a prolonged lull at Egmont. We were still in denial but we were witnessing the slow but sure demise of the region as a fishery. The coho had all but disappeared, and chinook were scanty as well. All this had happened in the space of about five years. Already there were fewer boats coming to try for them, and the marina's business was off. Some blamed the abundance of seals. Everyone knew it was more than just the seals but, just in case it wasn't, someone (I won't say it was Egmont Charlie, but most fingers pointed his way) went on a private hunting trip all winter and shot over a dozen.

We tied *Cormorant* to an outermost log. The plan was to fish until nightfall and spend the night here tied up to these logs and my dad was nervous about it. We were in true wilderness, more than ten miles by water from habitation of any kind, and not even our VHF radio worked in here. Nature truly loomed, sitting as we were in the dark bottom of a ditch of towering mountains. Secretly I felt comfortable enough, in that I and some friends had come here earlier that spring, not to fish but to spend the night in a place where we could raise some hell and not care about bothering any early rising fishermen with music or party shrieks, which might echo into the morning. (I recall that, under a full moon, I not only ate a live herring but first bit it in half, and took my time eating the two dying halves while someone photographed the event. We'd sworn a serious oath never to leave the boat and venture onto the boom. If you fell between two logs and they rolled or closed up even an inch, you weren't getting back out. We'd all seen the film of Ken Kesey's *Sometimes a Great Notion*.)

My dad and I baited our lines with the biggest herring the marina had to sell us. It was strange to mooch with logs on one side and open water on the other, because we both had to fish off the same side, usually a no-no because, with our live herring down there swimming at the end of long leaders, our lines could easily tangle without our knowing it. So I pointed my rod off the back, and my dad pointed his frontward. We didn't expect any luck, probably because it just didn't feel fishy. And with fishing so bad lately at Egmont we were used to long days where we sat and caught nothing. But not ten minutes in, I got a strike. That is, my line went slack. I reeled and reeled, caught up to the rising fish, felt some weight then hit it, my rod doubling as I set the hook. Then the fish took off, sounding—that is, swimming *straight down*—my reel screaming. Only big chinook sounded like that, straight down, non-stop. I'd caught thirty-pounders before and this was nothing like that, the power and speed of this run was of another order altogether, the reel screaming in a new way, overcome and ratchety like it might break. It kept going, straight down. My dad and I shouted confused instructions at each other about starting the boat and untying it and motoring away from the boom or we'd lose it for sure, untie the boat, no, start it first. The fish kept running. With a new, impossible lurch it picked up even more speed and then— nothing. Perfectly slack. I knew the fish was gone. I went through the motions of reeling up fast on the off chance it had changed tack and was coming fast at the boat. But, no, it was gone. Eventually, up came the one-ounce weight, and then the hooks. Two big trebles, the bottom three straightened out.

That was it for bites. It got dark, too dark to fish. In fact, with a cloudy sky and no source of light but stars, it got as dark as I'd ever seen dark. We sat on the deck and couldn't see each other. We laughed at how dark it was, and actually got spooked. What in hell might be crawl- ing at us across the log boom? We went inside to artificial light and some games of rummy, and when I semi-seriously locked the door behind us, my dad laughed, but I could tell he was glad I locked it.

That summer we had an even more extraordinary trip. Though I never did have many charters, rarely more than one a week, I was careful not to book anything during my dad's annual trip up. But that summer while my dad was there I got a desperation call through the marina office, some American fellow "who needed to charter *tomorrow*." Letting me use his phone to call him back, the marina owner instructed me matter-of-factly to charge the guy double.

I didn't charge the guy double but I explained that my father would be coming along. Jim wanted to take his new bride on a cruise north to Malibu Rapids for the day. No fishing. He just "needed to show her a special place." Having my dad on board was something I couldn't have even considered a year ago. They would've been listening to "Roll Over Mabel" five minutes in.

Jim proved a remarkable man. I was dubious when he showed up wearing pastels and white shoes and white belt, but that was the style for certain men at the time. He was maybe fifty, a bit younger than my dad. I was also dubious because his new bride, Rebecca, had to be twenty years younger. Tanned nut brown, she was all in white to show it off. They were fresh from their wedding in Hawaii and on their way home to Chicago and today was his "honeymoon treat" for her. He took his bride's proffered hand and helped her onto *Cormorant*'s deck as I scanned the deck for fish blood or hooks or dead herring.

Jim ran back up the ramp for the bagged lunch he'd arranged in the café, for which I later heard that he paid double, and then we were on our way. An old and tall but excellent first mate, my father untied *Cormorant* and cast us off.

We turned at Egmont Point and headed north up Princess Royal Reach. A cloudless, windless, perfect day. I steered from up on the bridge and couldn't hear over the engine noise what was said as, standing together on the back deck, Jim pointed out this and that. He appeared to know where he was. My dad bustled about, tidying, my six-five cabin boy. He stayed clear of the newlyweds. I had the sense of being watched, my skills as charter-boat skipper admired. Before long, though, he climbed the ladder to spell me from my job of steering, and suggested that I go "entertain the guests."

Jim was still pointing excitedly here and there, to either side of the steeply walled channel. He pointed to outcrops of rock and occasional clearings in the dense trees, and I began to make out patches of wildflowers. Jim had apparently planted them. They were modest patches, and Rebecca found them hard to spot, wildflowers lacking the huge blooms of their inbred cousins. But Jim was proud. I asked him how many places he'd planted.

"I Johnny Appleseeded the whole route." His "route" rhymed with *pout*, American.

"Really?" We were talking thirty, forty miles of steep wilderness.

"Any time I went up and back for supplies. If it wasn't too messy out." He saw my incredulous look. "Basically I just had to climb up and pitch a handful at some moss. Sometimes they took hold. Wasn't hard to do."

Unlike building Malibu, which was the rest of his story, and the reason we were on this trip.

I'd been to Princess Louisa Inlet once before, trying to impress a girlfriend. The hidden inlet was a mile long, surrounded by cliffs and, in winter, seventeen waterfalls spilling off their edges. At the far end was a glacier, and Chatterbox Falls. The inlet was sacred to the local First Nations: in earlier days, boys proved their manhood by climbing one of the cliffs, with the addition of a boulder attached to the skin of their back with bone spikes and cedar-bark cords. The inlet was guarded by a narrow entrance mouth, Malibu Rapids, passable only at high slack tide. Just inside was a collection of buildings, what looked like a lodge, a chapel, and an auditorium, plus other smaller structures, all rustically elegant cedar post-and-beam. It was doubly magnificent in that there was not so much as even a trapper's cabin for many miles. Simply called Malibu, it currently functioned as what I heard was a Christian youth camp.

I noticed Jim eyeing landforms, then checking his watch. Somewhat timidly he asked if we could possibly go any faster. Jim knew when high slack would be. I shouted up to my dad to pop 'er up a notch.

Twenty-five years earlier, Jim, an engineer, had been contracted to go up there and build a "Christian getaway," and he did so, single-handedly. Staying in a tent year-round, he felled huge cedars from the shores of Princess Louisa, and floated them to the site. He built a "tidal crane" that used steel cables and pulley and a bundle of float-ing logs as weight—when the tide went down, one end of a massive cedar log could be raised ten feet, wedged in place, then raised another ten feet with the next low tide, and so on, until it was lifted into position as a centre beam. Fondly and with articulate hands, his fingers as logs, Jim showed Rebecca and me how all of this leverage had worked.

He had a portable mill. Window glass was barged up. Wood stoves, a generator, tile, eventually furniture. It took him three years. He apol-ogized to us for bestowing the name "Malibu." He was from California and he'd been homesick.

Jim hadn't been back in twenty years, and he wanted to show his life's handiwork to his new bride.

Malibu's dock was in through the rapids on the Princess Louisa side and at slack tide we had to idle and turn circles while waiting for a sail-boat to struggle out, coming too close to the rocks. Rebecca climbed the ladder and delivered some sandwiches. Jim had bought lunch for four. Sandwich in mouth, I punched us through, and my dad and I marvelled at a first stately building half visible in the trees. I'd described Jim's engi-neering exploits to him and he sat staring in disbelief, he the former hardware department boss for whom pounding a straight nail was a feat.

Malibu's other structures came into view and we appreciated them silently. It could have been a high-end convention centre, or college. We idled just out from the dock. My dad was speechless. It was hard to comprehend what this man had done. Jim was speechless too, standing straight, humbled by his own feats, remembering things out of our ken. Rebecca stroked his wrist, taking in her husband as much as his handiwork.

Brightly clad young Christian campers sat in groups in the surrounding woods, playing games or, I imagined, enduring sermons. Somewhere the proud strum of a devotional guitar. I had just begun my approach to the dock, because of course we were going to disembark and enjoy a closer look at Jim's accomplishment, when a young fellow, blond, clean-cut as they come and no more than twenty, arrived at a trot to tell us we weren't allowed to come ashore. He had the air of having to do this at least once a day.

"This man," I pointed to Jim who stood silent on the deck, "built this place."

"Not a public dock. Bye." The blond lieutenant lifted a hand and walked away.

"He built it all by himself! He hasn't been here in twenty years! He lived here in a tent!" I hadn't stopped my approach and *Cormorant* nudged the dock bumpers, at the sound of which the guy spun around and came at us fast.

"You can't land. This is a private dock. You have to leave."

"He just got married and came all the way from Hawaii! He just wants to show his wife!" I might have said "goddamn" at some point. I'd seen Jim, who hadn't said a word, turn and go inside the cabin, tears in his eyes.

"*He built this place!*" I tried. The young functionary turned to leave again.

*Cormorant* drifted out from the dock, but my dad had got off. He looked up at me, waved me away too, and followed the blond guy.

"Hey," he called out. He really did have a nice deep voice.

As we drifted away I watched my dad catch up to the young man and briefly and gently touch his arm. They kept walking and went behind some trees. Rebecca had gone in to see to Jim. I could hear her murmurs.

My dad strode out from the trees and down to the dock, waving me in.

"They have ten minutes," he said, stooping with the ropes, working fast. "Just them." He was furious. "And they can't go inside anywhere."

He stayed furious, waiting up on the bridge with me, until Jim and Rebecca returned from their little tour and he saw the joy on their faces. When I asked him what he'd said to the guy, he said only, "I went over his head."

I don't think I've been more proud of my father than I was then. I wondered if money changed hands there in the trees, or if they bumped into the young man's superior. I didn't care. Though I don't think my dad was that poetic, only now does it occur to me that maybe the old Gonzaga student had "gone over his head" by reminding him of God and his Christian duty.

———

That non-drinking summer we fished more than ever because mornings came earlier. We cooked way more food than we needed, often two kinds of meat. He brought up multiple bags of Peek Freans cookies to feed his new sweet tooth, and he drank endless coffee. We played the same rummy game he played with my mother, "rummy 500," keeping score and standing to win twenty bucks in a week. We listened to the radio news, my dad leaning closer at the stock-market reports, something I'd never seen him do. He didn't feel like listening to music.

It was comfortable. For me, there was less sense of paying my dues. He was okay to hang around with. No deep or revealing conversations; we kept it light. He wasn't one to ask me about my life, other than the main things, like what year university I was in now, or would I be playing hockey again next year and for whom. He was too proud and too smart to probe me on subjects he had no clue about, like English literature, or my own writing. Just as I was too proud and smart to ask him about the business of corporate retail, or the details of sobriety after three decades of not.

I read him a poem once, though. I'd just had a few published in literary journals and happened to have one on board, and I didn't have it properly hidden because he found it and saw my name on the back cover. Bemused, he asked me to read the poem to him. He insisted, so finally I did. This is the poem I read him:

*Suddenly one Sunday*

*You, in pain again*
*from too much thinking*
*Here, I said, have some tea,*
*one herbal remedy dreamed up*
*by a lover from the hills*
*to give your mind time off*

*Stretching like a dog, then feigning sleep*
*on the bent couch,*
*you held the cooling cup*
*on the table*
*between your feet*
*Then—*
*within the smallest moment,*
*like music half-heard,*
*I saw you really trying*
*to die*

I didn't get much response, except for a crack about it not rhyming. I drove with him back to Vancouver when his visit ended, and stayed for dinner. Leaving, as I passed in front of the TV-room window, which was open a crack, I could hear my father telling my mother that I'd written a poem about him. He said, "He read it out to me." What struck me most wasn't that he thought it was about him, but the "he read it out," which was such an old phrase, a shortened version, I suppose, of "he read it out loud," and not something you heard much anymore. I see now that maybe the poem was partly about him. Poets can be the last ones to know what their poems mean.

One thing I did learn from that poem, though, simply from the speed with which he told my mother about it with me barely out the door, was his eager interest in this side of my life he knew nothing about. And continued to know nothing about, because we never spoke of it. He never asked. Some years later, when my books started to come—little-known, quirky things for the most part—he never mentioned reading any. My mother had her comments about them, and once over the phone she told me "how proud your father is." Of my work in general, the fact of it, I assumed. I never asked.

What strikes me about our sober summer was how quiet it was and how ordinary it felt. Nothing special. A father and a son who enjoyed each other's company because they were supposed to but also because they did. And we both loved fishing. Aboard the boat our long silences weren't at all uneasy.

At night before bed we were content to fill time playing cards. To save the house batteries, only one light burned overhead and we faced each other across a table that later would be flipped over to become my bed. The radio was on softly, FM rock, the weirdest songs he'd gently mock me for, as if I was responsible for them. The only biting insects were no-see-ums, which came in through the screens, and though we were rarely bitten they would land in numbers on the overhead light, be stunned, and fall into our game. My dad would spot one struggling on the table near his hand and approach it slowly with pointing index finger, say "Hello" in a high approximation of a female voice, then squish it out of its misery, if beings that small know misery. That summer, my father had a gently strange and inward humour.

Sober, he seemed no less content than anyone. I sensed an air of patience. Quietly waiting for something to arrive or for something to be over. He seemed to understand that he was leading a good enough life. Who knows why such a person goes back to drinking that life away.

———

Walking up the wide aluminum ramp, I remember it used to be bouncy wood, and I used to walk it many times a day. I need to arrange my moorage spot and find the marina office through a glass door in the side of the Backeddy, through whose open window I hear the odd solitary bellow and some clinking bottles. It's not quite dusk but it's a Friday night.

The marina owner is maybe forty-five, blond, an A-type who shuffles and sorts papers as we speak, not meeting my eyes. I suspect he's the owner because he looks ready to crack. In these parts, seasonal businesses are on constant life-support; he probably keeps minimal staff and does five jobs himself.

"Wow," I say, "things sure have changed since last time I was here!"

"What can I do for you?" Eyeing a calendar, he flips the page to next month.

"Well, I'm here for a little visit, just cruised across from Gabriola. Thought I'd moor here and maybe hang around a—"

"That you, blue canopy?" He jerks his forehead in the direction of the dock.

"Yeah, it's—"

"How many nights?"

"Maybe start with two? I thought I'd see what the weather did and—"

"There on the outside okay?"

"Sure, that's fine. I'll just keep it where it is." Though no other boats are moored on the outside. "As long as it doesn't wreck anyone's approach to the gas—"

"It's fine."

He takes my credit card and plugs it into his hand-held device. Other than the transaction taking twenty seconds to chug through, which I can see drives him crazy, this could be somewhere downtown.

"I really have to say it's wild being here. Came here, first time, forty-six years ago. It was a fish camp. Right here was a little café—" I stop myself. He's listening politely, that is, staring through my face and not registering a word. But I've just heard myself. I am now that old-timer who thinks his story is fabulously interesting, and whether it is or not, mostly he wants to talk about himself. Who cares if I used to pull thirty-pounders out of the Gap, right over this guy's right shoulder, through that window? Who cares if Vera, the gentlest person I ever met, daily used to walk the dirt road right up there like a knock-kneed six-four Aboriginal ghost. This guy, a busy man, probably sees one of me a week.

When I've pulled *Sylvan* a bit farther away from the gas pumps, tied the ropes more securely, and shut down the batteries, it's time for the luxury of a burger and a beer. I stand beside my boat and take another disbelieving look around. Across the way, all I can see of the reserve are a few weak lights. They're still on generators there, still boat-only access. To the far right are the brighter lights of the quarry. Maybe it's a little bigger. I think I can hear a distant clank and roar, which would mean they're working afternoon shift. Behind me, atop the steep embankment backing the marina, is a large structure I hadn't noticed. It could be a huge cedar-and-glass mansion. Or a lodge of some kind? I'll ask about it. Remarkable that in forty odd years it's the only noticeable change.

Except the Backeddy. I'm halfway through my first pint and waiting on my Skookum burger, *skookum* a Chinook word meaning big, or strong, or great, depending on who you talk to. (Even down in Vancouver a carpenter will slap his newly installed beam and say, "Skookum.") As for the Skookumchuck rapids, *chuk* means water, so, "big water." Personally, I think *skookum* means powerful. It makes the most sense.

My burger is merely big. One of those burgers that no living person, save those with a snake's hinged jaw, can get their mouth around. But I'll be powerfully full if I finish it.

"And how are those first bites?"

I'm startled to hear this citified phrase in Egmont. Also, my server isn't the cook or gas jockey or other dishevelled multi-tasker of olden days hustling out of the kitchen but a painfully attractive though heavily made up young Indigenous woman. She's about my older daughter's age, so I keep my eyes to my burger and don't smile charmingly when I say it's excellent. She probably knows I'm lying because she looks extremely savvy. She lifts her eyebrows at my empty pint so I lift my eyebrows back and she spins off with a smile.

I hate that I'm facing perhaps the best high-def TV screen I've ever seen. I hate that it's the B.C. Lions playing the Argos, and I hate most of all that I can't seem to pull my eyes away. Good high-def really is a sharp kind of magic. It rivals reality, it truly does. Am I that old-timer again, or am I properly worried that the screen's enslavement of the human race is now almost complete?

No, I like TV and I like football okay, I just don't want to watch a stupid CFL game in Egmont, where electricity used to feel like magic from afar. Where there were more eagles than people. Where twice a year to buy supplies a hermit would nose his kayak to the dock after a three-day paddle from up north, though nobody knew where, exactly, because he wouldn't say. Where I saw, down on that dock in front of where *Sylvan* sits calmly now, two ancient drunks rolling on the boards, weakly punching, looking to kill each other until Charlie strode down and got them apart with a paddle, and told me later they were long-time lovers. "Married" was the word he used, with respect. Where, my last summer in Egmont, certain of the Boston Bruins, overnighting here and loaded, provoked a fight with an equally loaded Egmonster, who got badly beaten up. It was a place where hockey didn't mean anything, and no one was impressed. Mostly, here was a place where nature felt skookum and humans felt small, and it was where I used to live.

———

My father made it without a drink for a little over a year. He did so without AA, which he never took to. He began one-year-on, two-years-off periods of sobriety. Not long after the rehab on Vancouver Island he retired from Sears. He likely was encouraged, or maybe even forced. It wasn't surprising. For a decade I'd been finding it hard to imagine how competent he could possibly be doing that job, the management of so many details, when at home he was so out to lunch, and doing worse and worse at faking like he wasn't. He was fifty-eight.

Over the years he'd become more isolated. My parents no longer hosted parties and went out rarely. His sober periods didn't help, because he would avoid social situations involving alcohol. The several couples they still saw, friends my mother had made selling real estate, lately weren't calling as much.

I loved it when, once every couple of years, my dad's old best pal Torg would drive up from Seattle with his wife Ilene and stay for a weekend. A few times it was just Torg and they'd go on a fishing trip together. Meeting Torg out in the driveway and looking genuinely happy for the first time in a while my dad became a loud American jock again, shoulder-punching, jabbing at the extra weight around his buddy's middle, and why the hell didn't you phone me for a whole year for cryin' out loud. Torg would greet my dad as "Gaspipe" but thereafter call him "Pipe." So began a weekend's beer-guzzling, and Torg kept up with him quite happily.

Torg was always interested in what I was up to and he made time to talk not just with me but about me. He'd tell me what my dad had told him about my hockey playing and, if a few beers had gone down, what a spectacular kid I was, and how "Your dad is the proudest man alive." Torg was funny and smart, a high school principal who knew how to talk to kids in a captivating way. I liked Torg. Mostly I liked that my dad had a best old friend who was funny and smart, and who liked my dad enough to travel up and visit. I can see the two of them out on the sundeck, my dad spinning some tale about salmon fishing, and Torg would lean forward at him, bug-eyed.

"Pipe?" he'd ask.

My dad would keep talking.

"Pipe?"

My dad would finally notice him leaning into his face and staring. "What."

"You're full of shit, you know that?"

And my dad would laugh and agree that he was full of shit.

"You're full of shit, but you're a good man, you bastard."

This routine would play out a few times near the end of the evening and then it was time to "hit the hay."

The last time I saw Torg I was still in Vancouver and came by doing my Sunday duty, which meant afternoon-TV sports and dinner. Torg and Ilene were packing up their car. Torg paused at the trunk, looked at me over his glasses and with a comic's timing thanked me for gracing them with my presence. I bet his students liked him but were also a little afraid of him.

Torg said he wanted to show me something. He turned and walked into the backyard. I shrugged at Ilene and my parents, and I followed him. Torg said nothing until we'd reached the back fence, and the bottom of my dad's garden. He pointed to the big-leafed plant at his feet.

"Have you seen this?"

"I have," I said. I nudged it with a foot. "Pretty cool, eh?" Torg was pointing at my dad's pumpkin, now the size of a grapefruit.

"So you've seen the WAG."

I nodded. "He does it every year." WAG were my initials. William Allen Gaston. When the pumpkin was the size of an orange he'd carve the initials in. By the time the pumpkin was the size of a pumpkin, the letters were glaring scars.

"Do you know how much your dad cares about you?"

"I do."

Torg was the kind of teacher who would peer at you, again over his glasses, with an insistent look saying, No, you don't. I didn't exactly enjoy being told something about my relationship with a man I saw way more than once every two years, and who this year had dragged me down here numerous times to show me the same carved and wounded pumpkin he'd shown me last Sunday, and the Sunday before that. How do you explain something this complicated to a teacher looking at you over his glasses?

"Anyway," Torg said, and looked away. Apologetic, he smiled and shook his head. "*God*, we went through a lot of beer last night. *Canuck beer*." He did look a little ragged. "I can't keep up to that man."

"Who can?"

"I'm worried about him."

"I am too." I tried to convey by my tone that I'd been worried for years.

"He's alone too much."

My mother had probably been away for most of their visit, weekends being prime time for realtors. And her work her prime excuse for avoiding her husband's drinking. I didn't know what Torg knew about any of this. All I knew was that I was being admonished for not spending enough time with my father. Torg, who didn't know certain things. I didn't have the wit, or the disrespect, to ask him whose duty it was, a best friend's or a son's, to keep a lonely man company.

———

I left the West Coast when he was sixty-three and I was thirty-three. Toronto, then Halifax, then a long stretch in New Brunswick. I flew back at least once a year, often at Christmas, often with my growing family in tow. So our time together was chaotic, more about the kids than the two of us.

Whether we first met at the door, or in the airport, it was usually evening and his style of greeting wouldn't change much:

"Just let me look at you." Sometimes he straight-armed and cupped my shoulder. Eyes squinting, teary. It wasn't clear if he had me in focus. Or if, like drunks are wont to do, he simply stayed within himself, staying with what he already knew.

But now he often said, "You're getting taller!"

"Still growing!" I'd say. This seemed weirdly true. I was almost eye to eye with him now. He stooped a bit but it was mostly his shrinking. That loss of cartilage between vertebrae can look especially dramatic in someone who used to be tall. Because I saw him only once a year, he looked to be aging in sad, shocking leaps.

He was more withdrawn. Even on the special occasion of my yearly visit, every morning he'd be downstairs in front of the TV at eleven precisely, which is when *Matlock* came on. Actually he'd be there ten minutes early, waiting. A Matinée Extra Mild burned between two browned fingers, or dangled from his lips, smoke rising into his eyes. Right above his left eye was a permanent yellow streak in his snow-white hair.

I smoked Matinée Extra Mild too. After years of coming over and stealing a pack or two from his carton, they became my brand. They were deemed "mild" because tiny perforations above the filter sucked air during machine tests, resulting in a lower, healthier rating, a lie. A smoker's lips automatically covered the perforations, giving a strong smoke.

I could tell he didn't want me to, but I would follow him down and wait with him.

"I get a kick out of that guy. *Matlock*," he'd say, waiting out five more minutes of daytime TV, usually colourful people with loud opinions, which he normally would not tolerate.

But his beer stash was down here and eleven was when he let himself crack his first one. *Matlock* could have been *Mannix* could have been *Columbo*. Whenever he disappeared mid-conversation to go downstairs because it was almost eleven, my mother would smile and shake her head and chuckle about how much he loved his *Matlock*. I almost admired how perfect denial can be, especially when it's been buffed and polished for forty years.

I can see him downstairs, in that straw-coloured chair, smaller in general, his shoulders closer to his ears. His pale-blue shirt, grey cardigan, and beige pants looking a bit big on him now, a smoke always going as he waited for *Matlock* to begin. Waiting for his beer to begin, in truth. Waiting to feel juuuust right. Waiting for relief. He was more content, even jolly, once a beer was in hand, but in these days there was a sense of him waiting for something else. Something far bigger. It didn't seem to matter that he was constantly alone. He had the air of an old man on his porch staring into the void. Waiting for what's coming next, waiting for *that*. It's not an unintelligent stare.

From the Maritimes I'd call every Sunday, timing it at least a half-hour before *Matlock*. My mom would answer, then shout for my dad, and he would pick up the downstairs phone. She and I would do most of the talking, my dad chuckling on cue. Once, devilish, I timed the call to coincide with eleven, and good God but I heard it, a brief vacancy on the other end, then a cough covering up a cracked-open can of beer.

When I turned forty and my dad seventy, I wrote him a letter. We'd written letters a few times before. This letter was different. I had grown more and more troubled that I had never told him, from my heart, what I felt about him. How I worried about him. How I worried about how he felt about his life that was almost over. His drinking. His apparent despair. How, on the several times I'd confronted him about his drinking, he'd responded, "What do *you* care?" Now, in a letter, with words written down, words he couldn't forget and couldn't deny, I told him I cared because I loved him. I told him that the people who loved him got angry when he drank because, over and over, they had to watch a smart man get stupid, and see a loving man grow distant. And that, to the people who loved him, his drinking felt like abandonment. When he drank he disappeared, and it looked like he was choosing to. I added that, since he had been abandoned by his own father, he would know what that felt like.

The week after, my father phoned me, a first. He said he got my letter, and it was a good letter. He said I was right about everything, and he thanked me. None of this was easy for him. I suspected my mother was behind it.

He said what he needed to say, and I thanked him, not filling it up with anything else, because I'd had my turn. But saying goodbye, I told him I loved him. He hesitated, the phone silence growing loud. Then he said, "I love you too." It came out quickly. It was weird for both of us. Weird to feel those words in your mouth, weird to hear them resonate in your skull.

My mother told me in a private call later that the letter had made him cry. I found out later still that my parents referred to this time of life as "Bill's honest period." And it seems they blamed it on me becoming a Buddhist.

The next visit we said "I love you" and "I love you too" in person. And now always at the end of phone calls. It did get easier, a little less shocking for both of us. But the words always jolted. He never said it first but he always said it back. I knew he meant it. In the moment, he probably felt the weirdness more than the love, but that was fine. It was better than us getting slick with it.

My younger daughter, Lilli, frequently says "I love you." When she's off to bed, or when I drop her off at school or the mall to meet her friends, she tells me she loves me and I say it back. I don't want her to stop saying it, not at all, but sometimes it does sound a little automatic. Like a topping up, or a checking in. It's said *easily*. Does saying it easily mean it's less felt? It sounds felt, as I hope it does when I say it back, the sound not feeling weird on my tongue anymore, hardly at all.

———

On *Sylvan's* deck I turn my back on the pub window lights to pee in a bucket. *Sylvan's* toilet's pump flusher has air in the line and is hard to get going and it's just easier this way. When I empty the bucket overboard, there's a burst of phosphorescence. A nice surprise, it always looks like magic. Like sparks of spiritual mischief, like the lights trailing Tinkerbell. It makes me love Egmont again if only for a moment. I lean over the gunnel and spit, and receive a modest sparkle. My dad and I used to marvel over it. We called it "phosphorous."

Phosphorescence scares me a little, especially here. If I stare long enough into the depths something big will go by, lit up. It'll be real but outlined in ghost-glow. Which somehow emphasizes the darkness. The gleam feels siren-like. Down there is dark pandemonium, and something wants me.

One time, living on this dock, tied up along the main walkway, in the middle of the night I was shocked awake by a thunderous boom against the hull, right beside my head. I woke in terror, breathing hard. Even though I soon understood what had done it, I was scared to get up and go out on deck. There in the faint light of the single dock lamp was a log, a massive one, pushed by the tidal current against *Cormorant's* hull. There was something eerie and looming about it. All was quiet and black and liquid, and night seemed too hauntingly real. It made me feel very alone.

I was naked except for my underwear but it was warm enough for me to grab my pike pole and go onto the dock and try to shove this big sucker away from my boat, though the tide was running pretty good. Phosphorescence rippled off the log. I planted the pole into a shallow knothole near the log's middle and started to push. Nothing. I gritted my teeth and strained and it began to move, but so, so slowly. I applied more muscle and changed my posture, really leaning into it, and it began to move more surely. It was almost clear. Then the log rolled the tiniest bit, the knothole changing its angle, and as I leaned into the final push the pole shot out and I flew in.

Instantly more than awake, the phosphorescence a flashbulb in my face, I knew that in two seconds the current would have me under the dock and into cables and chains and motor props and, well, sunken skulls and sea monsters. I punched up both hands and grabbed the dock edge before getting sucked under. My entire body was dragged and held parallel under the dock and it was at least as hard straining my way up and out as it had been pushing the log. But eventually I did heave myself onto the dock, where I lay gasping. And shocked, and afraid. I caught my breath, alone on the dark dock, hating the black water and the twisted spookiness of this place, and my stupidity. And my odd desire to live alone.

# NINE

*It's of no use trusting to friends,*
*or sons, or fathers.*

—MILAREPA

I'm dead asleep in *Sylvan's* V-berth when I'm thrown against the hull so violently I can't help yelling. I try to find my feet but can't, with waves hitting the boat broadside and rocking it badly. It pitches one way then yanks against its ropes on the other, testing their strength, jerking me across to the other wall. There's nothing to hang on to! When the rocking starts to ease and I see I'm in no danger, I start to laugh, because this is ridiculous. I know now why the marina owner asked if I was "okay mooring on the outside."

I get coffee water on to boil and stand rubbing my hands in front of the camp stove, wishing it were a bonfire. It's colder on water than on land, plus the tides here roil colder water up from the deeps, making for a colder place in general, Egmont a microclimate chilled by its water. Spooning coffee into a filter, I can feel the icy stuff come through the boat's uninsulated hull into my feet.

My second night's sleep aboard *Sylvan* was at least as bad as the first, back at Secret Cove. That cedar-and-glass place way up the hill overhanging the marina is some kind of convention centre after all, and a corny master of ceremonies' voice grew in corniness and volume as it introduced song after song into the night. It might have been a wedding reception and the happy couple's names might have been Don and Donna, and Don and Donna might have been old, because someone sure had a thing for Motown and the Four Tops.

Sipping a first coffee, things warm up. Another big boat goes by, a surprisingly speedy barge tug. Working on a Saturday? I brace myself and lay flat palms onto kitchen gear, but the waves aren't as big and violent.

I decide to go fishing. I'm in Egmont. Of course I'm going fishing.

Putting back two bananas for breakfast, I motor out past the unnamed islands, to the Gap. The back side of the second island has a new place—new as in not there forty years ago—with a seaplane but no boat at its dock.

The plan is to anchor and fish my old spot. Same spot, new method. But, oh my, how well I know this place. How well my *body* knows this place. When I reach the spot exactly between *that* duckbill point and *that* distant hill, throw the boat in neutral and it starts *this* speed of drift, the moon being a few days from full, I scramble to the bow to throw the anchor in exactly *now* because by the time it hits bottom the boat will be all the way over *there*, and it won't catch and hold till *here*, my spot.

Waiting for the pick to set and hold and the boat to straighten against the current, I hardly breathe. I know this feeling too. *Sylvan* points into the current, holds, and a loud wash comes off the back, almost a wake. I look up and take in the distant Skook, and circling mountains. My God, I'm twenty years old.

Water races past my white hull, jet black and cold. Anything could be under there. I get a sudden sense, also in my body, that something of my father is here, all the way down to the deeps. If he's anywhere, this is where he is. Nothing morbid in this notion at all. If anything it's the opposite. The cemetery of my father is grand and wild.

My idea is that I will troll while at anchor—the tide's that fast. I get the downriggers set up, and cannonballs clipped on, the rods rigged. A three-inch green Killy McGee spoon on one side and a Tiger Prawn hoochie on the other. I'm sitting over 120 feet of water, the current will take the gear down at an angle to where it's about 160. A prime spot. If there are any salmon near here, this is where they'd be.

Down go the cannonballs. I'm excited. I can't help but expect fish. As I always do, I visualize what it's like down there. One hundred feet down in the darkness. All a fish can see of these lures is the merest flash. A glimpse, a gleam of what might be food. Curious, a fish goes to it. Hungry, a fish takes it.

As always, I expect a strike right away. I expect a strike at all times. I am stricken with expectation, which is a state I must enjoy, because I think it's why I fish. It's like driving in your car and approaching someplace unknown but possibly wonderful.

I can almost see old Mr. Suzuki across from me, alone in his boat too—that ancient wooden runabout, painted red and white, sitting so low in the water that a two-foot wave might swamp it. (I just called him old; back then, he was likely younger than I am now.) Like me, he fished most every day and, like me, usually alone. A few times I saw him with grandkids, his manner with them reserved and quiet. He wore the shabby, grey wool clothes of a logger or commercial fisherman. Anchored sometimes thirty, forty feet apart, we never acknowledged each other. He never once initiated a wave or a nod, but he might have thought the same about me. No, he didn't seem the waving type. He looked like the kind of man who didn't deign to acknowledge a punk. And maybe he outright hated me, for what we'd done to him.

As rumour had it, Mr. Suzuki was an Egmont landowner and commercial fisherman when WWII broke out. He was interned, and the federal government sold his boat and land out from under him. A nice waterfront cottage, painted the same pink as Bathgate's store. Over the ensuing years he worked hard to re-establish himself, and by the time I got there he had retired and managed to buy a smaller place up the hill from his old place. No way he could afford waterfront. Rumour had it he could see his old place from his kitchen window.

My dad didn't like him, predictably enough. Because the Gap's prime spot wasn't all that big, we often sat in a fairly tight clutch of boats and close enough for my dad to keep an eye on him, which he did. It didn't help that Mr. Suzuki was the best fisherman around, likely the best I've ever seen, including Colly Peacock. I don't recall him ever getting skunked. Or, if everyone was getting skunked, he simply wouldn't show up, like he knew in advance.

Way too often my dad had to watch him drop anchor beside us, put his gear in, hook a big salmon, fight it for ten minutes, expertly net it, pull anchor and go home, when we'd been there all day with nothing. My dad, sitting there with glaring crew-cut, tilting a beer to his lips with an angry flick, called him "that sneaky Jap," almost loud enough for him to hear, the implication of "sneak attack" nothing but deliberate. Though not to his face, he'd refer to him this way at the cleaning table or the café. It didn't matter that Mr. Suzuki had been interned, lost his house, and all the rest. In case my dad forgot those details I informed him anew, plenty of times. It rankled. It reminded me how different our politics were, the gap so wide we sometimes couldn't see across to the other side.

The thing is, Mr. Suzuki *was* sneaky. Baiting his hooks, he would hunch forward so his low gunnel hid his hands. No one could see what size herring he used, or how big a weight, which told how deep he was going. Cupping both hands around herring and hooks and weight and leader, he lifted the whole hidden package over the gunnel and actually submerged his hands before letting it go. He knew we were all watching. I wonder if he knew how angry he made my father, or if he cared.

But many of the best fishermen are sneaky.

———

No strikes yet and I don't expect any. It's a beautiful day, a good time of year for the salmon to be running, and no one else is fishing. But I'm almost happy that I almost certainly won't be catching a salmon. I'm very glad I'm not using live herring for bait.

Just a little Buddhism.

It was a time of radical leftist politics, but also that of Eastern mysticism and suchlike, and those Egmont days also coincided with me becoming a Buddhist. It's funny how psychedelics were a gateway drug to religion. It was part of the era, but some of us stuck with it, for better or worse. Cults being all the rage in those days, and with me disappearing on retreats and sometimes during fishing season, I told my dad only enough to keep him from worrying. Though, unlike my mother, I doubt that he was. I think he knew that, like him, I wasn't a joiner.

I think I was skilful in presenting it. I didn't try to convert him. I probably said something like: "Buddhism isn't really a religion. It's a way to learn about your own mind. There are tools for this, the main one being meditation. It's hard because the mind is so slippery. Gurus are worth listening to if they're good at explaining the tools. But there are no rules, and you don't believe anything—anything—unless you verify it for yourself." I probably said less than that, even. He would have sat back in his chair, considering all or none of it, and said, "Interesting." But he'd ask, or offer, nothing more.

One effect Buddhism had on me was it made me question salmon fishing. Even in the Egmont days I pondered the killing. Not just the killing, but being the cause of suffering. Even worse, needless suffering.

Here I was, passionately hunting and killing salmon, employing a technique that used live bait. Out of thin air I'll guess that on average I killed a dozen live herring for every salmon I caught. Plus the odd grilse. Even harder to excuse: for every salmon I kept, I would also catch one or two rock cod that wouldn't make it back down to the bottom but get snatched up by eagles or—I don't like to admit this even now—would float along, inner ballast bag blown up like a balloon, flapping feebly, getting their eyes pecked out by gulls. To catch that one salmon, which I would club on the head for dinner or the freezer, I would kill a swath.

That's not all. The light-tackle, "sporting" way of fishing, favoured by passionate anglers like me, meant that I fought the fish for as long as possible—that is, playing it, extending the time I forced the fish to fight for its life, because its fight was my enjoyment.

Involvement in Buddhism took my views on killing to another level. Various schools have their own approaches to the subject, ranging from a sect that will sweep the bare earth in their path for fear of harming unseen insects, to those who simply refrain from eating meat. Tibetans and Mongolians, high-altitude people who adapted Buddhism to a climate where humans must eat meat or die, eat meat but won't kill the animals themselves. It's the taking of the life that's crucial, the idea being that if an animal happens to be dead it's fine to eat it. I've always found this approach a bit hypocritical, since it includes going to the grocery store and selecting a nice, cellophane-wrapped chunk of one of many of the animals in there that conveniently happen to be dead.

I broached this subject with more than one Buddhist teacher. What about taking responsibility for killing an animal you are going to eat? It was suggested that if I did kill something, I should try to bring my full awareness to the moment I stopped its consciousness. Mostly, I was told that I shouldn't turn away from its suffering.

"Suffering" being the key word here. Buddhism is at bottom a realistic approach and the rule is to cause as little suffering as you can. It counts that a fish's nervous system isn't very complex, and that it doesn't suffer as deeply as a mammal. I'm hoping that's the case, anyway. A fish in the wild lives in a constant state of heightened alertness, or call it fear—its big eyes that can't close are the very picture of this state—and I'm also hoping that its battle on the end of my line, a situation it probably can't comprehend, simply takes its constant state of panic up a notch. In other words, I'm banking on the science that suggests fish aren't capable of agony. Buddhism also says the fewer lives taken, the better, and that, to feed a village, kill one yak rather than fifty rabbits, because only one animal suffers. So it's better to kill one ten-pound fish than ten one-pound fish. It's also better not to use bait, which kills a bunch of little creatures in order to get the single one I plan on eating.

I tried it, the act of conscious killing. A salmon gulping air on deck, I brought as much awareness as I could muster to the moment. I stared at it, lying there alive. I felt the arc of the club coming down, the brute electricity of the *thwack*, the shock to my hand and arm. The suddenly empty, vacuumed quality of the fish, which I had just turned to meat.

I still don't know what to think about it, playing God. I still find it a challenge not to turn away from their suffering. It's still a work in progress.

In Egmont, I began to pull away from fishing. My dad and I never spoke about it, but I think the same thing was happening to him. We'd caught lots of salmon and it wasn't as thrilling as before. We were both tired of eating it. Often his freezer-load of salmon never did get eaten and he'd have to give lots away or throw it out. Sometimes his smoked salmon got mouldy in the fridge.

I remember the last time we fished Egmont together. Because the fishing was so much better near Pender Harbour we'd moved *Cormorant* there. But the fishing grounds weren't protected like Egmont, so one stormy day we decided to head back north up Agamemnon Channel and try good old Egmont again. We made the journey, bought some live bait at the marina, asked how the fishing had been lately, and were told that the Gap was still off, but yesterday some had been caught a hundred feet right out in front of the marina dock. We chuckled at this absurdity but cruised one hundred feet out and threw the anchor into thirty feet of water. We sat and sat, staring passively at our rod tips. We put on some music. We made dinner and ate it—the water so calm here it was like being tied at the dock already, so we might as well just stick it out till whenever. "We'll get the night bite," my dad added. I may have rolled my eyes.

Just as night was falling my dad tied into about a fifteen-pounder. It gave a spirited tussle in the shallower water. My dad loosened the reel's drag so it ran farther and the fight lasted longer, this the only bite we'd had all day. While I stood ready with the net, he got it almost to the boat. About six feet away it came partly out of the water, to its shoulders if a fish had shoulders, face pointing at us. It shook its head slowly back and forth, trying one tired last time to toss the hook. It did look like the fish knew a hook was in its mouth and the only way to free it was to shake its head exactly like that. I know it was my imagination, but the fish seemed aware of us too. Aware of the whole situation. But it was so tired. What head-shaking it could muster was too slow and weak to throw a hook. My dad and I watched.

"That's kind of sad," he said. He chuckled nervously. He was seeing what I was seeing. I knew then what I'd always suspected. He wasn't a natural born killer.

"It looks like it knows," I said.

We watched it watch us, slowly shaking its head.

"Kind of a shame to keep it," he said.

"Yeah."

"Probably wouldn't make it, though." Salmon this exhausted did not usually survive.

"No."

"The hook's down its gullet." We couldn't see either hook, only the line going into its throat. "Gullet" was one of my dad's words.

I netted the fish and clubbed it, and it ended up in my dad's freezer. I took a picture of my dad on the back deck holding it up, unconvincing smile on his face, man and fish lit too bright by a camera flash, because it was night now. For some reason I took the picture from a squat, which caught him from below, making him look fifteen feet tall and spectral, a looming ghostly giant raising a fish he didn't want.

Years later, when I was in town for Christmas and we were going through photo albums, I tapped the picture and asked him if he remembered that fish.

"That one shaking its head at us?"

———

How and why did I come back to killing salmon after thirty years? I don't know. It felt exciting again. I was back on the West Coast, I had a dental plan, I could afford a basic boat. But to tell the truth, it felt more like a second childhood. A primal urge came back.

I hunted around and cut a fresh club from the heavy wood of a fallen arbutus. I bring awareness to its moment of impact with a fish's head. Now when I keep a salmon, I try to use the whole creature. There's the grilled or smoked meat, of course; the guts are crab bait. I sometimes even boil the head for stock, because I make a mean Marseillaise stew, so good I might pause in the slurping long enough to thank the fish. Trolling with downriggers lets me use artificial lures, and no killing of bait anymore, even here in Egmont, as I fish the Gap.

I've tried different depths and lures now, even clipping on an old dare devil, red and white as a barber's pole, one of my dad's old standbys for pinks. But nothing doing. "Not even a smell," as he used to say. It's been a pleasant enough time sitting out here on *Sylvan's* deck, watching my two rod tips, my head on a swivel. But after a few fruitless hours I'm reminded of the Zen monk who was so filled with compassion for all sentient beings that, though he had nothing else to eat and lived beside a pond filled with carp, he could not bring himself to bait a hook and catch one. Instead he sat beside the pond holding his pole with line dangling over the water, unbaited hook a foot clear of the surface. The fish, so moved by his compassion and worried for his health, leapt out of the water to bite the hook, sacrificing themselves to be his dinner. It's a technique I have yet to try.

So the legendary Gap is fishless. And feels fishless. I'm not surprised but it's a bit depressing. I wonder how often Mr. Suzuki got skunked here and then how long he persisted before he gave up trying.

Pulling the anchor, I'm amazed at my reluctance. I'm always reluctant to quit fishing. I think I have a sickness. If God came down while I sat fishing and told me, officially, there were no fish swimming within one hundred miles of this spot, I suspect I'd be reluctant to reel in my line.

Back at the marina dock I manoeuvre around one end of it, wary of a low-tide rock on the left, and make for an inside berth, remembering this morning's crazy jostle. It wasn't fair of the owner not to warn me, so I'll brook no complaint from him about my grabbing a new spot without consulting him.

The dock fingers are small, the tide running. I'm not a good docker at the best of times. But I was always a bit better at it than my dad, I suspect much in the same way Gilligan was probably a bit better than the Skipper. I was living back east when my dad eventually sold *Cormorant*, largely because he had trouble docking it by himself, sober or not. In our defence, it's difficult to manoeuvre an inboard, because something called cavitation dictates that in reverse it turns only one way. So I'll blame cavitation, not vodka, on what apparently happened the third and last time my mother ever ventured out on *Cormorant* with him, an innocent cruise around Deep Cove—somewhere in his attempt to dock she flew over the bow railing, bounced off a creosote piling and landed on the planks, on her back.

I once got laughed at while aiming *Cormorant* at exactly the small span of inside dock I have *Sylvan* aimed at now. Coming in, closer and closer, with the tide running, instead of curling sideways to the dock in the proper manner I managed only to bump *Cormorant*'s nose into it, dead on. The hooting was instant. From the timbre of the owner's son's honking wheezes I could tell he was stoned, as were his two friends. I could also tell that they had seen me coming and had ventured outside for the sole purpose of watching me try to dock my boat. There wasn't much to do in Egmont and I was their entertainment. All three were bent over their knees. My dad, draining a beer and getting the lines ready, didn't notice them and I didn't point them out. I was a pretty bad docker, but still.

*Sylvan* doesn't cavitate and no one laughs at my dock job this time, though I think luck was on my side as I curl it in sideways, leap out and tie it up quickly, trying and largely succeeding to resemble a studly former charter boat operator.

The massive TV screen is showing the finale of what appears to be the America's Cup sailboat race. *Sailboat* should be in quotation marks. These craft are so high-tech they are steered by computer and their sails aren't even sails, but the wing of an aircraft, standing on end. I take a seat farthest from the screen. From tired chatter at a nearby table I confirm that last night's DJ Motown ranting was a wedding reception.

I have the menu cracked open, wondering if it's my imagination that I'm still feeling some faint reflux from last night's Skookumchuck burger, when a waiter spots me from behind the bar.

"You Bill?"

For the briefest moment I wonder if I've been recognized as a studly former charter boat operator, but then I know it's Dede calling, because she can track me effortlessly, everywhere. Then I'm worried something's amiss. She'll track me to a grocery store to add couscous to my list, but this is no trip to a grocery store.

It is in fact Dede and she wants me to call. I'm one of the last cellphone holdouts, and I do not want to ask the owner for the loan of his office phone, because that will truly nail me down as a codger. I wonder if it's possible the pay phone is still around back at the top of the boat launch and indeed it is, looking like abandoned equipment that's easier to leave alone than properly get rid of. I climb in, squeak closed its old door, and feel powerful déjà vu within its cramped glass walls. Back in the day I spent a lot of time in here. Tonight, standing in the silence before the call, I can feel exactly how lonely I was.

Dede needs some reassurance, and I try my best to give it to her. Should she be worried, she asks. Vaughn is up fighting wild fires in B.C.'s northern interior and today in the news was the story of the Hotshots, nineteen firefighters down in Arizona who got trapped when the wind shifted. They dug fast holes to climb into and covered themselves with space-age heat-deflecting fabric, and all were burned alive. It takes me a moment to speak, and then I remind her what Vaughn told us, that they always have two escape routes, and monitor any shift in the wind. She asks why is it they bother putting out forest fires anyway, and I spout out half the truth, which is that fires endanger local communities. I keep mum on the other half, which is that the timber's worth something to some corporation somewhere. Dede believes my reassurances about as much as I do.

She asks what Egmont is like, is it the same. She knows why I'm here, and doesn't ask for more when all I can tell her is that it's strange. I don't know how to describe that, here in this phone booth, time folds back on itself. Nor can I explain, though I'd like to, how I've just learned that I'm not lonely now like I used to be, decades ago. It's about having children, and her, and it's a difference I can feel in my body. Mostly I want to talk to Vaughn, hear his voice. I picture him at work and he's content enough, facing a wall of fire. He's wearing a protective suit. From our single conversation about it I know that he feels the heat mostly on his wrists, and neck.

———

I grew used to it, but for a while I was bothered that my two boys didn't take to the same stuff I did. Fishing in particular. That my two girls seemed to like fishing certainly helped, but not completely. My older daughter, Lise, can take it or leave it and I think she fishes because she knows it makes me happy. Only Lilli appears to love nature in the same mindless way I did, and do. The test is that she's curious even about the hidden and the ugly and the slimy. She's wanted to be a vet since a young child and nothing's changed. She volunteers at a local animal hospital, and though just fourteen had the job of administering anaesthetic and the little gas masks to all the famous wild bunnies trapped on the University of Victoria campus, so they could be sterilized then trucked away to live out their days on distant farms, one of which is in Texas.

But this spring Vaughn, nineteen, asked me to take him out and teach him to operate *Sylvan*. Needless to say I was excited, partly because I plotted to sneak in some fishing. I still have this notion that if he wins a long battle with a big chinook, he'll be hooked, so to speak. It's a foolish notion, because around Gabriola the chances of that kind of action are slim.

He was doing it for love. A long-distance girlfriend was coming from Australia and he wanted to impress her. We set out and he had fun cranking *Sylvan* up over twenty-two, twenty-three knots and leaning into some high-banked turns. He said it reminded him of a video game, but I think he was being ironic, as he knew that would be the last thing I'd want to hear. He was less thrilled with all the details I imposed on him—how to work the sonar, how to avoid the local reefs, how to set the anchor. But he had to know all this stuff, because he admitted he wanted to take his friend boat-camping. He got me to write all the details down, and asked if I knew of any sheltered coves.

Boat-camping is exactly the thing I'd love to do with Vaughn myself, but probably never will. I have only to take a breath, think back and picture myself at nineteen, and consider the question of who I'd want to boat-camp with—a girlfriend, or my father? Of course it's no contest. It's not even a question. It would be worrisome if my son chose me. It would be doubly worrisome if he did come and I had one too many beers and kept him awake all night with amplified snoring from the bow.

It's enough of a joy simply to have a son's attention. It's a rare thing to be able to tell a young man to turn due east, watch him do it at speed, and feel his appreciation. So I enjoyed the day. And after showing him how to rig the rods for cod in case Alice wanted to fish, I snuck in some angling. We hauled up a nice, dinner-size ling. And after demonstrating how to slice two fine fillets off the spine, I described the very best way to cook them: dredged in flour, fried in half butter, half olive oil, then lemon, then salt.

Vaughn is the only one in my family who looks like my father. Big eyes, a triangular face, high cheekbones. A face that exudes a wary privacy. He looks nothing like me. One day while grocery shopping in Fredericton, when he was one, I was wearing him in a front-pack when a drunk around fifty did a theatrical double-take on seeing him, and then me. He checked us both out again. Then the asshole chortled, "Must have been the mailman." I trust Dede completely, but there was some relief, if only so people wouldn't be suspicious, if only so Vaughn wouldn't be suspicious, when he began to look so much like my dad.

Genes are such tricksters. We know we aren't our parents, but sometimes we're made to wonder.

The Gabriola cabin has a massive sundeck on two sides—so big it's hard to know what we're supposed to do with it. Still leaving room for a wedding or a few dozen sunbathers, what I've done is line the perimeter with pots for my container garden. (In public I call it my "pot garden," and no one on Gabriola bats an eye.) I grow a variety of vegetables in fifty assorted pots.

Dede has jokingly worried about how much I seem to be turning into my father. There's the fishing, of course, and the sports, and the smoking of salmon, and also I used to smoke heavily, and there's been the sporadic over-the-top drinking, any bout of which sets her back into wary silence, despite the months and often years that go by without an incident.

Now there's the gardening. When my dad retired, two years younger than I am now, his main occupation became his garden. His sprawling backyard had always had a raspberry patch, but then he bought the best rototiller Sears could supply and turned the main slope into a garden. Over the next decade he grew tomatoes, beans, corn, peas, green peppers, cayenne peppers, pumpkins, squash, garlic, lettuce, red cabbage, and kohlrabi. He tried but had less success with broccoli and cauliflower. I remember all of this because, whenever I had dinner on my parents' deck on a late-summer evening, enjoying the bounty from the garden down below, my dad was loud about it.

"Whaddabout those beans?" he'd say.

"They're good," someone would answer, nodding, chewing.

"From the garden," he'd say.

He had a wooden shed installed against the bottom fence. In it he kept his supplies, including beer and sometimes bottles of the strong stuff, always hidden. And magazines on gardening. Once when I dropped by I found him tossing wooden matchsticks into a dozen fresh holes. It was for green-pepper transplants, he explained, and would "give them some phosphorous." Once I found him snipping string on a cauliflower plant he'd bound up, and him startled by the size of the tiny white head. He looked suspicious, like he'd been misled by the instructions he'd read.

"Whaddabout that cabbage?" he'd ask, up on the deck.

"It's good, it's great."

"From the garden." Brow knit, empty fork poised in the air, chewing carefully to test, he'd add, "Succulent."

His inability to taste led to a few disasters. Once, he decided to turn a large tomato crop into spaghetti sauce. He simmered it all day, stirring and tasting, murmuring "succulent," then jarred and froze ten quarts. I heard about the time the first jar was used, and can see it. It's summer, the sundeck.

"Whaddabout that sauce?" Nobody says anything, so he adds, "From the garden." And it's true—he's grown not just the tomatoes but the garlic, green pepper and cayenne peppers. Still no comment, so he supplies it. "Succulent."

No one speaks because they're standing up, spinning around, rushing inside for something cold. In his day of mixing and stirring, perhaps in an attempt to add something he could actually taste, he'd thrown in handfuls of cayenne peppers, red as tomato.

Another time, he followed a recipe for garlic-stuffed salmon, and used six bulbs of garlic because he thought "clove" meant bulb.

I love hot food myself, and grow several kinds of peppers in my deck pots, including habaneros and ghosts, both of which are too hot to actually cook with. It's hard not fishing for compliments. I probably chew the romaine with furrowed brow and poised fork, and ask what people think. Because I *babied* that lettuce, I plucked slugs, I rescued it from a week of no watering. Of course it's good. I know the voice of humourers. And I'm mocked, exactly like my dad was, by questions as to whether this pork chop or sausage was from the garden too.

My hair went grey prematurely, as his did, and now it's white, as was his. I'm the same height he was when he died. I often wear the last grey cardigan sweater that he owned. It all feels weird and comforting. Improbably, both.

I never met either of my grandfathers. But I feel I know my mother's father, who died when she was sixteen. He'd been a social activist, and my mother once used "the Wobblies" in discussing him. He was Jewish, something he hid, as did my mother, but one only had to look at my mother and her brother to think, well of course. One photo is remarkable. He has that manner of babyish face where you can't tell if he's eighteen or forty. He's dressed in a WWI uniform, the hat that of a Boy Scout leader. I'm taken with his eyes. They aren't relaxed; he's making them wide. They are bright, liquid and pleading. He's looking right through the lens, and it seems he can also peer through time, because he appears nothing but alive.

I've never seen a picture of my dad's father. Ozro. I don't know if a photograph even exists, or, if so, where it might be found. It's possible there isn't one. You have to wonder what kind of life has been led where no one cares to keep an image of you. I have no idea who he looked like. I wonder what part of me looks like him, because there's no doubt something does.

———

Trying to decide what kind of burger to get this time, I order a pint of something called Fat Tug. It's strong. Best be careful, it's only afternoon. Out of principle I never get a salmon burger, I suppose the principle being that it makes little sense to buy something you can make as well yourself. But I'm tempted to ask them where they get their salmon from, if only because it might give rise to a display of my snappy facetious wit, as I turn into a codger bragging about his exploits, stabbing a finger at the window—*right out front, right there, it was called the Gap.*

Saturday mid-afternoon, gone is the well-heeled lunchtime crowd, here at all because of last night's wedding, and the yachting race is now baseball. It looks like a few locals have come in specifically to watch the Blue Jays, which strikes me as strange, though I don't know why. A couple of rough-edged guys a bit older than me appear to be settling in for the long haul. One guy's unshaven, eyes suspiciously glassy. He could well be an Egmonster.

More casual in jeans and T-shirt, the same server as last night takes my order of a halibut burger. I've never caught a halibut, and in fact I don't know how.

I gaze out the window at the deliciously calm water of the Gap. One late afternoon about this time of year, and probably a Saturday because of the number of boats, a runabout full of local ruffians—Egmonsters—came out to terrorize us fishermen, our small fleet anchored there in the narrows. My dad and I were content aboard

*Cormorant* in the calm but crowded company of other boats because, fish or no fish, where would you rather be? But then out from the village dock roars this boatload of five or six maniacs. They looked down-and-out and in their late twenties or even thirties, too old for this sort of thing. You could hear their yelling and screaming over the noise of the outboard, no easy feat. They roared to the edge of the pack of peaceful fishermen, screamed nonsense, waved bottles, threw a few empties over a bow, did water doughnuts, and zoomed dangerously close to a boat or two. Mr. Suzuki was there and he calmly regarded them as they roared close.

A more macho type in another boat, I think also into the beer, brandished a gaff hook and stabbed the air with it, which only inflamed the drunks and their boat quickly swung round and came alongside, almost like a pirate ship positioning itself to fire cannons and hurl grappling. A guy in the drunk-boat used a paddle to fence with the guy's gaff. In a gesture of solidarity all the other boats began sounding horns and yelling at the brigands. My dad and I didn't. The bad boat pulled away and did a few more doughnuts and, tired or maybe just out of booze, the Egmonsters turned and headed back in the direction of the government dock. Doing so they crossed twenty feet off the stern of *Cormorant*, giving us the finger as they did.

Due to the Egmont tides our lines trailed way out behind our boat, right near the surface. When their boat passed over them, our lines got taken by their engine leg and suddenly both our reels were screaming as line peeled off at the speed of their boat. My dad and I stood, breathless, barely holding on to the crazy, screaming rods—it was as if the bad, monstrous energy of that boat had leapt to the small machines we held in our hands. The boat diminished with distance, the Egmonsters' fingers still up—fishermen themselves, they knew what they were doing to us. My dad was standing tall, not angry, too surprised to be angry. We held on. In the nine or ten seconds it took to strip our reels of the rest of their line, before snapping off the spindle, he briefly met my eyes. He was thrilled, gentle, and didn't have a clue, and his eyes were nothing but a child's.

# TEN

*Perhaps, in general, dying men make poor navigators.*
—D.W. WILSON, *Ballistics*

The Backeddy halibut burger is to be recommended, not fishy at all. And it isn't so huge that my pint of Fat Tug doesn't feel like one more. But it's too early for another, and anyway I don't want to. I'm happy when I decide to go for a walk.

The marina's dirt driveway up to the main road is steep and makes me feel my burger, my beer, and my age. I've decided to hike the trail to the Skookumchuck rapids, despite the amazing news of a grizzly being shot in the area last month, the first grizzly in living memory here. No one knows what to make of it. Carla, my server, told me that on a hike to the Skook I had way more chance of getting mauled by "a pack of Chinese tourists."

Up on the road, I'm literally walking on my old footsteps. Despite the decades, it feels only familiar. It's not just the road or trees, many of which, the big ones at least, I remember as individuals. I'm also feeling my old self. This is exactly how I felt—walking alone, just like this, a little lonely, passing this big cedar stump. Shouldn't I feel different? Shouldn't I know more, at least?

I reach Vera's campground but its sign is gone. There's just the dirt driveway up into a thick stand of alders I can't see beyond to determine if it's still a campground or not. Wouldn't there be a sign? A little farther along the alders are still too thick to let me see anything. I decide to decide that Vera's is someone's private property now and my search would be unwelcome. Nor am I sure I want to see my tent's sad metal skeleton, twenty-foot alders spearing up through it.

Following more old footsteps I turn right at the junction—the tiny post office standing all alone next to a weedy baseball diamond—and head up to the lake, after which I'll find the trailhead to the Skook. I did this walk so many times I could do it with eyes closed.

Here's the lake where I washed my hair, and my scalp would no longer itch. I think it was because I was so alone and the day so silent that I can still feel the itch, then the difference after soap. Then the smell of my skin drying in the sun. The wide mouth of an empty afternoon. I can feel my time in this place as a time I was seeking to find myself, or make myself into someone, I'm not sure how that works. Or worked. But, alone, I got to know well my main urges, and the array of voices in my head.

I knew that friends thought I was a bit weird, because I fished all the time and because I was so often alone. Living alone was downright strange. What was my problem? Stranger still, I had a recurring fantasy. I dreamed of being even more alone, going even farther away, north, farther into the bush. I loved all back-to-the-land stories of communes, or squatters. I loved hearing about hermits, living "up there" all alone. I absolutely loved meeting that hermit, not much older than me, who kayaked down to civilization—that is, Bathgate's store—twice a year to pick up and cash a government cheque, buy flour and sugar and hooks, then off he'd go. I buttonholed him once in the produce section, and he let loose a waterfall of words, describing how he made his shack out of plywood from an abandoned logging camp, though he wouldn't say what inlet, and how he had lifelong disability cheques for his schizophrenia—I'm sure I heard the wink in his words as he said this—and that he spent his time mostly reading, and fixing up his shack, and how once he broke his leg falling off a small cliff but had accelerated the healing of the bone through a concentration of will. He held my gaze saying this, and he seemed perfectly at ease and sane.

I dreamed of building a shack, or living on a boat, even one as small as *Cormorant*, way up some nameless inlet, no one else around. I would be happy, if not enlightened, and never bored. The only recurring factor in all of these daydreams was that there was no one else around.

The entrance to the Skook trail now has a tourist information building. An arched sign announces the Skookumchuck Narrows Provincial Park. Vehicle parking has been carved into the woods on both sides of the road, and two dozen cars sit in orderly rows waiting for their owners. Four young people, Asians, are disappearing into the darkness of the trailhead, the size and density of the trees making quite an impressive tunnel. One guy snaps continuous selfies of his group, and shouts commands excitedly, with his free hand choreographing them into his viewfinder. To my chagrin I see I've been hearing their language as Japanese, though I'm pretty sure it isn't.

———

Recently we put down our dog, Blackjack. He never did get to see our place on Gabriola, which is a dog's paradise. He wouldn't have done the car ride well, and he was too old to enjoy the place anyway. It might have killed him, trying to chase a deer, or duck. Come to think of it, it would have been a better way to go. *Bark,* down.

We got him, for free, at a farm in New Brunswick, a place called Tay Creek, a rural crossroads where, incidentally, the major-league baseball player Matt Stairs is from. Sometimes, watching baseball on TV, I'd see Stairs come to bat and say to Blackjack, "There's your daddy." I'd say this only with someone else besides Blackjack in the room, of course. Usually no kid cracked a smile, having heard my joke once too often.

A vet came to our house to do it. We'd set the appointment a week earlier, and naturally in the meantime Blackjack was extra-sweet, wagging his tail like mad at any sight of you, and once he tried to romp, which looked pathetic, given the withered back legs. If anything, we'd let it go too long. He was incontinent, and our living-room carpet had become his big sprawling diaper. Some friends didn't understand our letting him live this long; others understood completely. A mix of the three most intelligent breeds of dog, Blackjack had a kind of clairvoyance about each family member and their moods. He was part of the family, to be sure, and he loved protecting us. It was horrible to end his life. Sobbing, I fed him a fistful of cheese as his leg was shaved and a needle inserted. He died chewing cheese, with a mound of lovely cheese-to-come waiting on the floor in front of his one good eye.

Putting Blackjack down reminded me of my dad in three big ways. Even in the midst of my sobbing I thought of him, dead twelve years.

First I thought of Ricky. Ricky was my main dog growing up, and the name of my dad's childhood dog in Mukilteo—he revealed this as we were trying to name this new dog we'd just bought in a pet store near the Sears in Burnaby. She was a border collie–German shepherd cross, soiled with her own shit as she sat cutely in her cage, her big eyes prime bait for anyone out buying a dog. All of us were suckers for her, my dad most of all, though he tried to hide it.

We named her Ricky even though she was female. Any detail from my dad's boyhood was so rare. That he'd had a dog named Ricky was one of the only things I knew about him at that point. He appeared to like our choice of name for her.

Another reason Blackjack's death reminded me of my dad was because, when our well-loved Ricky got cancer and was taken to the vet to be put down, it was the one time I saw my dad cry. When I returned from my mission to the vet, where I said goodbye but didn't stay to watch, my dad had in the meantime come home from work and met me in the front hall where we hugged and sobbed in each other's arms. Over Ricky, though it felt like it was for more than just Ricky. It was the only time my dad and I did something like that. I could smell booze but didn't care. Chests heaving against each other, helpless against it. When we parted we walked in different directions.

There's a third reason I thought about my dad, though here something feels ungracious to be comparing my dad to a dog. I was driving with Connor the day before Blackjack's scheduled euthanasia and I asked him if he wanted to be present for it. He thought awhile, then decided he wanted to pass. He didn't seem all that broken up about it in general. He added, "He hasn't been much of a dog lately." This was perfectly accurate. Blackjack hadn't done much more than sleep for a long time. Awake, he was deaf, almost blind, flatulent, demented, and he barked in a geriatric rasp non-stop for no discernable reason. He couldn't go for a walk, let alone play. He'd been slowly dying for some time now, and passing from view as he did.

———

Aging does speed up. We will grey and stoop and squint with a gathering velocity that looks weirdly vigorous. During the dozen years I lived in the Maritimes, my father aged and diminished in ways I wasn't around to witness daily, so my yearly visits were a shock. More stooped, more wizened, more *an old man*.

Both my father and mother were always so proud of his height. A man who could not fit in a plane to fight WWII. Who always made a big deal of not being able to fit "Jap cars" and complained proudly of not being able to borrow my mother's Toyota when his car was in for repairs. So it had come to pass that, in the deeps of some anonymous night, I had reached *exactly* his height. And then I was taller.

In those years he diminished in my mind too. With two, then three, then four children of my own, and living four thousand miles distant, and chasing part-time teaching jobs and freelance writing to keep the fridge full, I didn't dwell on my parents' lives as much. Our sole contact was that Sunday phone call, trading the week's details. During these calls I gleaned what I could about my dad's developing dementia—"vascular dementia," brought on primarily by decades of two- and three-pack-a-day smoking that squeezed off oxygen to his brain. That alcohol had also taken its toll was a given, but never elaborated on in medical terms.

I'd always call, my mom would always instantly answer, and she would always call my dad to the phone. My mom and I would cover some basics, often involving Sears-catalogue birthday presents for someone in our house, and eventually we'd hear my dad pick up. Then my mother would quickly say, "I'll let you two talk," as if we had some special father–son issue we couldn't wait to share, and hang up.

"How're the kids?"

He'd ask this because this is what is asked. It got me talking for a couple minutes, listing recent triumphs. I'd sneak Dede's in too, and get going on mine, but somewhere along the line my dad was no longer listening, I could tell. All his energies were spent maintaining the sounds of conversation, saying "right" and chuckling. He seemed bored in the way a stranger might, but knew he had to feign attention to this person who was his child. It got to the point where nothing I said on the phone had a chance of piquing his interest, let alone sticking. Not even that his grandson's middle name was, legally, not Robert but Bob, in his honour. I saw that the death of a brain was definitely a kind of death. When I realized he wouldn't find amusing the cool story about little Vaughn's first multi-syllabic word, spoken at the dining-room table the night before in front of company—the word was "bonesy-fuckin'"—why even tell him? I did tell him, but with a certain dullness of voice, almost a talking-to-myself. It reminded me of the days when I wouldn't bother telling him stuff because he wouldn't remember for another reason.

Yearly visits gave me harder evidence of his waning. He'd always done the Vancouver *Province* crossword, a fairly easy one, and did it fast and confidently, with a pen. On one visit I found one, still done in pen, but with blank squares and mistakes, corrections penned in darker. A year later I found one with a single letter penned into a single box. And it was wrong. This was the trip when my mother whispered all the sad developments to me, like how he'd forgotten the way the coffee maker worked, and how—something I'd already noticed—his favourite noun had become "thing." *Bring me that thing.* *Put the thing in the thing.* He'd often say it with a wry little smile, as if he was being ironic and could say the right word if he wanted to.

Literally at a loss for words, my dad showed me the process I would later witness in my mother, and to some extent, already, myself. It's a fuller-blown version of the tip-of-the-tongue phenomenon, the one we all experience when we can't "find" someone's name, yet we can see them perfectly and know what they were wearing the last time we saw them. I grew used to my dad, his expression now one of lessening humour, impatiently trying to say *mailbox* and describing it as "You know, that thing, it's red, it's on street corners, there's one there in front of the Raes' house, and you walk to it, and you've written this thing to somebody and put *stamps* on it and you shove it through the *slot*. You know, *that* thing." Evidence of the main culprit were two fingers stained dark brown, and the centre of his white forehead cowlick above stained blond. A cigarette still dangled from his lips.

One night Dede called me to the phone. My mother. It wasn't Sunday. My father had fallen out on the driveway while fetching the Vancouver *Province*, where the paper boy had thrown it, and his hip had broken. She was home from the hospital, where Dad awaited surgery. He had fallen five, six hours ago and I was vaguely angry that she'd waited this long to tell me.

"What's the prognosis?" I asked. He was over seventy. He had dementia. He wasn't in shape. I knew what broken hips did to some old people.

"The prognosis is that he gets better. What did you *think* the prognosis would be?" I could hear the fear in her voice, but it was her turn to be angry. She insisted there was no need to fly back.

I did anyway. Things had gone sideways. Hallucinating while suffering both DTs and severe nicotine withdrawal, he wasn't properly restrained by belts and he clambered from bed and fell, rebreaking his hip, and during the operation suffered a series of small strokes. Now he was strapped to his hospital bed, mostly unaware of where he was and loud about it, hated by the nurses for being unruly. My mother tells me on the drive in from the airport to the hospital that he seemed mentally out of control.

And it was true—even asleep he was nothing but restless with demons. A heavy smoker and sometime quitter now myself, I raced off and returned with the strongest nicotine patch I could get, stuck two on him, and he settled right down. (There is so much genius in the medical profession, but this was also around the time hospital workers finally solved the mystery of why so many post-op patients developed such mysterious headaches: a forced withdrawal from coffee.)

Not many months later I miraculously landed a job back on the West Coast, in Victoria. Dede and I were both self-employed and tired of it; we had a fourth child on the way and at least one of us needed a job with security and a dental plan. It was great luck that this job happened to be in a pretty city a two-hour ferry ride from where my father was hurrying toward his end. We moved, and a year went by with as many ferry rides and visits as I could manage. There wasn't much quality time or in-depth communication. He was at home, in a hospital bed moved into the TV room, right under the "Gaston Makes All-American" picture. Eyes open, he'd stare puzzled at his fingers as they straightened invisible sheet edges, or swept off invisible insects. He improved a bit and could walk with a cane but couldn't progress beyond an odd, exaggerated shuffle. He never again dressed in anything but pyjamas, bathrobe, and slippers.

My mother worked hard as his only caregiver, taking years off her own life. He called his hip a foot, and no way he could come up with the word *coffee*, or *water*, or even the name he used to be able to put to your face. Channel 2 was "two two two." And over the months he drifted and drifted, a slow fade, not just for him but for anyone who knew him. One Sunday my mother called Victoria and reported finding my dad standing beside his bed, shuffling on the spot, crying because he'd forgotten how to move forward.

Then he wasn't talking anymore at all. It got harder to get him out of a bed, or a chair. After encouragement from all sides my mother finally let him go, to live with three other old men, all immobile stroke victims, in a room in extended care. She donated the extra-tall hospital bed. She had to order and buy a special wheelchair, one that was longer and could fold down almost into a lying position, which was the only position he could tolerate now without moaning angrily and flailing his left arm. My mother was proud buying a special chair for someone extra-tall, though that no longer described him.

I visited from Victoria. I thought he looked handsome and young and aware compared to his three roommates, two of whom were staring mouth-breathers. One visit, the timing was right for me to take him for a spin around the grounds in his long wheelchair, though he moaned reprimands at me if I took a corner too fast or hit a rut. I fed him, bringing soup to his face, which he'd lower an inch to accept the spoon, an act that felt as awkwardly intimate as the first time I told him I loved him. More intimate, even. Flesh and blood. Life and death.

No longer walking, no longer talking, occupying less physical space—surely this is a kind of dying. But none of it prepared me for the real thing. That one invisibly explosive *moment*. I'm still comparing a dog's death to my dad's, and I apologize to anyone offended by that, but these two deaths—my father, my dog Blackjack—are the two I've witnessed. That last breath. That endless gap between the last breath and the one that never does come. That gap is incomprehensible.

———

He was seventy when we last fished together. I was visiting from down east and he chartered a boat and guide near Pender Harbour, out of the Jolly Roger Inn, where we stayed. He'd always liked the Jolly Roger, the pirate flag that is, with its skull-and-crossbones logo, and once he bought one, a small pennant, for *Cormorant*. He explained to me in his formal Sears voice that any pleasure craft displaying this flag while anchored, or at dock, signalled an open invitation to come aboard for a drink. He did raise our Jolly Roger once or twice, when he was well into it and wanted a fellow pirate to *har* with, but no one came aboard. Nor have I seen this flag in action at marinas elsewhere. Maybe it's American.

Dad brought along his good mooching rod and reel, the reel in its original padded case, and the rod, a Shakespeare, broken down and stowed in a long carry-case, identical to what pool sharks use to transport their cues. He made a big deal about his gear while assembling it in front of Mike, our guide; he sex-whistled when he tested the drag.

Mike, muscular and bespectacled, was the kind of local I thought of as "bush Marxist," an unschooled but highly intelligent guy who worked in resource industries, mostly logging and fishing. They tended to harbour opinions. Mike lacked a sense of humour, or at least my dad's brand, and spent much of the morning smiling politely for him when he had to, and then eventually not smiling at all. My dad explained that his reel was his "special lefty reel, hard to find." It was a good reel, a high-end Longstone, but if you simply unscrewed the line guide and reassembled it on the opposite side, it became a right-handed reel. All mooching reels were made this way. What would be rare is a mooching reel that *wasn't* also a lefty. My dad sort of knew this, but also sort of didn't, depending on his "mood." In any case, Mike didn't know what to make of him.

We zoomed across to the southern tip of Texada Island to begin our six-hour charter. Anchored in a little bay, Mike began a long-winded explanation about what mooching is and how he had his own customized version. Though I'd never fished this particular bay before, we were near my old stomping grounds and to tell the truth I'd been competitive with this guide from the moment I woke up that morning. My dad had already done my bragging for me, fishing instead of hockey this time, and Mike was patient while enduring his exaggerations about my guiding exploits of twenty years before.

Mike demonstrated baiting the hook. His mooching technique was quite different, in that, instead of using two treble hooks he used but a single small hook and inserted it—*plick*—through the herring's nostrils. So lightly punctured, the herring could stay alive and swimming down there for hours. But Mike's main technical difference was patience. Just like a goldfish, he explained, salmon will suck food in then quickly spit it out. In, out, several times. Then if he likes it, he'll swallow it. Because of this single, small hook, the salmon won't feel anything odd, it'll feel like a yummy herring. So the main thing to do if you think you're having a bite, is simply to wait. And wait and wait. Let the salmon tell you when it's swimming away with the herring down its throat. He urged us to *please* not waste any strikes by reacting impatiently—fishing had been slow these last weeks and we might only get one chance at a salmon.

He asked if we wanted to handle our own rods, or have him play the bite, set the hook, then pass it to us. I probably chuckled and rolled my eyes. It's what I used to do for clients and friends—see the rod tip go slack, reel like mad, set the hook, hand the rod off. My dad and I assured him we'd handle our own rods, and I might have made noises to the effect that the only reason Mike was here with us at all is because we needed a boat.

To make a long story mercifully shorter, I blew my one chance. Mid-morning, I had a bite, some nibbles that came and went—the sucking in, the spitting out. It was so hard not to react. In my day, I'd have begun reeling like a bastard, feel the weight, set the hook, fish on. Why was I letting this fish spit out the damn bait? I angled the rod tip into the water, reeled in just a little, thought I felt some weight, and struck. Nothing. Fish spooked. I looked to Mike, who turned away to gaze back to the mainland. I could hear him breathing, in and out.

I got no fish that day but happily my dad got two, one of them about fifteen pounds. He was content as we zoomed back in, not just for the nice fish, and not just because he was quite pissed by then, but because he could mock me.

"So you thought you could take on your Old Sea Father."

"I guess I'll never learn."

"That might have been a nice one there, right at the start. But you missed it."

"I guess I did."

"So you thought you could take on your Old Sea Father."

I'd had two beers, but only that. I knew it would be our last time fishing together, though nothing had been said. Mike had been offered beer perhaps six hundred times, and only the first several times did he bother explaining that he never drank while working. But his mood was fine on the trip back to the Jolly Roger dock because he'd found us two, and if you counted mine, three good fish and his workday was done.

The instant we docked my dad said to us both, "I have to ske-daddle up to the bathroom. Must be the damn beer. Really have to go," in the loud and over-explanatory mode that meant something else entirely.

I watched Mike clean the fish. He was more expert at that too.

"Your dad's quite the character," he said, not looking up, elbows jigging out as he parted flesh from bone as smoothly as a sushi chef. His tone communicated appreciation but also sympathy.

"He is," I said. I don't know why, but I added, "He grew up troll-ing for salmon from a rowboat, with the line wrapped around his foot."

My dad came back down quite drunk. As he watched Mike finish up he teetered back on his heels, breathing heavily.

"Really had to go," he said.

Mike bagged the red-orange fillets and handed them to me. My dad came up to him and held out his rod and reel, which I had taken apart and put in their cases.

"Take this," he said to Mike. "My special lefty."

"What? No." Mike looked to me for help. "Hey, no thanks."

"You're a great guide," my dad said. "Thank you. You're just great."

"Don't give your stuff away, Dad."

"Here," he said, staring down at it and giving it a shake. "I don't need it anymore." He was on the verge of teary and dramatic.

"Thanks, but I have lots and lots of gear. And you'll need it," he said.

"We'll go out again, Dad."

He ignored me. He lifted the reel and gently waggled it. "You gotta have one for a lefty."

Mike didn't know what to say or do. My dad brushed past him, went to his boat and stooped down, almost falling. He tossed the rod and reel onto the front seat. Straightening up, he gave us his dramatic profile of looking out to sea, then he turned and kept walking, back up to the Jolly Roger bar.

———

When I think of death, when I get close and touch the icy truth of my coming non-existence, I'm terrified. It's a common terror, I understand. If you happen to be free of it, if you're comfortable with death, I envy you more than I envy anyone. I'm not as afraid of the dying part—the disease or accident, or the pain. There are drugs for that. I think I could "survive" that, so to speak. It's more the death part I'm afraid of. I don't want to leave this place. I can't bear leaving my children, my wife, my body, my mind. I don't want to non-exist. This self that exists simply cannot conceive of not.

Life is the most miraculous thing imaginable. Sandwiched between two eternities, we are glorious mystery meat. As Vladimir Nabokov mused, isn't it interesting that we aren't concerned or even curious about the first eternity, before our birth, while the second one ties us in a knot. It's scary as hell. Fear *is* hell. If ever you need sobering up, listen to Woody Guthrie's "Little Black Train." It's coming.

I never asked my father about death or what he thought of it. If he thought there was an afterlife, for instance. If he was afraid. None of my kids have asked me about these things either. Maybe it too obviously doesn't matter what I think, since they know I can't possibly know anything more than they do, and why even ask? Anyone who's loud and certain about heaven or hell is the least convincing. We're all ignorant, frightened children here, we're together on this one. We have this biggest thing in common, no hierarchy possible.

It would be wonderful someday to announce to my children that I don't fear death, and then say something wise and convincing. I doubt this will ever happen.

Maybe children don't ask a father about death because he's the last person they want to see afraid.

My dad did joke about it. He'd hear of someone's deathbed struggle, or on TV see someone kept alive with wires and tubes, and say, "When I get like that, chop me up for the bait bucket." It's no surprise we almost never talked seriously about death, since we talked seriously about virtually nothing, except, sometimes, the Canucks' playoff chances, or when the bite might come on.

But there was one time. It wasn't really a conversation. He was ten years retired and his dementia had started up, though we didn't know yet that dementia is what it was. He was sunk heavily in his recliner, dulled from more than his daily quota of beer, his cause for celebration my visit from back east. We were watching TV, not saying much. He began mumbling, mostly to himself.

"I'm gonna die, you know," he said, apropos of nothing. The almost singsong quality sounded like he said this often, and to himself. From his tone I could tell this was different from one of his brain tumour announcements.

"Yeah, I guess you are," I said. "Me too." I wanted to swing it away from the maudlin, or the made up.

"No," he said. "It's gonna happen. I really am." He stared harder at the TV, seeing it less. I could tell he was feeling its reality and was afraid.

"I guess so," I said. "But not for lots of years."

He didn't respond. Then he said what I've never forgotten, and what I would remember, not that many years later, on the day he did die. What he said to himself was a soft, intense, *"I wonder how I'll do?"*

———

I'd seen dead bodies, but I'd never seen anyone die.

I saw three bodies when I was younger, all within a five-year period. Each incident was sad but colourful. First, I was hitchhiking back to Vancouver from Long Beach, on Vancouver Island, light was falling and it was storming out, and three guys squeezed in the front of a pickup stopped for me. It was a work truck, Canadian Coast Guard, and I'm still not sure if it was actually a practical joke. Rolling down his window, a guy in a uniform yelled something about a fish boat and this very storm, and I was welcome to ride in back if I didn't mind riding "with the body." He hooked a thumb to indicate someone lying in the back of the truck, zipped into a cloth bag. I hopped in, sat against the cab wall and off we went. The cloth was thin enough for me to make out the poor guy's nose, brow, chin. The head bounced inanely during washboard stretches of gravel road, and swayed almost coyly when the truck took corners. I rode with that body until Port Alberni, where the truck stopped under a street light, the driver rapped on the window, and I hopped out.

The second body resulted from a violent event. Late one night a friend and I were playing board hockey on the living-room floor of a house we rented, and an explosion outside rattled the house, a horrendous collision of two cars right in front. We raced out to encounter one guy, maybe twenty, bloody-faced, climbing out of his black

Mustang, moaning about his ruined new car, which steamed loudly through its crumpled hood. He was drunk. He'd hit the driver's side of a station wagon, which was empty, windows blown out. I searched the vicinity and saw the top of a head doming the water of the roadside ditch. A neighbour helped me drag the man out. He was missing a foot, and one look at the boneless bag of his collapsed abdomen told me he was dead. I remember his empty khaki pant-leg and that there was no blood coming from his footless leg.

The third body was the strangest. Travelling solo through Europe after the winter playing hockey in France, I was enjoying lots of beach time in Rethymnon, on Crete. In the hostel I'd heard talk of the town's well-known witch, an eccentric who always wore a gold chain-mail dress. One hot day, lying on the sand half-asleep, I was roused by a pair of bare female feet inches from my nose, and weird shouting. I rolled over to see a woman dressed neck-to-ankle in gold chain mail. She pointed at my face and shouted, "Boy in water! You help!" Emphasizing the *you* she jabbed her finger at me.

She pointed down the beach where a group had gathered. Somehow I knew what had happened. I also somehow knew that she had chosen me out of everyone on this beach because I was a lifeguard, or used to be. How *she* knew, I had no idea. I got up and sprinted to the crowd, broke through to two men making clumsy attempts on an unconscious young man, pumping his knees into his torso. I knelt on the sand at the fellow's head, pinched his nose and started mouth-to-mouth. I took his pulse with my free hand, felt none, and began CPR. The only other time I'd done any of this was during my lifeguard exam, when I performed mouth-to-mouth on the other guy being examined, a friend of mine, who rhythmically flicked his tongue into my mouth as a joke. This Greek fellow wouldn't be doing that. His eyes were partly open, skin cold, no pulse. As a result of the leg pumping, on the sand around his head was a halo of chewed feta, cucumber and olives from his lunch, which now I could also taste. The witch had arrived and cleared a space, giving me room to work, shouting at men in the crowd who shouted back at her. I kept working, though I didn't have high hopes, and through my sideways glances I saw her begin circumambulating us, shaking some kind of rattle and warbling a chant. Not knowing what else to do, I persisted. After maybe five minutes a doctor was kneeling across from me, and he took over the chest compressions. A minute later he put a hand on mine and gently got me to stop.

That was what I'd seen of death. But, as many people know, to see life stop is another thing altogether. My father is the only person I've seen die, and as he was dying I remembered him asking, *"I wonder how I'll do."* I was to be alone with him in a room for six hours while he did it.

———

We fished so much together and, looking back on it, I have to admit that he sometimes did pull a rabbit out of the hat.

I was fifteen when we entered the annual Sears fishing derby in Horseshoe Bay. There were three stores in the lower mainland and one across in Victoria, and over a hundred Sears employees entered. The first prize was a small boat and motor. We launched our old Winnipeg lake boat there in Horseshoe Bay and the derby boundaries didn't extend very far beyond. Even in those days that part of Howe Sound was getting fished out, so expectations weren't high.

Everyone trolled. Trolled and trolled, following each other in circles over old hot spots. Half the boats were rentals, the blue SEWELS logo plastered on the side. You could tell from the way many of the rental-boat fishermen handled their rods that they didn't know what they were doing. Instead of keeping the rods in holders, and as far from the other rods as possible, preventing tangles, they held the rods carelessly, swinging them around, crossing them over, even play sword-fighting. I couldn't imagine the birds' nests they were dragging behind the boat. But you could see bottles swigged and passed; they were having a good time. It was just my dad and I in our boat, and he wasn't drinking. I'd already seen that he never drank in front of employees.

We saw hardly any nets come out. The few salmon we did see boated were "tiddlers," as my dad called them. The weigh-in deadline was two. It was past noon and getting on one.

"We have a shot here," my dad said, seeing nothing much caught. "I should throw down a cut plug."

We were trolling just off Bowen Island in front of a white-house-with-flagpole, a famous spot for springs. We reeled up and he took the flasher and big weight off his rod, replacing it with a small weight and single large hook. He laid a fresh herring on a board and pro-ceeded to decapitate it.

"You *bevel* it," he said, enjoying the word. He cut the head off at a particular angle, inserted the hook near where the head used to be. He dropped the rig in the water, picked up the rod and pulled it along to get the herring to roll and flash.

He whistled the whistle, then, "Sexy."

I ran the motor. He'd say "neutral," and let his line down to the bottom. We had no depth sounder; it was all by feel. Hitting bottom, he'd say "forward," and I kicked the motor into gear, which raised his line, a slow troll. Then back to neutral, the line fell, then forward, and up it came. This was "motor-mooching," he explained. He was all intent now, holding his rod carefully in hand, poised with it as if he actually expected a bite. Why had we been trolling all this time if this was how you did it, I wondered.

He got a strike. At least he said it was a strike. Judging from his rod tip, it was more like the nibbles you got fishing for pickerel. But then the rod bowed and he struck back, and he had a fish on.

He caught a spring, not huge, but bigger than the tiddlers we'd seen. It was a quarter to two.

"Whaddya think?" he asked me. "Keep fishing or see if this wins something?"

I wanted to see if it won something. We roared in, pulling up to the weigh-in dock with two minutes to spare. A few coho were up on display, with tags on.

"Jeez," he whispered to me, dismayed. "This might *win*."

I asked him what was wrong with that.

Carrying his fish, head down, he approached the crowd at the weigh station. "The boss shouldn't win. I already *have* a boat." Already spotted, he couldn't turn back. Seeing us, a few hopeful faces fell.

Our spring was only nine pounds but it won. We were handed a glossy photo of our new boat and motor, a ten-foot fibreglass with a five-horse Evinrude. I never did see the boat in the flesh, because my dad sold it that week. I suspect someone got a good deal. He didn't enter the Sears derby again.

But he did sometimes look expert. Motor-mooching, the bevelling of heads to win a derby. Yet so much else was clearly malarkey. Ferries chewing up the herring? Salmon slapping your bait with their tails. The night bite?

My last summer in Egmont, Ray, the new friend who had shown me the ropes in previous summers, fishing in his car-topper and testing lures professionally, appeared at the marina with a big new boat. It was his uncle's twenty-foot Grew. He'd bragged about it, calling it the Cadillac of boats, and now here he was docking it in sunglasses, sitting tall. He had some new gear to try out. He invited me aboard "the Grew."

First he had to show me everything about the boat, from high-end spark plugs to the "velvet drive" gearbox. He didn't smile when I asked him what happened if the velvet wore out. Ray was likable but straight-ahead. When we were doing all that fishing together and two of my crazy friends came up to party, he faded into the background and I knew he saw me differently thereafter. The thing is, he'd had an interesting, hardscrabble life, a frail white guy growing up on the reserve under the Lions Gate Bridge, and had stories of knifings and worse. Hard liquor was ordinary sin to him, but when weed was passed around the campfire he went silent. Some people just didn't trust artist types or hippies.

But fishing buddies are like teammates whose lifestyle quibbles are easily cast aside in the common passion, all eyes on the prize. Ray and I went out in his Grew. It was evening, the bite in the Gap was long over, so we went over to Egmont Point to drift with live herring and shoot the shit, in particular discuss what had just happened at the marina café. We'd just had Bev's ling cod and chips and Helen's famous clam chowder. As we finished up, Bev approached us acting strangely shy.

"You two are like sons to me," is what he said, for starters. It was odd seeing Ray as a brother, him a foot shorter, fine-boned and dark and hirsute, everything I was not. The previous summer Ray and I had frequented the café, supplying it with fresh fish in return for meals, and on occasion Bev, probably sixty, sat at an adjoining table and told us tales from his youth in England. They weren't that interesting as tales go, and Bev had the self-conscious air of an old man telling young men, well, some tales.

"If you agree, I want to name you both executors of my will."

Neither of us understood, so he explained. The upshot was that he and Helen had no children and, as executors, we'd get a portion of his estate when he died. He didn't have much, he said, no house or anything like that, but he had "savings." He grew teary as he said this. I knew that Ray was feeling as weird as I was. Bev was just not a person you felt close to. It was sad in spades that we were two he felt were the most like his sons. When he finished we voiced our loud sentiments that we sure hoped this wouldn't come to pass for years and years, decades. It was all awkward. He didn't appear to have anything more to say, and no special liqueur came out to mark the occasion, so we paid the bill (Bev taking our money, looking stern!) and left to go fishing. Explaining our haste, Ray told Bev we had to get the night bite.

Ray gunned the Grew carefully, like a kid his first motorbike.

"You think there's actually a night bite?" I asked him when we reached Egmont Point and he cut the throaty engine back.

"For sure there's a night bite."

He had the fastest hands. In maybe five seconds he had a live herring hooked in two spots and was pulling line off the reel. We sat close to shore in only fifty feet of water. A warm August evening, it was as tranquil as sunrise, though richer with light. The Grew was embedded in a mirror.

"People like fishing the evening because it's so nice," I said. I remembered my dad saying it was when the big ones come out, which made no sense in several different ways. Come out from where, being one.

"Who knows," he said, dismissive. "You think we're actually in his will?"

"I sort of hope not."

We talked, we drifted. Ray could talk fishing endlessly. That winter, anchored in the Fraser River and using for bait "intestines filled with guts," he'd caught a seven-foot sturgeon. His new passion was fly-fishing. Which made sense because he did look edgy mooching like this, sitting still. Otherwise he had quit drinking, not that he ever drank much to begin with. He'd just seen too much crap. Something about a sister. He'd seen two good friends go at it with knives. I told him I'd quit too if I saw stuff like that.

The light fell and sundown was upon us. Other than a random mudshark I'd wrestled off my hook, no action. We drifted within spitting distance of the treed shore, not really fishing. We sat in no more than ten feet of water. Ray powered up to kick us out a little and the instant we moved something grabbed my line. From the erratic head shakes and the way it came at the boat, making me reel fast to catch up, I knew it was a salmon. It came right up. There was my weight and there was— It exploded onto its side and took off. My reel screamed. Because of its size and charcoal hue, at first I thought it was a seal. But I realized what I'd just seen. Ray was hooting and dancing.

"That's *fifty*. That's *sixty*!" Ray yelled as the fish ran. "*That's a big fucking fish.*" He raved that it was the size and colour of the derby winners he'd seen. Ray made special trips to marinas just to see the weigh-ins. Before they find their spawning river, Ray added, the giants turn almost black, just like this one.

"*Sixty*?" I yelled.

"I don't know! *Seventy!*"

It stopped. More erratic head shakes. We agreed it couldn't be seventy. Maybe sixty. But even a fifty-pounder was freakish.

"Let it run. Don't hurry it," Ray hissed. He had me by the arm. "We have all night." We stared out onto the calm water, under which a gigantic salmon was, it seemed, scheming. "Baby it. Baby it."

I assured him I would baby it. Then I told him what I'd been worried about since the fight began.

"Remember that little dogfish?"

"Oh Jesus," he said. "Same leader?"

In answer I just looked at him. Dogfish, or mudshark, have razor teeth and routinely leave a leader frayed, and greatly weakened. Not expecting any salmon on the agenda tonight, not believing in the night bite, I hadn't bothered changing the leader. As it was, the leader was only twelve-pound test, which a big salmon could break with ease if I misplayed it. I had no idea how much weaker the leader was or if I had any chance of getting this fish to the boat.

"Jesus. Baby it," Ray said, his voice falling to a deadness, knowing what a frayed leader meant. "Baby it. We have all night."

I babied it. I forced it hardly at all, keeping just enough pressure on the rod to turn its head toward the boat, but letting it run all it wanted. Scariest were the violent head shakes, when a fish could most likely break a frayed leader. Ray had slowly motored out to deeper water, in case of snags or kelp the salmon could get hung up on. After a couple more long runs, and retrievals, the fish mostly just circled the boat, forty feet directly below. The rod tip dipped in rhythm as the salmon opened and closed its big mouth to breathe. Fifteen minutes went by. A half-hour. I babied the monstrous fish. It was almost dark. Its runs grew shorter. Ray kept assuring me we had all night.

It took another run, maybe fifty yards, then stopped to shake its head. An extra-violent shaking. It felt like a last-ditch attempt to throw the hook. More shaking, then— Nothing. Dead slack. Ray saw the slack and yelled at me to reel, but I knew. I reeled in, knowing I'd see only a two-ounce weight trailing a broken leader. And that's what I saw, though it was almost dark now.

A classic fish story. Back at the dock people only half-listened to me, not believing the story, in particular the size of the fish, even with Ray excitedly confirming all. I've been telling this story for years, not adding to the size of the fish because it's unbelievable enough already. I don't know if anyone has ever really believed me. Because, yes, the punchline is: You should have seen the one that got away. And it's true, you really should have seen the one that got away.

But the real punchline is, the night bite is indeed when the big ones come out.

———

The rapids are still amazing. Despite the chain-link fence and warning sign, despite the dozen or so tourists gathered here on the bald rock point. Over this roar I'd still have to shout to be heard. Beneath my feet, I can still feel the solid rock shudder, and stare dumbstruck at the universe of water rushing by, a sensation not unlike the sense-sucking tumult of Niagara Falls.

How can I begrudge the crowd? It was only a matter of time. The roar and turmoil is a pebble's throw away. It's the biggest tidal rapids in the world. The water height on one side can be nine feet higher than on the other. On the hour's hike in I passed old people ambling carefully along, then I was passed by professional hikers walking faster than I can run. I heard accents I couldn't identify. It was only a matter of time. Egmont couldn't keep such a thing for itself.

I hate the fence. And the interpretive sign, anchored in its cement pedestal, blocking what it explains. What I dislike most of all are the daredevil kayakers. Maybe *kayak* isn't the word; it's a five-foot kayaky thing they kneel in to surf a standing wave, not moving in relation to the land while water rivers under them. Using the paddle as leverage they flip themselves to point backwards, or plunge under for an Eskimo roll. I watch two kayaky surfers work the standing wave, hooting and yelling, though I can't hear them over the roar. On the next rock over another half-dozen share a joint while taking off or pulling on wetsuits. Good healthy fun, but their boats are garish red, blue, or yellow. Helmets are black or neon orange. I see a turquoise vest. The backdrop of forest green and cloudy sky doesn't stand a chance against their candy-coloured aesthetic, the beer ad urgency. They're hogging all the focus.

To the left is the small cove, more a timid indentation in the shore, where my dad and I tied to the floating bull kelp and fished. We stayed a little nervous. We were probably more than a little stupid. Aside from two divers who dared that cove for twenty minutes on a slack tide, quickly filling a garbage can with speared ling cod, I never saw anyone else fish there.

Most of the tourists are Asian. They would've watched us fish, pointed at the crazy boat tied to seaweed, took selfies with my dad in the background. I can't imagine what he would have made of that.

On the distant shore across from Egmont where the little reserve is, what looks like an old wooden scow pulls up to the lone dock. It looks unhurried and inconsequential. It's the dock where I would sometimes buy live bait, because they often had it when the marina did not. It was cheaper too, a dollar a dozen instead of two. But you'd tie to the dock and it might take ten or fifteen minutes for someone to wander down the trail from one of the scatter of modest dwellings, modest because they were without electricity and accessible by boat only. I liked buying bait there, if only because the herring had all their scales, having been less molested by a dip net.

One hot summer day when my dad was with me on *Cormorant* we ran out of bait and I thought to try the reserve dock because it looked like someone was manning it. We putted up and my dad looked dubious. The dock was half-sunk logs bound by logging cable, topped with wonky plywood, and the dock shack was a canvas shelter. We were attended by a man I knew as Jerry. A heavy-set fellow, Jerry could have been twenty or forty, and I was tempted to see him as mentally challenged while knowing that this might not be the label for him. He was so soft-spoken as to be difficult to hear, and he wore mechanic's coveralls, though they were off-colour with dirt, not grease. That morning I noticed Jerry moving extra-carefully, and he had bloody lips, and dried blood on the back of his wrist. He clutched a crumpled paper lunch bag tight to his chest, and moaned—if it's possible to moan in a whisper—while he dipped out herring for us, one-handed.

Not counting them and giving us more than the two dozen we

asked for, he tipped the herring into our bucket, then said, "You wanna see?" He lisped the last word badly.

He didn't wait for our answer. Moving slowly, almost suggesting ritual, he brought the bag from his chest and daintily fingered open the top. He moaned quietly on each breath. It might have been a mournful song.

Whispering, "Muh teesh," he opened and angled the bag so we could see in. Clustered in there were over a dozen teeth, mostly molars, each tooth a mix of white enamel, black rot, and red blood. I caught a brief whiff. He clutched the bag back to his chest protectively, as if to keep the teeth close, still a part of him. He moaned, or sang, ignoring me when I tried to pay.

My dad and I cast off and motored away from the dock, back to the Gap. He sat staring into the middle distance at something I couldn't see, softly shaking his head, his look of incomprehension not so different from Jerry's.

# ELEVEN

*Those who have never had a father can at any rate
never know the sweets of losing one. To most men the
death of his father is a new lease on life.*

—SAMUEL BUTLER

*Sylvan* has a pot, a frypan, a plate and a bowl—I had big plans to buy my food at Bathgate's and make meals on board, like before on *Cormorant*. Yet here I am, in out of the cold, scanning Backeddy's menu again. I vow not to make it three burgers in a row.

The seafood platter—prawns, scallops, salmon, halibut—is pricey by pub standards. This is gastro-pub. I wave Carla over and ask her what, if any, of the fish is fresh, not frozen. If you're going to pay almost thirty bucks for a meal in a pub you buy the right to ask some basic questions, but she looks miffed when she turns away, saying, "I will go and ask Chef," irony on the last word. I know who she reminds me of now in the route she's taken with her makeup—Elizabeth

Taylor as Cleopatra. It's more playful than sultry. But I'll bet she scares any young Egmonsters into shyness.

I've got the pulse of the place now, this new Egmont. It's a Saturday evening, late summer, and the pub is less than a quarter full with no anticipation of more bodies arriving. The wedding brought a crowd and they've dispersed. Skookumchuck hikers have driven back to southern towns, no place here to stay. Random yachts tie up, but not many. I've learned that the two sleek boats moored side by side are jet boats that take tourists to play in the rapids. It's a weekend with good wild tides, but there have been no customers.

I'm leaving tomorrow. When I got back from my Skook hike I untied and went for a little cruise up past Egmont Point into Prince of Wales Reach, which narrowed north in the distance and beckoned with the darkest solitudes. A favourite little island, its bald head growing a single huge fir tree smack in the middle, like a child's drawing, is now totally bald. Who would do such a thing? I hope a storm and not a heartless vandal took that fir. The third bay along I tucked in for a look at a beach that at low tide used to be covered in oysters, "covered" being no exaggeration, the whole beach white with them and often several deep. I motored in and saw a seafood clear-cut, no oysters, just tawny gravel. But then on seeing the beach and its verge of dense, dark forest, I remembered why I left Egmont for good. It wasn't just the fishing gone off, or the isolation. It was more visceral.

Indigenous people everywhere seem to share an understanding about the environment, and its character. They believe it *has* a character. Any given place—forest clearing, cove, river—has its own quality distinct from any other clearing, cove or river, emanating a spirit that's anything from bland to kind to siren-like to malevolent, or any combination in between. The word *ambience* is our surface sense of this. Japanese call it *kami*, Tibetans *drala*. To cite one example, before

Europeans came, the dramatically lovely valley that now contains the township of Banff was used for hunting forays but never for living. Today, many visitors report that it's hard to get a good night's sleep there.

Anyway, long ago I came to this beach for oysters and learned something about Egmont. That day, following the urge to be even more alone, I was on the water hunting real isolation. I thought I'd have lunch. I anchored *Cormorant*, launched the dinghy off the stern and rowed to shore, beaching into the crunch of oysters. I picked enough to make room for a fire, which as it happened was also about the right amount to eat. I made a fire within a ring of rocks on which I laid the dozen big oysters, still in their shells. I loved them this way, popping open when done, sizzling in their own juice, otherwise unadorned, just salty enough. What's more flavourful than an oyster?

I stood humming to myself, fidgeting, nudging oysters closer to the flames with the toe of my sneaker. It wasn't a deep beach, maybe thirty feet to the wall of trees, and I kept glancing up at the silent, dark wall every ten seconds or so. It was a beautiful blue-sky day, windless, so why did it feel almost cold, and why did the bright light seem somehow dark? I nudged oysters. I glanced up at the forest. Why weren't the oysters opening yet? I glanced again. Why wasn't this fun? Why did it feel so absolutely shitty? Why was I afraid? Why was I *this* afraid?

I could no longer stand it, a looming blackness of spirit I finally admitted I'd felt *glaring* at me from the moment I set foot on land. It was time to get right away from here. I didn't stop to put out the fire. I didn't stop to grab oysters to take. I shoved off the beach, rowed quickly, boarded *Cormorant*, pulled anchor and turned the key. I never once felt foolish or cowardly. I felt like I'd escaped something real.

Who knows. There are endless deserted bays up the coast all the way to Alaska, each with its own personality. Rarely, but sometimes they're inhabited. It's not hard to imagine how a place might trigger and then over the years cement a hermit's madness.

The thing is, I discovered Egmont's darkness in general, maybe its heart, and I've rediscovered it this trip, remembering. The feeling is that humans really aren't welcome. That is to say, *I'm* really not welcome. Maybe I'm crazy, but I think I was told not to go alone into the haunted woods.

And yes, maybe I simply encountered my own darkness, one that has nothing to do with this place or that.

Carla comes back with news from Chef and it's no surprise. Nothing on the seafood platter isn't "fresh-frozen at sea." I order it anyway, because now I'm too shy of Carla not to. I almost fall to codger mode and blurt to her unsmiling profile that I used to supply fresh ling cod to the café that in olden days occupied this very spot, but hold my tongue. I've been a seafood snob all my life and I really should get over it, because fresh is just getting too hard to find. Unless we're talking farmed, but then you might as well just go suck the lead paint off an old windowsill.

I'm also too shy to ask Carla why she came back to live in Egmont. Clearly she's lived elsewhere. Wise beyond her years, she has big life changes, maybe survival, written all over her.

Lemon and salt and gastro-pub tartar sauce are so happy on the tongue that even fish that's been frozen is an excellent chew.

Halibut, salmon, scallops, prawns. I've just eaten four kinds of meat.

I will definitely leave tomorrow. Done my second pint, I try to come up with a good reason for ordering a third. No other bodies have come into the Backeddy, and the Blue Jays game is long over. I decide to buy a six-pack and go have a beer on board *Sylvan* for the first time ever.

Egmont is where I started writing, aboard *Cormorant*. I guess I should thank this place for that. Or blame it. But maybe tonight, gazing across the darkness of the Gap, I'll be inspired to jot some notes. I wonder if anyone here heard my old orange typewriter clacking away in the dark.

———

What really happened to my father?

Back when we used to troll, if fishing was slow my dad would rifle around gently in his tackle box, wary of hooks, and lift out a flat, bronze lure called a Tom Mack. "This'll knock 'em dead," he'd say. Salmon were often about to be knocked dead in our boat, especially when nothing was biting and he resorted to the baits of his childhood.

He'd tie on the lure then pull it through the water, checking its action, and do his sexy whistle. The Tom Mack was a homely thing, not nearly as bright or colourful as any of today's lures. I had the notion that only a really old fish might be knocked dead by it.

"Mukilteo," he'd say softly. And he'd tell me again how the Tom Mack used to knock 'em dead, especially coho, when he'd troll from a rowboat, the line wrapped around his foot. And how, to conjure more deadly action in the Tom Mack, he would jerk his foot up and down, which he demonstrated by flapping his hand.

"How old were you?"

"Twelve. Thirteen."

"Did you fish alone?"

A pause. "Sometimes there'd be a friend."

"Why didn't they row, so you could use a rod?"

"It was the Depression! Nobody had a rod! Couldn't afford it!"

That's all I heard from my dad about Mukilteo, aside from his dog Ricky. And the time he caught the huge ling cod off the wharf and couldn't eat it because of the worms. The rest I heard from my mother, though her details changed over time, her lifelong habit being to protect her children from cruel truths. For instance, one evening when I was twenty and over for the weekend she announced in her cheerful voice as she tossed a salad, "Grammie died yesterday." This would be her mother, my grandmother. I knew Grammie had been sick but didn't know it was that serious. Also, I'd been there all weekend, and why my mother waited that long to tell me, and in her cheerful voice, I had no idea, and still haven't.

When my mother began her own slow journey into dementia, I learned lots of new things. In certain moods she would talk and talk, often repeating a story I'd heard the day before. But sometimes I'd hear a curious word or phrase, almost like a flash of bait, and I'd lean in and get her to expand. One Halloween night, helping her with trick-or-treaters, despite her condo being out of bounds to all but a few kids with grandparents in the building, she took and unwrapped her fourth or fifth mini–candy bar from the bowl and said, "And of course this was Mother's favourite night."

"What do you mean her 'favourite night'?"

She looked at me like someone who'd forgotten his own middle name. "Well she was the Halloween lady."

"The Halloween lady?"

"We were the House of Horrors!" She looked her idiot son up and down.

I persisted and got more from her and learned something remarkable, that my grandmother was a Halloween lady famous throughout Everett. A lineup of thrilled families at the door, Grammie herself a ghoul leaping from the pantry. Sitting at a card table inside the door, my mother collected a nickel per person.

This violated in a wonderful way the image I had of my grandmother—dour, critical, not smiling much, except when she rolled a

Yahtzee and she would bellow, truly exited, pronouncing it "yachee." Playing Yahtzee, she made everyone use the rolling cup, not our bare hands, which for some reason was cheating. But my Grammie was a Halloween lady!

One day, visiting my mother five years after my father had died, I was treated to new information. Lately she focused mostly on her teenage years. Sometimes her girlhood. Sometimes early years with my father.

"It was sure good," she said, and I almost missed it, "when they got hell and gone from that place."

"Who, Dad?"

"When he escaped," she said, giving me that look, like I was wilfully forgetting these things. She had been going on rapturously about admiring him from afar in high school and then finally dating him in college, Bob Gaston, how he was so tall and handsome and how her girlfriends were jealous. I'd heard this a hundred times, but something was new.

"Escaped?"

"That father of his. And that place he lived." She visibly shuddered.

"When did he move to Everett?"

"Well, when he went back and forth." My mother's stern look. I should know these things.

"Back and forth?"

"Well, in those foster homes."

"What?"

"When he was fostered."

"Dad was in foster homes?"

"Well, when his mother couldn't afford to keep both Margaret and your father, so your father was sent off to the foster homes."

"What?"

"He'd get violent and that would be that. She'd kick him out and—"

"Who'd get violent?"

"Your father's father!" Why was I being deliberately stupid?

"He'd get violent?"

It was here that I heard about the restraining order denying Ozro Gaston entry into the State of Washington.

"The worst time was when he tried to get at Bob's mother and Bob would have none of it and he picked up that fireplace poker and he stood there in front of her waving it at him—that man sure made him pay for that one."

"How old was he?"

"He was ten." She is teary now. "I can just see him standing there swinging with that poker. He was so thin. Your father had his nose broken, and his arm."

"He never told me any of this, about his dad." What he'd told me was that he was ten when his dad died sitting on the curb getting hit in the head by a fire truck's loose ladder.

"Well he didn't tell me either! I learned it all from your Aunt Margaret. She said if your father had been any bigger he would have killed their father with that poker because he sure was trying."

I stood up at this point, though not to go anywhere.

"No, the *worst* time was once when your father brought home a big fish and nailed it to the laundry post. His father got at him for that one too."

"For what? Why was he mad?"

"Well maybe for putting a hole in the laundry post!" She shook her head at me. "I really couldn't tell you."

I remembered the story of him proudly hauling the monster ling cod home in his wagon. And him telling me how he had cried after seeing the fish had worms and was useless.

"Was it because it was full of worms?"

"I really couldn't tell you. It was the luckiest thing in his life when they escaped that man."

"But then he was in foster homes."

"One of them, oh! . . . It was so bad. I hate to even think of it."

"How do you mean, 'bad'?"

She looked at me, and actually saw me for maybe the first time. "It was bad exactly how you think I mean bad." She looked away, and fresh tears came. "There was this other boy at that place. He was a grown man I think. He was really bad to your father."

———

It probably goes without saying, but to learn what happened to my father was to forgive him. Forgive him everything—his drinking, his distance, his weakness that disgusted a teenage boy. All I need do is conjure an image of a sickly skinny kid, not yet twelve. The kind of kid who's a head taller than his classmates but always looking down and off to the side, fear the one obvious thing about him. He knows where his mother and sister live, but he can't join them. Walking away from the school every afternoon, he can't go to someplace called "my house." It gets lonelier at night, despite him having to share a room. There's no place to hide.

I don't know why I waited so long to call my Aunt Margaret. Maybe I was afraid to find out more. We are not a communicative family. When I did finally make contact, Margaret was not only willing to answer any question I had about my father, she was glad to. She was warm, generous, and articulate. She admitted, though, that during "the trouble years," she was a little girl and didn't know much, or remember much, and her brother, being six years older, didn't want to have much to do with her either. What's a twelve-year-old boy going to tell his six-year-old sister? And in those years they weren't living in the same house anyway. Because, yes, it was true that their mother couldn't afford to keep them both.

Other things I learned:

The worst trouble was in Portland, Oregon, not in Washington, not Everett or Mukilteo. They were living in Portland when the worst abuse took place, and where my ten-year-old dad would have killed his father had he been bigger. Yes, Bobby was badly hurt that night. Would he have lost a tooth, I asked Aunt Margaret, a front tooth? That later was framed in gold? Margaret didn't know about a tooth. Did she remember him losing the tooth in Madison Square Garden? No, she didn't recall that. But the three of them fled Portland in the middle of the night and made their way to Monroe, Washington, and some relatives there. It was the Depression, and everyone was poor. It was in Monroe where my dad was farmed out, broken arm and all.

My grandfather, Ozro, was called "Oz" by friends. He was an accomplished violinist. It was true that he was from a respected and well-to-do family, but he was the black sheep. A restraining order from the State of Washington was news to Margaret, but she was a child and there might have been. However, she did know that Ozro was warned by his wife's Monroe relatives that trouble awaited if he ever tried to see his wife or children. The one time Oz did try, showing up at the front gate one day, he had his eyes blackened and he fled back south.

Ozro worked for Burroughs Business Machines, "maybe even second in command." Then he became an unemployed drunk, in Portland, and he died when my father was twenty-two and in the navy, apparently while at sea fighting the Japanese. Yes, my aunt assured me, my dad would have been made aware of his father's death, probably in a letter. I've tried to picture his expression when learning the news, and can't. It's even harder to fathom what he might have felt, likely something complex beyond my ken—if he felt anything at all. While telling me about his father being killed by the fire truck his face was nothing but animated, even a little pleased with the story.

Margaret was glad to have learned, and fairly recently, that for the last year of his life her father had gone sober and worked as a longshoreman on the Portland docks. Then he got sick with cirrhosis but never sought treatment for it, not even painkillers. I suppose I'm looking for some kind of redemption for him, and I wonder if in that last year he took up the violin again.

Margaret told me that she and my dad never spoke of their father. Not once.

Mukilteo was my father's favourite place, though it was just a gas station and a few stores, a clutch of houses, and the ferry dock for Whidbey Island. But it was here he was able to live with his mother and sister again when, Margaret calculated, he was fourteen through seventeen. He had a trombone and played in the Everett school band. He made all-state in basketball, which attracted the scouts from college. She never saw him smile much, but he had friends. "Pals," she said. And, yes, they had Ricky! In Mukilteo, he did lots and lots of fishing. Eventually, someone gave him the gift of a fishing rod. It was already old, made of bamboo or cane, and she remembered him keeping it in a special place. He would borrow a neighbour's rowboat and, if no one else was available, sometimes he let little Margaret row the boat while he trolled. She rowed with all her might, afraid he wouldn't ask her again.

And it was Mukilteo where their mother lost her high school cafeteria job, unable to stop herself ladling Bobby too much food. And, yes, fired twice.

———

I try to sleep but I'm haunted by seals barking in the night. I saw a couple today sunning themselves on a cluster of islets just off the Gap and it sounds like it's coming from there. Last night, the wedding and the Motown probably outshouted them.

It's literally a drag, losing a salmon to a seal. I lost a few that way out there in the Gap. It's always a shock. You're fighting a salmon, it's made a couple of runs, your heart's going pretty good, you're wondering how big it is. Twenty? Twenty-five? Other boats are watching. It stops a run, gives a bunch of solid head shakes, and then—somehow it's become a submarine, slow and steady and stubborn. Line drags slowly off your reel, like you've hooked the bottom and it's steadily walking away. After ten seconds of denial you admit to yourself what it is, because it's happened before, exactly like this. You utter the swear word of your choice, clamp down on your reel, and the line snaps—gone are seal, salmon, and gear. The first couple times you didn't clamp down, you patiently waited for your line to be almost gone and you watched the seal, a big bugger, hump itself onto the islet, dragging your twenty-pound fish. Your twenty-*five*-pound fish.

Though these midnight seals keep me from slumber it's a welcome sound, because it's wildlife, and coming back, much like that mysterious grizzly. It's so sad there are no salmon here anymore, and no herring, and because of no herring, no seabirds. Though it's hard to see these seals as wildlife, somehow. They sound like sloppy old granddads in grouch mode, capable only of whisky-voiced vowel sounds, no consonants at all. Old salts on Gabriola call them rock sausage.

I had one beer on *Sylvan*, is all. I couldn't get comfortable, sitting in the captain's chair, which keeps you too erect. And I'm still planning on leaving tomorrow, and didn't fancy a headache. And I didn't want to keep getting up to pee in the night, Egmont's too cold. And, and, and. Just didn't feel like drinking, I guess. Drinking here.

I admit to feeling a bit maudlin. Seals aren't all that's keeping me awake. I can feel my father, see him vividly. He's keeping me up. Which isn't a bad thing.

Hearing about his childhood, I not only automatically forgave him, I can get weepy thinking about this little kid, beaten up by his father, abandoned by his mother, made morbidly shy and afraid of virtually everything as life keeps coming at him. His size, his booming voice, doesn't fool me now for a second. So my forgiveness is automatic. The question remains, do I forgive myself?

At night, like now, I'm haunted by some things in particular, a gallery of events I torture myself with. We first moved to Deep Cove when I was fourteen and we moored our Winnipeg lake boat out in the bay near our house. One new friend had a better boat we waterskied behind but it was broken and I volunteered ours. My dad, not sure if I could handle it, or not trusting my friends to drive while I skied, offered to drive for us. Maybe he just wanted to come.

These guys were pros, and the idea was to ski without ever getting wet. From the dock they took off in a standing position, single ski, jumping when the rope snapped to maximum pull. Unless they tried new tricks they never fell, and would complete their dry slalom when the driver towed them at full speed past the dock and the skier let go fifty feet out and cruised in ropeless to catch the dock with both hands, wet only to the knees. Indian Arm was deep and very cold, and there were lots of stinging jellyfish in late summer, but the real reason for the dry ski was the macho one—you came in dry, you kicked your ski off while yawning, then lit a smoke, already bored. I was the new kid and had completed a dry ski not once.

My friends watched from the dock as my gangly dad and I rowed our dinghy out to our moored boat then cruised over to meet them. The first skier got rigged up, and I stayed on board, the spotter. The procedure was to motor slowly away from the dock then gun it when there was fifteen feet of slack rope.

We motored out, I yelled "Gun it" at the right amount of slack and my dad, a careful driver, eased the throttle up a little faster, then a little faster, slowly pulling the incredulous screaming skier into the icy water.

"*Gun* it, fucking *gun* it!" the sinking pro yelled, thrusting his thumb in the air, the signal for faster.

I was yelling at him to gun it too and he did, and our lake boat eventually did pull the struggling skier out of the water. He did a few pissed-off slalom runs and then signalled that he wanted to go back to the dock. I told my dad what to do, to circle past at full speed, and he started to, but as the skier got close to the dock he kindly slowed right down, I guess so the skier wouldn't have to swim very far. He just didn't get it. There was more swearing, not just from the skier but from all the pros on the dock, and the gist of their outrage was that my father should not be driving.

So he was shamed out of his own boat. I had no choice but to stay with my new friends and I guess my dad knew this, but it felt like betrayal and I didn't enjoy dropping him at our buoy then watching him row in, knees up, elbows out, alone, and walk up the bank, especially when he paused halfway up to watch us ski.

It was bad enough at the time, this vivid image of him on the bank, shunned, watching us. Watching me. It was a singular memory, one that always got me in the gut. But when I got the new information, when I think of his abuse at the hands of "an older boy" about the age of these heroic water skiers, it's doubly hard to take. There's something about the crude, grabbing, scornful authority of boys that age.

Here on *Sylvan*, listening to the croak of seals, I'm hungry again. I hear him wryly suggest that we have hamburger with our chicken, being funny but also not.

I think of that birthday party and my mother's best friend Doris passing out and soiling herself at her own doorstep, the smell of it, and my dad's unforgivably stupid insult to her, hissed into my ear, that she was faking. I hated him for that. Why did it take me so long to realize that not only couldn't he taste, he also couldn't smell? So, while he might have insulted her, he wasn't stupid.

I think of him leaving on that fishing trip a day after his mother arrived in Winnipeg, the only time I met my grandmother. I don't think I saw them speak. I don't know if I was ever told when she died.

I think of his meekness in the face of any authority. Any "father figure" might be seeing it in too simple a light. But how is it possible to hate someone for simply being afraid?

The constant lying. I see now that it wasn't lying, exactly. If the only goal, moment by moment, is to avoid more possible pain, truth holds no more value than anything else. And he was such a bad liar. I always knew. But would I rather have had a father who was a good liar, slick and successful at it? Or a bad one, clumsy, transparent? It's obvious to me now that I'd rather have had the bad liar, because it means that lying was not in his nature. Not that I could see this at the time.

Mostly, I think of his unreachable sadness. I didn't know how to fix it then, and I don't know how to fix it now.

———

I didn't know much about his past on the night he died.

On his deathbed, my father taught me the lesson of my life. He didn't deliberately share wisdom. Nor was he witlessly making a mistake, teaching what not to do. His dying taught in a third way.

I got the call from my mother at noon. My father is in intensive care. He has aspirational pneumonia, and because he has a DNR—do not resuscitate—order, it is going to kill him. He is not expected to live out the day.

I pack three kids in the car and drive to the Vancouver ferry. My heart is going pretty good, but I'm vividly empty of thoughts. There is shock in the air; it feels like a drawn-out car accident. No one close to me has died. My father is going to die. *Dad is going to die.* This is *It*. I realize that part of me has been fearing this day my entire life.

What's very odd is that Dede is with Lilli back east in Virginia, because exactly one week earlier she had an identical call about her father. I'd spoken to her that morning and he was apparently rallying. What is almost funny is that her father had a weak heart and was expected to die ages ago. My dad's vitals are hale and hearty, and yet here he is, dying. We were making funeral travel plans last week, but for the wrong father.

In an otherworldly drive, ferry ride, and crawl through Vancouver traffic, I have a heightened sense of my children and enjoying everything about them. I cherish their words, which are few—I've told them what's about to happen, and that this has never happened to me before, and they don't know what to say.

We park at the hospital. Three hours has passed since the call, three hours to prepare myself, but there is no preparing for such a thing. We step inside his hospital room and my kids get one quick look at their dying grandfather, their grandmother standing at his side. His large bulk is covered in a blue sheet and he is breathing monstrous breaths, each one an enormous gasp that rattles the bed and fills the room. It is frightening and I usher them back out into the hall, where a nurse takes over. My mother will be taking them back to her house now, the nurse explains, because my mother has explained it to her. I learn that my brother is camping with his family somewhere in the Gulf Islands, and no one has been able to contact him.

I go in and stand across the bed from my mother. The room is too electric for me to hug her, and she doesn't want to be hugged. She looks manic and exhausted. She holds one of his hands lightly, talking non-stop in her cheerful voice, a smile frozen on her face. Her manner is that of talking to a baby, who might or might not be able to understand.

"And here's Billy! Remember how you two would go fishing? Remember how much you used to enjoy that? And your boat? You had a lot of good fishing trips with your son. Remember how you used to fill the freezer with salmon? And you'd smoke the salmon and give it to neighbours? And we'd eat it too. We sure loved that smoked salmon. And here's Billy! Remember how he'd swim in the pool and you'd watch? You had such good times in that pool! And remember—"

His body convulsing hugely every twenty seconds or so, Dad's eyes are open and he looks terrified.

While she talks, my mother gestures me over to her side of the bed, where she hands me my dad's hand as though it were a torch that couldn't be laid down. When I take his hand my mother stops talking and looks at me as though I am supposed to pick that part up too. As though this is what one does.

"Hi Dad," I say. "It's Bill. Can you hear me?"

He gives my hand a quick, terrified squeeze. Here is a man who hasn't been with us for half a year, but now he very much is.

As if he weren't here, my mother explains that the nurse said it would be good to talk to him about how good his life has been. Then she says she is going, and taking my kids and she will take them to A&W for dinner. Her manner makes it clear that she will not be coming back. With that, after fifty years with him, she walks away. No goodbye to my father, no pause at the door for a last look back. She is exhausted and panicking and needs to flee, and I shouldn't have judged or blamed her for anything right then but it's odd—perhaps the word is *tragic*—how these things go. At a deathbed, you'd think that family things could be mercifully smooth for a change, to allow the honest and the heartfelt to take place. But dying, it seems, is chaos. It's only natural to feel it as an emergency. All this time, for hours, my mother has been standing and talking, but somehow she hasn't understood that my dad knows exactly what is going on. He is terrified that he is dying, and she thinks she is talking to an uncomprehending baby. Seeing the two of them together, yet two worlds so far apart, is grotesquely frightening to me.

My mother is gone and in the new quiet I tell Dad that Mom has left and that I am here with him and won't be going away. There is no squeeze, but I think I feel understanding and relief. I tell him I'm getting a chair and lay his hand on his chest.

And so I begin hours of sitting and waiting for him to die. The rhythm of his huge breath—body lurch, bed rattle, gasp—becomes the heartbeat of the room.

Lurch rattle gasp.

Lurch rattle gasp.

Eyes open, he glances fearfully this way and that, seeing things not in the room. Whatever's here is immediate. He doesn't blink.

A nurse comes and goes, checking on us, and every hour or so a doctor. I go and find a pay phone and call Dede in Virginia, to tell her the funny coincidence, that her dad cried wolf and the real dying dad is right here. She sees the humour and laughs for me, but hearing something in my voice she reminds me that it's also okay to cry, and I do.

Back in the room, I watch him. I study him. Lurch rattle gasp. His eyes open, his fear. I don't say much. I remind him that I'm here with him and, uselessly, to not be afraid. At one point a nurse beckons me outside, where a doctor, one I haven't seen, waits. He introduces himself, then informs me, in practised tones, that it doesn't look good.

"What doesn't look good?"

"Your father. I'm afraid the prognosis is that he won't survive twenty-four hours."

"Oh. Well, I knew that."

The doctor seems surprised, and doubtful.

"My mother told me that on the phone. Hours ago. He has aspirational pneumonia. And he has a DNR, so. . . ."

"That's right." He seems a bit irritated that I know these things. A colleague hasn't told him, or written it down, or something, though I couldn't care less, because my father is dying. "Well, we've done more tests and it seems his heart is very strong, and we are more or less waiting for it to give out."

I go back in and sit and take Dad's hand and wrap it around my index finger and ask if he can hear me. A quick squeeze. He glances fearfully this way and that. He is still panicking. He knows what's up.

Seeing his terror for the first time, the nature of it, a thought strikes me. They are giving my father painkillers for physical pain, "keeping him comfortable," they informed me. But he is anything but comfortable. Isn't fear pain? *Isn't terror a horrible pain?*

I race out to find the nurse. I tell her what I've just realized and ask her to please give my father some morphine because he is in terrible pain. He's *afraid*, I explain. The nurse gives me a long look then tells me that they do not euthanize patients here. I get angry, I start crying, almost hysterically, burbling out that my father is terrified and he shouldn't have to be, it is torturing him. I scare the nurse, I think, and she turns away and says she needs to get a doctor's permission. It strikes me as the height of absurdity that my dad is dying, and that there are rules. I go back to his side, still crying softly, finding it hard now to look at his frightened face. Lurch, rattle, gasp. Lurch, rattle, gasp. The nurse comes with her permission, and a loaded syringe. She is all cheerful as she inserts the needle into the elbow of the tube feeding fluids into my dad's arm.

"*This*'ll make you feel a little better." She plunges the plunger. "There."

It does. His eyes settle a bit, though they remain watchful, and cautious. I stand up and watch him again. I feel better now too. The nurse leaves.

It's here that I see it. I'm standing, watching his face, and the hair rises on the back of my neck. I see into his darting eyes. It is, yet it isn't the man I thought I knew. It's my dad when he was young. Here he is, a child, and he's afraid. Deathly afraid. I see that this boy has never not been present and vital in the centre of this man, my father. I see, so clearly, that the man I thought I knew is but a layering of buffers. He wove a cocoon with ploys, with feints, with masks, to keep fearful things away, the biggest of which has caught him at last and is overwhelming him now. His personality is what he built. His joking, his business savvy, his camaraderie, his whistles, his moods—all what his ten-year-old spirit placed around itself, cushions against life's onslaught. What I knew of my father was none other than a spectacular suit of armour.

It's not some kind of theory or concept I'm seeing but a fleshy truth, a process lying here in its entirety in the shape of my father. I see it all in a flash, the kind of knowing that is irrefutable.

And what he is showing me grows simultaneously much larger, because I see how I made myself in the same way. I can feel, deep in my core, how, especially as children, we react to pain by growing protective scabs or calluses, the collection of which, over the years, becomes our personality. So instant is my understanding that it will take me years to catch up and comprehend more fully, even as my visual memory of the moment grows less and less sharp. I'll never fully comprehend, or be able describe it well enough, even to myself.

It's a teaching unlike any other I've had. What my father showed me has let me not only understand him, but everyone. And, with no effort involved at all, to forgive. This understanding, and its forgiveness, includes myself.

He continues his dying. Lurch, rattle, gasp. The morphine lets him settle down more, and whatever he confronts seems to have become more dreamlike, or at least less fearsome. His eyes shoot off less quickly, and if anything he appears more interested. I have a jolt of guilt and wonder if by insisting on giving him morphine I have denied him some kind of final awareness, or sharpness of vision, or even redemption, if there is such a thing. But I don't think so. His level of panic, literally scared to death, just didn't seem at all right, didn't seem to allow anything remotely worthwhile.

Time has passed. I've been with him for hours. They bring me a recliner and a blanket, and I set up near the foot of his bed. Occasionally I reach out, touch his leg, and tell him I am here. I notice his breathing, and the lurch and rattle, has grown less explosive. The doctor said he would weaken, and get less oxygen, and weaken more, and eventually his brain would die, and then his heart.

In this strangest of all nights, one thing doesn't feel strange: the close proximity to my father, over all these hours. I'm comfortable with him this close, through the night. We're about the same distance apart as we were on *Cormorant*. Touching distance, if we reach across. He's not yelling snores this time, but he's still a loud bluster. He'd find this funny. If he could, if he could see his own fear, he'd make a bait-bucket joke.

Another discovery I make is that, even in a crisis like this, the crisis eventually somehow becomes normal. It's actually possible to grow bored. I study the room. I smell pine cleanser. The buzzing lights and sleek, blinking machines look a little bored themselves. Even my dad seems inured to his lurch, rattle, gasp, which is simply a new kind of breathing. My mind wanders, and when I come to in the middle of a fantasy about Chinese food, I'm amazed at myself and guilty. I tell my dad I'll be right back, that I have to phone Dede again. I go and do so. When I return I settle into the recliner, lurch, rattle, gasp, and start to read a *National Geographic*. Immersed in life on a Pacific atoll, I keep coming back to the reality in the room, lurch, rattle, gasp, the reality of the dying body of this man who did his part to give me life, who raised me, spent time with me, adored me, was friends with me in the only way we could both manage.

I realize I have dozed. It's the middle of the night. Gasp, lurch, rattle, gasp—but softer. I am amazed I slept, it was probably only a few minutes, but still. I see that part of me wants to "get this over with." Another wash of guilt. But, no, why prolong this? Why in the world?

The breathing spasms grow quieter, and more time passes and soon enough I can barely hear him. I don't want to touch him, or disturb him now in any way. And then I realize I can hear nothing at all.

A nurse comes in softly. She leans over him, does something professional.

"He's passed," she says. To me, and to herself.

———

A last thing about his death. I have no idea what to make of it. I have a good imagination, this I admit, but it felt only real. What happened was: The nurse turned on all the lights. She mopped his brow and closed his eyes. I asked if I could please spend time alone with him and she kindly nodded and left. I stood beside him. I said his name, so loud that my own voice surprised me. I put my hand on his chest, feeling warmth there, and then I bent and kissed his forehead. My heart was beating fast and I felt very, very good. It felt like he was still in the room, but a presence that was more richly my father than any I'd experienced in the years since he'd begun diminishing, and even before. It was like another light had come on, but one I experienced more in my body than my eyes. It felt extremely good in the room—wonderfully bright, and soft, and wise. It felt like a splendid awe, and I truly don't know whose awe it was.

———

Up at dawn, my plan being to head back down to Gabriola today, or at least make a start. Maybe troll Bjerre Shoal? Then stay a night in Pender Harbour? Finish that six-pack?

Egmont is so tucked up into mountains and sheltered from prevailing winds that I haven't bothered keeping up with the weather out there in the strait. So I down the first of my last two breakfast bananas while waiting for coffee water to boil and listen to the *Continuous Marine Report*, fuzzy on my radio.

My bananas are speckled with black dots, though not quite overcome. It's funny how at this stage they're too sweet. How can anything, let alone fruit, ever be too sweet?

Eventually Audrey comes on with her automated buoy reports and I pay attention as I pour steaming water into the filter. Her smooth and tawny voice. I hear my dad's sex whistle. It turns out Merry Island is calm—so calm that Audrey pronounces the *l*. But who knows what it'll be like a few hours from now? On cue my stomach gets to churning again, that stomach of a wind chicken.

I need to fuel up. Because the tide is running so fast and I'm such a lousy docker, I take ten minutes and hand-bomb—that is, pull my boat with its bow rope—around the perimeter of the dock and tie it up in front of the gas pumps. I stand for a moment facing the marina office, hands on hips in my best "where is everybody" pose, have no idea if I've been seen, then go in and finish my coffee and the second half of my sweet breakfast.

Mechanical things, especially boats, apparently know us well. They're in touch with what might be called karma, and also humour, because when I finish fuelling, draining my bank account in the process, I turn *Sylvan*'s key and am greeted by the shriek of shrieks—the alternator belt is yelling at me anew. I know its language now. It's yelling, *I dare you!*

It's way too early in the day to bend over into cold metal and get greasy but I lift the engine hatch. It's especially galling because any mechanic with the right socket wrench could fix this properly in two minutes. The bored young gas jockey, who looks suspiciously like the son of the speedy marina owner, can't help sneak a few peeks at me as I go through my YouTube list of alternator belt fixes. The bar of soap held against the screaming belt doesn't work at all this time. Eventually I resort to my new can of WD-40, despite the warning that it eats into the belt material, which is how it makes it grabby and why it works at all. Now my alternator belt is quiet again, but might decide to be karmically hilarious and snap on me out there on the Salish Sea.

———

I'm fishing Egmont one last time. I think maybe I want to give my trip, and my dad's story, a fairy-tale ending. I want to catch a big one, a monster, and then release it unharmed in an act of compassion while I recall my dad's gentle spirit. Or, maybe I'm just a fishing addict and part of me refuses to believe that Egmont could be void of salmon.

One cannonball I send down to 150, the other to 90, a forest-green spatterback hoochie on the deep line and a three-inch Cop Car spoon on the shallow. First I try trolling the Gap, going with the current. It's ridiculous, the speed at which *Sylvan* moves along the shoreline, easily ten miles an hour. I'm trolling in a river. I'll be in the rapids in five minutes. Four. I go as far as the quarry, where it shallows right up, and over *Sylvan*'s engine I can hear the rapids though they're a half-mile away. Picturing a fraying alternator belt, I pull the gear and head up to the more benign Egmont Point.

After ten minutes of trolling there, and nipping dangerously close to shore, almost to the spot where I hooked that sixty- or seventy- *eighty*? pound salmon, I eye a wiggle on a rod tip and pull up to check for seaweed. Impaled and thrashing on the end of the Cop Car's big single hook is a tiny chinook. Maybe six inches long, not much bigger than the lure. Hooked through the gill plate and throat, it won't survive. So, there are salmon here in Egmont. And I've just needlessly killed one.

After tying on a seven-inch pearl plug, too big for babies to bite, I aim *Sylvan* toward the nameless twin islands. I don't know why I'm delaying this departure. I've been pretending to gaze around at my youth one last time, but it's just hard for me to stop fishing. And it's fun, I must admit, trying all these new spots here; trolling lets you do that while anchoring did not. Heading toward the first nameless island, I bungee-cord the steering wheel for straight-ahead, and go below to make another coffee.

Both downriggers go off at exactly the same time and I race back up. It's not a strike. The two metal arms are bouncing, both cables dragging out. I've snagged bottom. I glance at the sounder and see I've hit a reef, only twenty-five feet down. The boat comes to a complete stop, everything trembling, then, *pop, pop*, both cables break, and *Sylvan* lurches forward.

I stop fishing for the day.

What sounds better: "I snagged both balls on a reef" or "I lost my balls on the bottom"? My dad would have approved either one. He would have loved saying it over and over. And this is as close to a fairy-tale ending as I'm going to get.

The downrigger winches pull up two lengths of shredded, slack cable, ball-less. I feel it in my gut, much like when the eagle killed the heron. If losing my cannonballs was an omen, I really don't want to know what it means.

Time to go. *Over* time. Just like that first departure from Egmont felt overdue.

It was good to be gone from here, particularly the charter-business part. After four years we moved *Cormorant* to Irvines Landing, where salmon could still be had at nearby Daniel Point, Quarry Bay, and Bjerre Shoal. It was a busier time for me, due to word of mouth but also the brochure we printed up and put on the Horseshoe Bay ferries. And there was a decent grocery store in Garden Bay, and a couple of fun hotel bars in the area, one of them the pink hotel Joni Mitchell sang about. Five minutes away, a garbage dump with guaranteed bears. It was always exciting to see one from behind your windshield, thirty feet away, and I took full advantage of that dump to impress any visiting girlfriend. If the wind blew in the right direction it didn't smell too bad and, on cue, enhancing any budding romance, up in the cedars a chorus of ravens sang haunting bear warnings. Or maybe they were human warnings for the bears, who's to say. But it was a better place to be. More people, more fish. The light was way brighter. My dad liked it better there too. Sometimes his two weeks became three.

Maybe I'll anchor and check out Garden Bay tonight, see what memories come. There's no hurry—I'll keep reminding myself of that. I nudge the throttle forward, get *Sylvan* up to speed, turn south. Then throttle right back again, down to idle, and switch on the radio, wait for Audrey to come on and tell me about any dangerous weather out there. I hear that it's still calm at Merry Island.

Sylvan gets to speed again, and though the heating gauge climbs and the belt might go, it's already lighter ahead on the southern horizon. In all likelihood I'll emerge from the darkness of Agamemnon Channel into a brighter light, and a calm Salish Sea, another blue and windless day. It's a beautiful place to have lived and I'm lucky, as was my father. At any moment I might slow down, set up the gear and try for salmon. Ball-less, I can motor-mooch.

There's no hurry. Ahead lies a world that feels chaotic and beyond my reach. But I'm happy enough. From what I can tell, though their waters are foreign to me, my children have learned to navigate.

When we die, we should all be understood, by someone.

## MUKILTEO, EPILOGUE

*Angling is where the child, if not the infant, gets to go on living.*
—THOMAS McGUANE

My daughter Lise is in Berkeley, California, finishing up her degree, and I'm a proud father en route south to load the car with her books and bring her back north where she belongs. I took a detour at the Everett, Washington exit and now here I am occupying a window seat in a café in Mukilteo, a place I've never been.

Open on the table between my coffee and slice of bumbleberry pie is *Mukilteo Days*, an old, red picture book, a hardcover of a size that usually adorns a coffee table. After my mother died, going through her small mountain of storage I found it in a cardboard box so old the packing tape disintegrated to my touch, the box sitting unopened for twenty, thirty years. Inside the book's front cover is an inscription from my Aunt Margaret to her older brother: "Happy Birthday Bob— Remember the good times and <u>forget</u> the rest." The underlined word speaks volumes, as they say.

I thumb through Margaret's gift to him, study the black and white photos, circa 1934, of this one-street village that served as the ferry terminal to Whidbey Island. There's a wooden lighthouse. A small school, and classroom of big-eyed kids at their wooden desks. An antique gas station with its lollipop-headed pumps. A drugstore, which likely had a soda fountain. A small grocery. It's bittersweet imagining a reedy boy tugging a wagon half full of food. Was that here, along this road outside this window?

I always thought he was saying "Mukilteeall," ending with an *l*. Is it possible he thought it ended with *l*? I don't see how. There would have been a sign as you entered town; it would have been on the post office. The brochure I picked up from the Visitor Center rack explains that in the local language Mukilteo means "where the water narrows." But an identical assertion in my aunt's book says the name means "good camping place." How is this possible? I wonder if these two qualities are somehow the same, or can be conjoined, and the name means "this is a fine place to stay because the water narrows and the fishing is good."

Used to be good. The café's window affords a great view of the channel across to Whidbey Island, and there's not a fishing boat to be seen. Other than this view, and the old lighthouse (built in 1906, says my brochure), nothing in Mukilteo is as it used to be.

In the Visitor Center a bizarre surprise awaited, because I learned that, just down the road, was "the biggest building on the planet," a Boeing factory. I drove over to have a look, parking across the street from a windowless wall that went on and on and on for blocks. I read in the brochure that it covers 98.7 acres. I contemplate the vast wall, and what's behind it. A colour photo shows an assembly line for jumbo jets, a string of them, nose to tail. I read that there are over one million light bulbs burning in there, and dozens of cafés, a daycare, a credit union, plus miles of tunnels underneath, along with three thousand bicycles, for workers to get from A to B. Finally, there's a microclimate *inside* the building—it actually used to cloud up and rain a bit in there until they installed proper fans, which one assumes are also the planet's biggest.

The bumbleberry pie isn't very good. It takes like chain pie, nothing homemade about it. Nothing *Mukilteo* about it. Mostly, I just can't get over the strangeness, the hilarity, that my father's tiny Mukilteo is the site of the biggest building on the planet.

The brochure says Mukilteo is one of Seattle's wealthiest suburbs. Its population is in the mid-twenty thousands. When my dad lived here, it hovered around five hundred.

This café could be anywhere. Out the window, other than the lighthouse and the view of Whidbey, nothing is what my father saw. The ferry itself is immense. Not that I expected differently, but I hoped for something, some trace. Maybe it's because of this flipping through my aunt's antique book, then looking up at so much proof of passed time, that *I* feel old, sitting here. One thing that's been said about parents dying is, when both parents are gone, you experience a weighty generational shift. It's not that a burden of family responsibility has suddenly fallen upon you, because you're probably almost old yourself and have already been living a heavily responsible life. This new weight is more emotional than practical. But it's tectonic. When your parents are gone, you are now the old guard. You are next in line to disappear. It's your turn.

———

To get closer, to make a connection, I decide to go down to the cemetery of my father, to the water itself. I pay for my snack, the king's ransom charged by airports and ferry terminals everywhere, and pick my way through a car lineup and chain-link fence and reach the manufactured waterfront of bulldozed rocks where I find one big enough to sit on. As he must have done, I stare across at Whidbey Island. He must have yearned to go there, to be someplace else, and at some point he did. But really I have no idea how he felt here, or what he thought about. When he was this close to the water, he probably just wanted to go fishing.

I get up and clamber even closer. The tide is out a couple of feet and there's seaweed-slick rock to negotiate. It's identical to the Canadian seaweed I'm used to. There are also barnacles, and I know enough to step on these to keep from sliding, though I can hear I'm crushing some of the little creatures. When I get to the water's edge I stoop and slide a hand in. It's so cold.

I think of "a mother's love." Not that all mothers are the same, but there seems to be agreement on what the phrase means. A recognition of a kind of love absolute. "A father's love" conjures a less general notion, if it conjures a notion at all. We might think of pride, or camaraderie, or judgment, or even distance. The other day a friend, who'd borne up under a difficult relationship with his father, volunteered that the word best describing what his father's love felt like was *inferred*.

Here at the cemetery, I think I can feel love, and though it's faint, and maybe imaginary, it feels stronger than inferred.

———

I have to drive down the shoreline road south almost to Edmunds before I find what I'm looking for. A faded sign beneath the marina's main one reads SALMON FISHING CHARTERS. I don't want to go on one, I just want to talk to somebody. At the desk I learn from a perilously old woman with a flesh-coloured bandage covering one entire cheek, who for some reason has a thick Southern accent, that they have no charter boats on site, but they can "arrange" for one. I ask if there's anybody around who might know something about fishing in the area and she rolls her chair a half turn and points to the back door and says, "Find Rod. He does." I see that she's wearing baggy jeans, which endears her to me further. She might be in her nineties.

It turns out that Rod is a mechanic, about the same age as me. I find him in the paved yard full of big boats—boats "on the hard" is the expression—working on the back end of a cabin cruiser that still sits in the boat-hoist sling. He's wearing mechanic's coveralls and matching cap. One of the boat's two engine legs lies on a tarp, and Rod is poking around in the transom cavity with a finger, which he withdraws from time to time to examine closely. I know what he's doing, checking for water in the leg oil. This spring I watched a mechanic probe *Sylvan* identically.

"Any water?" It's not often that I get to ask a mechanic an intelligent question.

"Oh, I'll find some," he says, not looking at me, then turns to give me the stage wink. I'm not fond of winkers, but he had to cover for his outrageous joke. Finding water in leg oil would mean hundreds of dollars of work for him.

I tell him he's been pointed out as the resident fishing expert, and would he mind being pestered for some information. He seems quite happy with all this, so while he prods I ask questions of his back. The sun has come out, and it's pleasant out here amid these big boats, all being prepped to travel to great places.

I ask him how far you have to go to find salmon these days and he says not far, because a few big runs come in and hang around on their way to the Columbia River.

"So these would all be hatchery fish?"

"*Oh* yeah."

I know about these Columbian fish, because they make up the bulk of the fish that pass Gabriola, and after joking with him about us Canucks trying to pick off as many American fish as we can before they get down this far, I tell him that my dad grew up in Mukilteo and used to fish there as a boy.

"Those would *not* have been hatchery fish," says Rod, turning around and smiling for me.

I describe my dad trolling from a rowboat, the line around his foot, all that.

"You mean he was mooching," says Rod.

I pause, then explain what I thought mooching meant, the anchoring and the live bait. I can barely contain the urge to tell him that I used to mooch professionally.

"He was mooching," Rod says. "Mukilteo *invented* mooching."

"What, the word? Or the actual, you know, the mooching part?"

"Well, mooching began there," he says. It wasn't clear that he understood my question. But then he adds, "Guys in rowboats."

"In rowboats!"

He turns to show me everything with his hands. "Rowboats. The stop-and-go part," he rows, then stops rowing, "it gets your bait down," he starts rowing again, "then up, so it changes your depth all the time. The stopping was basically just a guy resting." He smiles for me again.

"So mooching probably started out as a kind of lazy trolling?"

"That's probably how it started."

"What about motor-mooching?"

"That probably started when guys could afford a motor." He turns back to probing the oily leg cavity. "They also called it cut-plugging."

"Cut-plugging. I've heard of that."

He tells me how you take a herring and cut off its head, just so, "on the bevel," and hook it just so, and when you mooch it, it'll spin and flash and resemble a wounded herring, and salmon can't resist. He didn't say "sexy," but it's what he meant.

"So they invented cut-plugging too. It's sort of the same thing."

I have another question for Rod.

"Okay, so, would there be any truth to the story of, in the old days, that ferry"—I point north to Mukilteo—"chewing through schools of herring and the fishing being really good if you could get right in behind—"

"It's *still* good like that." Rod spins to me in a way that tells me he's done it himself. "Only when a big spawn is on. They pack in there, the water gets white with their stuff—" He lifts his chin in the direction of Mukilteo too—"and the birds are everywhere going just nuts, and you try to get in behind and, yeah, it can be bang-bang-bang." His face falls again. "Never get herring come through like that any more though."

I have one more question.

"So is it true that salmon slap bait with their tail?"

Rod turns and sees that I'm a tourist and a fool after all. He shows me with wavy hand.

"Couldn't happen. A salmon slaps its tail, it's already gone."

## THANKS

First, to my brother, who chose to opt out of this, and who has his own story to tell.

To my mother, for doing her best to keep the family together.

To my children, and there are no words.

To Ozro Frank, Ozro Claire, Alexander, and George B., fathers all, none of whom I met in the flesh.

To John Gould, Eve Joseph, Patrick Friesen, and Dede Crane, for early reading and wise counsel through this book's fits and starts. To my agent, Carolyn Forde. And to the fine folks at Hamish Hamilton for their good work, especially Nick Garrison, for believing in this.

Finally, to my father, whose default was always kindness.